Academically well researched, Neil Martin offers a reading of Galatians that reveals one of the key challenges of the churches in Paul's era, one that is often overlooked. I recommend this book to academics, pastors, and gospel workers who are interested in the shaping of communities that reflect great accommodation despite differences in the gospel community.
—*Rev Tayo Arikawe, International Director, Langham Partnership International*

Neil Martin has accomplished something to which few writers in the crowded field of Pauline research should even aspire: saying something both new *and* significant about as foundational a concept as the reason for Paul's sharp invective in Galatians. Appropriating the best insights of the old, new, and radical new perspectives on Paul, Martin comes down squarely in none of those camps. Instead, he argues that Paul's biggest fears were about *Gentile* believers adopting Jewish laws and regressing to their previous *pagan* attitudes of trying to incentivize the gods to bless them. Searching questions arise about how Christians today may be unwittingly doing the same things when they imitate cultural forms in church practices that do not invite new Christians to make clear breaks from their past. Here is a book to read slowly and reflect on in detail.
—*Craig L. Blomberg, Distinguished Professor Emeritus of New Testament, Denver Seminary, Littleton, CO*

Might cultural habits and convictions of their pre-Christian past affect the way converts discern rival interpretations of their new-found faith? In this compelling and original study, Neil Martin argues from a wide range of ancient primary sources that this is what lies behind Paul's puzzling warning to Gentile Galatians: having come to faith in Christ, their additional adoption of Jewish observance would for them entail going back to problematic patterns of their pre-Christian past. An excellent case study in how to bring the rewards of careful historical scholarship to the service of contemporary theological, pastoral and missional engagement!
—*Markus Bockmuehl, Dean Ireland's Professor of the Exegesis of Holy Scripture, University of Oxford*

In *Galatians Reconsidered*, Neil Martin builds on the vast scope of Galatians scholarship and offers a new lens for understanding Paul's arguments. Martin reframes the problem Paul is addressing in Galatians: not Jewish legalism or

D1558213

nationalism but Gentile regression. In this proposal, Paul is deeply concerned that Gentiles who have followed Jesus will take a stance toward the Torah that mirrors their own former, pagan law-keeping. A fresh and important contribution to the conversation.

—*Jeannine K. Brown, Bethel Seminary, Saint Paul, Minnesota*

Neil Martin interprets Galatians giving due weight to the fact that converts inevitably employ their existing cultural and religious resources to help understand and live their new faith. It makes a very significant difference, allowing Martin to illuminate the puzzle of Paul's linking of the temptation for the Galatians to place themselves under the law with regression to their previous pagan religious practices (Gal. 4:8-10). In the process critical questions are raised about Paul's relationship with Judaism and a fresh discernment proposed of the contemporary significance of his struggle in Galatia. All interpreters of Galatians will benefit greatly from engagement with this stimulating and thoughtful perspective on the letter.

—*Stephen Chester, Lord and Lady Coggan Professor of New Testament, Wycliffe College, Toronto*

Neil Martin offers an innovative and subtle interpretation of a number of the thorniest interpretative quandaries in Galatians. Along the way, he also provides a map of the main schools of Pauline theology, an introduction to the probable religious habits of the Galatians before their conversion, and an investigation of the contemporary relevance of Paul's pastoral theology. Students of Paul's letters (including those of us who have been reading Paul for years) are certain to come away wiser.

—*Nathan Eubank, Rev. John A. O'Brien Associate Professor of Theology, Notre Dame*

Galatians is a puzzle in many ways, partly because Paul is so angry about encouraging Jewish practices that he is unconcerned about elsewhere. Neil Martin has more emotional intelligence than anyone I've ever met, so I'm not surprised he has found this solution to the conundrum. His suggestion, that Paul is concerned about the insidious effects of old habits, is so obvious once it's pointed out, it becomes difficult to read Paul's letter in any other way. In this work, he shows how churches in all cultures - not just those in first century Galatia - suffer from similar serious problems.

—*David Instone-Brewer, Senior Research Fellow, Tyndale House, Cambridge*

How can Paul say that for the Gentile Christians to keep the Jewish law would be for them to return to their pagan past? Without either taking Sinai to be a covenant of works or denying the threat of legalism in the human heart, Neil Martin offers a fresh reading of Galatians that explains why keeping the good law of God would have been so dangerous for these converted Gentiles. In the course of exploring the context and content of the letter he communicates deep exegetical and historical work with engaging clarity and the pace of a whodunnit. But the real sting comes at the end of the book when he brings Paul's warnings as he has explained them to bear upon the contemporary church. This section will open up new vistas of application for preachers far beyond the standard quest for the contemporary Gentile equivalent to circumcision. Taken seriously, its searching critique has the potential to upturn our entire approach to evangelism and Christian discipleship.

—*Garry Williams, Director, Pastors Academy*

To some modern readers, Paul's letter to the Galatians may appear to be more of a battleground for divergent perspectives within Pauline scholarship than a piece of pastoral communication. In *Galatians Reconsidered*, Neil Martin offers a fresh reading of Paul's remarkable letter then engages carefully with the letter in its historical and literary context so as to highlight its pastoral and missiological impact. Martin argues creatively that Paul addresses not primarily the actual teaching of the Jewish 'agitators' but the way in which that teaching might have been *understood* by Galatians who were tempted to 'regress' to former pagan patterns of thought and behaviour. This is a fascinating study combining engaging prose with attention to detail. It has significance for understanding Paul's ancient letter and for contemporary missiological practice. Students, preachers, and other serious readers will benefit from careful reading of this book.

—*Alistair I. Wilson, Lecturer in Mission and New Testament, Director of Postgraduate Studies, Edinburgh Theological Seminary*

When writing on Galatians, scholars face two temptations. The first is the conceit that, despite centuries of interpretation, you have, at long last, finally discovered *the* interpretive key to Paul's most controverted letter. The other is to get so buried in minutiae that you lose touch with its life-changing relevance. In *Galatians Reconsidered*, Neil Martin admirably resists both temptations. Creatively drawing on an understanding of the power of habit and applying this insight to the concern Paul has for the Galatians' regression to the patterns of their pagan past, Martin offers a reading coherent for Pauline scholars that is also compelling for twenty-first century readers. Galatians is so much more than sophisticated soteriology; it's an actionable vision of Christian discipleship—as needed in Paul's day as it is in ours. While one may take issue with Martin's interpretation, this is a brilliantly executed argument and a pleasure to read. Highly recommended!

—*Todd Wilson, PhD, Cofounder & President, The Center for Pastor Theologians*

GALATIANS
RECONSIDERED

Neil Martin

APOLLOS (an imprint of Inter-Varsity Press)
36 Causton Street, London SW1P 4ST, England
Email: ivp@ivpbooks.com
Website: www.ivpbooks.com

First published 2022

British Library Cataloguing-in-Publication Data
A catalogue record for this book is available from the British Library.

ISBN: 978-1-78974-389-0
eBook ISBN: 978-1-78974-390-6

Typeset in the United States of America
Printed and bound by CPI Group (UK) Ltd., Croydon, CR0 4YY

Produced on paper from sustainable forests

*Inter-Varsity Press publishes Christian books that are true to the Bible and that communicate the
gospel, develop discipleship and strengthen the church for its mission in the world.*

*IVP originated within the Inter-Varsity Fellowship, now the Universities and Colleges Christian
Fellowship, a student movement connecting Christian Unions in universities and colleges throughout
Great Britain, and a member movement of the International Fellowship of Evangelical Students.
Website: www.uccf.org.uk. That historic association is maintained, and all senior IVP staff and
committee members subscribe to the UCCF Basis of Faith.*

For Ruth

Contents

Contents

Part II
GOING BACKWARDS IN GALATIA

Contents

Part III
GOING FORWARDS WITH PAUL

Contents

Preface and Acknowledgements

I like stories that return at the end to the place where they started, and this book is that kind of story. By the time we reach the final page, Christianity, and Paul, and the particular slice of Paul's thought we're going to be training our attention on here – his claim in Galatians that men and women are not justified by 'works of the law' but by faith in Christ – turn out to be, at root, the same things the church has affirmed them to be, by and large, since the earliest centuries of its existence. Justification is a movement from God towards people, offered to all and needed by all, a great rectification of our estrangement from him – crediting righteousness to the unrighteous through union with Christ in his death, resurrection and glorious ascension.

But like those stories, the reassuring familiarity of the final outcome gives a rather false impression of the journey that has led there. This book documents a seven-year adventure through the intricacies of Pauline theology chasing an intuition – a hunch – that the 'Old' and the 'New' and the 'Radical New' Perspectives on Paul *each* hold pieces of the 'justification' puzzle and yet *none* of them accounts for it all. Paul does indeed dichotomize salvation by faith and salvation by works in Galatians, but that doesn't necessarily make his opponents legalists or undermine the fact that he himself upheld 'the works of the law' and joyfully participated in them among his fellow Jews with absolute consistency. For Paul, the problem with these works was their propensity to reanimate the *pagan* religious presuppositions of his Gentile readers – presuppositions which, as we will shortly see, have survived and continue to thrive, spelling danger for Christians today in much the same way they spelled danger in the past.

Moving from the archaeology of upland Anatolia to painstaking lexical research in the bowels of the Bodleian library without the safety net of subscription to pre-packaged theological syntheses, *Galatians Reconsidered* weaves harmony out of dissonance by returning to the letter's original historical setting and to the exegetical strategies of its earliest interpreters. In the process, Galatians emerges not only as a touchstone for the apostle's understanding of Christ and the significance of his achievements but also as a potent case study in pastoral wisdom, deeply challenging superficial modern concepts of Christian discipleship.

Galatians Reconsidered is at once distinct from and intimately related to my doctoral thesis, published in 2020 as *Regression in Galatians*, and written under the supervision of Professor Markus Bockmuehl at Oxford University. The two books share almost nothing in terms of their actual text but almost all the ideas developed and applied in the chapters ahead were formed and tested in that earlier project. This, as I can now see clearly, is the book I was *trying* to write all along. But I am grateful for the wise hand that slowed me down and made me think, and rethink, and revisit the argument before beginning to locate it in the landscape of its larger consequences. I am grateful to my examiners, Professors Nathan Eubank and Cilliers Breytenbach, for their encouragement and careful scrutiny; to the members of the New Testament Seminar at the Faculty of Theology and Religion in Oxford for their stimulating company and searching questions; and to Markus, in particular, for his patience with a natural pastor itching to *apply* ideas that needed time to mature in the rich soil of academic rigour before emerging into the daylight. The work is gigantically better for his input.

When the time came to approach potential publishing partners, I couldn't have asked for better support in my corner than my former colleague and sister-in-creative-arms at HarperCollins, Belinda Budge, who lent her vast experience, insight and energy to the project, steering the proposal towards our erstwhile teammate, Sam Richardson at SPCK, and through Sam to IVP/Apollos. Tom Creedy at IVP has been an outstanding editor, guiding me through the acquisitions and editorial processes with consummate skill and good humour. This book is very much *our* project now and *we* very much hope *you* like it!

I am significantly indebted as an author to friends and colleagues in each of the three ministry areas that have occupied my attention in the years since I completed my research.

Special thanks are due to Professor Garry Williams at London Seminary for his willingness to support my almost total devotion to writing through the summer of 2021, and for his careful, thoughtful, insightful and encouraging interaction with both the first draft and the final edited version of the manuscript. Bill James, Matthew Mason, John Benton, Malcolm MacGregor, Steve Bowers, Phil Raine and Hadden Turner all played valuable parts in creating the supportive and encouraging environment in which this project was completed. Two full cohorts of students at the Seminary unwittingly endured incompletely digested versions of the material that follows, and I am grateful for their insights, for their good questions, and for several memorable penny-dropping moments along the way – both for the class members and the lecturer.

This project would simply not have happened without the encouragement, friendship and support of the church family at Oxford Evangelical Presbyterian Church who patiently tolerated my withdrawal from teaching and pastoral responsibilities for several months during the final stages of writing and demonstrated a bottomless willingness to pray for my progress. Our pastor, and my good friend, Andy Young, continues to amaze me not only with his stamina and interest in this and every other project being incubated in our congregation, but with his relentless determination to practise the grace that he so faithfully preaches. Andy's enthusiasm and belief in me, and his incredibly high tolerance for reading raw draft chapters are the main reasons why the third part of this book exists.

While writing *Galatians Reconsidered*, I have also overseen the emergence of a small Christian charity called 'B-Less', focussed on identifying and equipping graduate students to serve as mentors and encouragers among Christian undergrads in British universities and helping them reach out to their friends with the gospel. All three of the brilliant B-Less scholars who served with us in the first year of the Charity's existence – Noel Cheong, Andrew Cowan and Alberto Solano – read through the first draft of the text and offered insightful comments in our biweekly colloquia. I am particularly grateful to the trustees of B-Less – George DiWakar, John-Mark Teeuwen, Nick Wu and Andy Young – and to our ministry board in the United States – Tripp and Kelli Corl, Derek and Tiffany DeLange, Don and Lynn Howe, Tony and Mary-Ellen Kubat, Justin and Marguerite Sellers, and Dan and Faith Van Enk – for their unfailing support for this project, and for generously sanctioning the use of time and resources necessary to bring it to completion.

Several other friends and colleagues generously devoted time to reading and commenting on large sections of the text, among whom I particularly want to thank Stephen Chester, George DiWakar, David Instone-Brewer, Herald Gandi, Bethany Lucas, John-Mark Teeuwen and Taman Turbinton.

My wife, Ruth, and our four amazing children – Ginny, Willow, Sam and Robin – have been cheering me on along this journey with Galatians for longer now than most of us can remember. I'm so grateful to all of them for their unfailing belief in this project and for our shared commitment as a family – weak and less-than-ordinary though we are – to the health and vitality of God's church and to the aspiration that his message of undeserved favour from heaven to earth would land with its full force and impact in a world much more like Paul's world than most of us imagine, a world vulnerable, as a result, to many of the same spiritual dangers. We offer this book with a prayer that, where its contents are good and true, God might use it to encourage and to challenge and to lift his people's eyes to him, renouncing self-confidence and discovering, in practice, the truth of Paul's famous words, 'I no longer live but Christ lives in me.'

Oxford, June 2022.

Prologue

Introduction

This is a book about the power of habits – the surprising tenacity of our habitual assumptions and their potential to reassert themselves whenever we return to circumstances similar to those in which they first formed.

I buy an electric toothbrush. My dentist tells me to hold it *steady* and glide it *gently* across the surface of my teeth. But when I stand in my familiar bathroom and squeeze out a blob of my familiar toothpaste and bring the brush up to my mouth in my familiar way, irrespective of my dentist's advice, my hand jerks involuntarily back and forth so uncontrollably that I literally have to grab hold of it with the other hand to make it stop.

Why? This disturbing experience is not in fact the onset of Parkinson's disease but the visible manifestation of an entrenched connection between a certain set of circumstantial cues and a behaviour that's become associated with them through years of repetitive reinforcement. I've stood and brushed my teeth *manually* in that same posture, back and forth, back and forth, every day of my life since childhood. Put me back in that same situation, put my hands back in that same position relative to my face and equip them with a toothbrush – *any kind of toothbrush* – and they repeat that familiar behaviour without conscious direction. Perhaps I'm on my own here, but it's taken me several years of determined effort, including some very deliberate changes to my stance and the order in which I do things, to erase that piece of programming from my mind and body.

What has all that got to do with Galatians?

From the earliest days of Christian reflection on the documents of the New Testament, Paul's letter to the Galatians has claimed attention as one of the prime sources for our understanding of the gospel. What is it that we affirm about the coming of Christ? What is it that we believe about his life, death and resurrection, and what consequences follow? Despite its obscure origins in a dispute about Gentile converts embracing Jewish laws, the church throughout the centuries has found a touchstone here for thoughtful, believing interaction with these questions. And it's been exposed to an extraordinary degree of scholarly scrutiny as a result.

Where were the Galatian churches? Who were the 'Agitators' who were causing all the problems there and where did they come from? What does Paul mean by justification by faith? How does it relate to his bold statements about union, indeed co-crucifixion, with Christ? Do we see continuity, discontinuity or both in Paul's journey from zealous Pharisee to bold advocate for the gospel of Jesus? How do his negative remarks about 'the works of the law' integrate with his positive remarks about 'the law of Christ'?

The problem with all these questions, and with all of our answers, is the problem of *coherence*. Credible solutions to individual parts of the puzzle are legion, making sense of Paul's text piece by tiny piece. But if the goal of all good interpretation is a holistic reading, the problem with this procedure is the pieces that stubbornly refuse to fit. Tidy Paul up in one place as a total opponent of Jewish legal observances and problems break out in another with, say, his willingness to partner with law-observant Jews in the wider proclamation of the gospel (Gal. 2:9–10). Package Paul up as a polemicist against legal observances functioning as a means to define the boundaries of the believing community, and now the severity of his warnings seems out of place (Gal. 5:2, 4).

In this book, the goal is not to tear up the various 'solutions' on offer and declare a new day, but rather to show how the best parts of them integrate when we stop and take notice of a single neglected element, an element by no means unique to Galatians but common to Paul's letters more broadly and central to his pastoral theology: the simple fact that his readers, like all of us, were creatures of habit.

Paul wrote Galatians to a church of immature Gentile converts with muscle memory already established in the sphere of religious devotion. When he makes – and then doggedly repeats – the seemingly bizarre assertion that embracing *Jewish* norms is going to involve a return to their *pagan* religious past, he isn't claiming that Judaism is somehow equivalent to pagan worship. No, he's worried that if his readers continue along this path the assumptions they've imbibed in their past lives as pagans will reassert themselves in the present, even at the cost of distorting the very Jewish customs they now claim to follow.

Food laws, sacred calendars and costly personal sacrifices like circumcision held no fear for Jewish Christ-followers like Paul who had learned at their mothers' knees that 'a person [was] not justified by the works of the law, but by faith...' (Gal. 2:15–16, cf. 3:6–9, 11). But for believing Gentiles, these things were powerfully associated with equivalent practices in their former religious lives. Give them *new* religious laws to keep, and the assumptions that went along with their *old* laws couldn't fail to be reawakened.

This is the insight we'll be chasing in the chapters ahead. And as we do so, I hope to show that *coherence* is the result. With regression to the Galatians' habitual expectations about religious behaviour and what it achieves reinstated as the problem, the letter emerges as a compelling whole – both in its original context and as a pressing challenge to the church today.

Prospect

Taking Paul's regression language seriously in Galatians and reframing our understanding of his argument accordingly yields an exciting and much-needed reassertion of its unity and contemporary relevance. Does the classic Pauline dichotomy between faith and works intentionally deny the possibility that humans can oblige God to bless them, as the Reformers argued? *I believe it does.* But does that mean his Jewish opponents saw works as a way to impose such an obligation? *Not necessarily.* Noting the risk that *pagan* religious expectations could be reactivated when immature converts embraced *Jewish* religious practice brokers a refreshing compatibility between Paul's positive attitude to law among Jewish Christians and the extremity of his concern for Gentiles.

In Galatians, Paul presents justification by faith in relief against *pagan* attitudes to religious works. He surely had opinions about Jewish 'legalism' and 'nationalism', but Galatians isn't the place to go to see them clearly. Paul's problem with his audience had to do with the fundamentally *Jewish* concept of divine–human interaction that *he had taught them* being displaced by pagan alternatives that made the gods dependent on their human worshippers, capable of being incentivized more or less effectively to give them what they wanted. We don't have to believe Paul opposed Jewish law *itself* to see his gospel in its true colours in Galatians. All we need is the realization that he opposed 'the works of the law' *as they were being misappropriated by his recently converted readers.*

Re-establishing the problem of pastoring recent converts at the heart of Galatians opens our eyes to the apostle's positive vision for Christian maturity. His correspondents' former pagan devotions were casting a long shadow over the present – a shadow so long that, for Paul, the only safe response was immediate, outright rejection of the superficially similar practices they were being urged to adopt. But he didn't want his readers to *stay* in that fragile place. On the contrary, his extensive exposition of the theme of life in the Spirit outlines a path towards growth and stability, enabling Gentiles and Jews alike to 'fulfil the law of Christ' (Gal. 6:2), freely affirming with Paul that 'neither circumcision nor uncircumcision means anything; what counts is the new creation' (Gal. 6:15).

Christian community too is an important thread in the fabric of our story, but with regression re-established as its central motif, previously muted implications are brought to new prominence. Yes, Jewish laws marked ethnic boundaries in Paul's world, and the negotiation of those boundaries was a significant issue in the emergent mixed communities of the early church (Gal. 2:11–21). But the primary focus of Galatians is nonetheless subtly and importantly different. Jewish Christian teachers in Galatia wielded law as a means to shut Gentiles out (Gal. 4:17). But, for Paul, the collateral damage was a more pressing concern. It was their failure to grasp the importance of accommodation more than their failure to understand the finer points of soteriology that drove Paul's strident response to his opponents in the letter. They failed to take the weaknesses of their hearers into account. They failed to moderate their enthusiasm for the law in the light of the damage it could do to others, driving them unwittingly into the arms of 'another gospel' animated by deep-seated pagan assumptions. With regression as our guide, accommodation attains a new and overdue prominence in the letter, emerging as a key point of connection to the larger landscape of Paul's life and theology.

Beyond the confines of the New Testament, intriguingly similar patristic interactions with Paul's argument resurface from obscurity. Circumstances akin to the Galatian situation in settings scattered from fourth-century Carthage to the furthermost reaches of the Carolingian Empire illustrate the churches' waning sensitivity to the letter's original context and the disastrous pastoral consequences of failing to take habituated religious attitudes into consideration as part of the process of discipleship. Deepening blindness to the ongoing importance of entrenched *pagan* norms is exposed in the emerging Protestant tendency to misattribute medieval Catholic perspectives on works to Paul's *Jewish* contemporaries.

Christian converts today are no longer recruited from past lives of worship in the temples of Asclepius and Cybele, but the conviction that 'religious' actions make it possible to secure the futures we believe we deserve is still very much alive. Readings limiting the scope of Galatians to an intramural debate between first-century Jewish sects enforce a false sense of distance from the text on scholars and pastors alike. In reality, quasi-pagan attitudes to health, wealth, image and career dominate the landscape of modern Christianity, and Galatians has them squarely in its sights. Paul's warnings about practices with deep-rooted associations to pre-Christian and extra-Christian norms aim directly at forms of Christian discipleship that have become conventional across our increasingly globalized world. Christians in secular societies today don't think about works in the way Jews did, they think about them like Paul's Gentile readers did, and they need the same medicine. Accommodation is a pressing need in multicultural congregations where the priority of listening to and understanding the implications of our actions for believers from other backgrounds has rarely been so important. Read with regression at its centre, the urgency and polemical edge of Galatians snaps back into focus and the letter finds its church-changing, life-giving voice.

Now, the danger with a project like this, of course, is that it degenerates into yet another revisionist attempt to prove that 'everyone was wrong about Paul before *I* came along'. I don't know about you, but I've read too many of those books and this is not going to be another. *Galatians Reconsidered* is about working *with* the great teachers of the church. Certainly, there are new things I want to suggest, and old things I want to recover. But at its core, the argument hangs on the realization that Old Perspectives, New Perspectives and Radical New Perspectives alike *all* hold parts of the larger puzzle. The contribution I'm seeking to make here lies in the realm of *putting them together*. *Galatians Reconsidered* doesn't pretend to be 'the answer' – some kind of mythic passport to *complete* understanding. It joins with God's people through the centuries in the work of faithfully *seeking* understanding. If it proves useful in that larger endeavour, in whole or in part, and if it's surpassed by subsequent books that see further as a result, I will be more than content.

Part I

OPENING UP THE TEXT

1

The Problem With the
Problem in Galatia

Introduction

One of the reasons Galatians remains such an intriguing text is the fact that it stubbornly resists simplistic attempts to articulate the underlying problem it was written to address. That a problem existed is clear enough – Galatians is the only letter in the New Testament where Paul dispenses with his characteristic introductory thanksgiving formulae and dives straight into the fray:

> *I am astonished that you are so quickly deserting the one who called you to live in the grace of Christ and are turning to a different gospel – which is really no gospel at all.* (Gal. 1:6–7)

His appeal is urgent, his call to action absolute. Galatians reads like an attempt to snatch a child from in front of a speeding car. But what *is* the car? What is it that, in Paul's mind, is about to smash the faith of his vulnerable Gentile Christian readers to smithereens?

All we have left to guide us as we seek an answer to this question is a single letter affording a fleeting glimpse into a relationship with a larger history that both the sender and the recipients could assume but which, to us, remains stubbornly inaccessible. Acknowledging these limitations and the tensions and ambiguities that exist within even the incomplete snapshot of the situation that remains to us is an indispensable first step if we want to see the underlying problem more clearly and, aided by that clarity, to speak with more confidence about the gospel that Paul was seeking to defend.

1 Knowns and Unknowns in the Context

Galatians was certainly written by Paul and that makes it *early* – earlier by some distance than any of the other extrabiblical sources of insight into the life of the emergent Christian movement to which we might

3

turn.[1] Quite where we should position it relative to the rest of the *biblical* data, however, and where its composition fits in along Paul's larger biographical timeline, are debated questions. Early estimates place it in the late AD 40s, late estimates ten or more years later – with implications either way for the maturity of the church's approach to Jewish and Gentile integration and, in some reconstructions, implications for the maturity of Paul's own thought.

Recent developments in Pauline scholarship have tended to favour dates at the earlier end of this spectrum. Computer reconstructions of ancient travel routes have enabled improved approximations for the duration of Paul's missionary adventures.[2] Archaeological and textual studies have narrowed the range of chronological options for certain key events in his life.[3] Scholars debate whether or not the meeting in Jerusalem described in Galatians 2:1–10 should be equated with Luke's portrait of the Jerusalem Council in Acts 15, forcing the Galatian crisis into the period after Paul's separation from Barnabas (Acts 15:36–41). But whatever conclusion we come to about the relationship between the epistles and Acts, there's still no reason to assume the composition of the letter transgresses the boundaries of the AD 40s or that the gap between its composition and Paul's original encounter with his readers was anything other than short (certainly less than five years, perhaps as little as eighteen months).[4] Whichever way we put the data together, the error bars for Pauline chronology are set quite narrowly by ancient-historical standards. But, for all this progress, much remains shrouded in doubt and we do well to remember that our launching point for this investigation is still not as secure *in time* as we might ideally like it to be.

---

1 That Galatians was indeed written *by Paul* has never been seriously disputed – although this probably says more about its preoccupation with the theological themes that preoccupied the minds of early critical scholars than it does about anything intrinsically 'less Pauline' in the letters that *were disputed* (the point is drawn out with entertaining clarity by Harold Hoehner in his article 'Did Paul Write Galatians?' – Hoehner 2006: 150–169). Galatians, of course, famously highlights the distinction between material taken down by Paul's amanuensis and material written 'with [his] own hand' (Gal. 6:11) – a distinction that might have led to questions about authorship akin to those surrounding 2 Thessalonians (see esp. 2 Thess. 2:2; 3:17) along some hypothetical alternative critical trajectory (see Betz 1979: 1).

2 See, for example, the Stanford Geospatial Network Model of the Roman World, ORBIS (www.orbis .stanford.edu).

3 Note, for example, the discussion narrowing the window of probable dates for Paul's meeting with the Roman Proconsul of Achaia, L. Junius Gallio, as recorded in Acts 18:12–17, to a period lasting as little as a few months in the summer of AD 51 (see Jewett 1979: 38–40, Murphy-O'Connor 2012: 15–18).

4 For a more thorough exploration of the relationship between Acts and Galatians, see Martin 2020: 13–47.

Neither is our launching point entirely secure *in space*. The letter was certainly written to churches in the Roman province of Galatia which accounted for a substantial swathe of eastern central Asia Minor in the first century, stretching from Ankara in the north almost as far as the Cilician coast in the south. Quite where within this vast area 'the churches of Galatia' (Gal. 1:2) actually were, however, is another debated question. Some claim that Paul used the term 'Galatians' (Gal. 3:1) as an ethnic identifier – and that the Galatian churches must therefore have been located in the north where Gaulish mercenaries had settled three centuries before, giving the region its name.[5] But this argument is inconclusive, and even if Paul's audience *were* ethnic Galatians, there were plenty of them living in the south by the time the letter was written, thanks to their widespread deployment as soldiers during the convulsions that gave birth to the Roman empire.[6]

The alternative, and increasingly dominant, view is that the Galatian churches were located in the south. Early Christian inscriptions cluster around southern cities, including an unusual concentration of epitaphs to individuals named Paul.[7] Evidence of Jewish communities, whose presence in the orbit of the Galatian churches seems necessary to make sense of the letter as a whole, is sparse in the south but this does at least compare favourably with the situation in the north where it is completely absent.[8] 2 Timothy and Acts both speak about Paul's activities in this region – referring to the churches he planted (Acts 13–14) and to the persecutions he endured (Acts 13:50; 14:5, 19; 2 Tim. 3:11).[9] Paul may even allude to these persecutions in Galatians itself if the reminiscences about his first meeting with his readers in Galatians 4:13 and the 'illness' (lit. 'weakness of the flesh') that gave rise to it refer to the same events described in Acts 14:19–20 – viz. his flight from Lystra to Derbe after suffering such a brutal stoning that the onlookers thought he was dead.[10] None of this, however, is made *explicit* in the text.

In addition to the identity and physical location of the Galatians, the identity of Paul's opponents in the letter is also in doubt. In and of themselves, efforts to solve this problem represent a substantial seam in modern New Testament scholarship. Indeed, whole edifices have been constructed on the slender

---

5   See, for example, Martyn 1997: 16.

6   See Breytenbach 1996: 154–159.

7   See Breytenbach et al. 2018: 73–91.

8   See Breytenbach 1996: 127–133, 144–148.

9   Even sceptical accounts of Acts and the pastoral epistles have to wrestle with these data as credible early testimonies to the extent of Paul's missionary endeavours (see Martin 2020: 18, 23–25).

10 See Hays 2000: 293–294.

evidence afforded by the text, most notably F.C. Baur's hugely influential hypothesis that the Jewish teachers in Galatia were part of a militant, organized anti-Paul faction from Jerusalem whose telltale fingerprints can also be detected in Philippians and other Pauline contexts, and whose existence discloses an irrevocable parting of the ways between the Gentile and Jewish churches led by Paul and Peter respectively.[11]

As we will see in the next chapter, the quest for conclusions here is complicated by the fact that Galatians is a polemical text. Paul does not sit down and calmly introduce his *dramatis personae* with names and addresses before setting out the issues to be discussed in a measured list of bullet points. Paul is tearing his hair out, and everything he says about the people now influencing his readers has to be read within that context. Strict limitations must be observed as we try to move from the text we have to inferences about the actual underlying situation. I will assume only that Paul's opponents were Jewish Christians, that they challenged the adequacy of his apostolic credentials, that they insisted on circumcision and observance of the Jewish law, and that they made their case with reference to the Abraham story in Genesis.[12] Beyond that, we will leave the question of their identity open. Indeed, it will become clear as we move forward that the question of their identity is less central to our understanding of the letter than is normally imagined if, in fact, Paul's critique was not directed at what the opponents themselves thought but rather at the impact of their thinking on their recently converted pagan hearers.

2 Incongruities in the Text

Alongside unresolved questions about its historical context, Galatians also exhibits incongruities and tensions within the text itself.

2.1 The Integrity of Paul's Argument

First, we note a tension affecting its thematic and pastoral integrity. Whoever Paul's opponents were, and whatever their motives, there is little doubt about the essence of their demands. Submitting to circumcision and embracing Jewish law were requirements for them, indispensable conditions of integration into the Abrahamic family. And for Paul this was totally unacceptable. 'If you

---

11 See Baur 1878, vol. 1: 44–60.

12 Here, I am consciously working within the guidelines established by John Barclay in his classic 1987 article 'Mirror-Reading a Polemical Letter: Galatians as a Test Case', which still sets the benchmark for restrained exegetical sanity in a field plagued by overambitious reconstructions of the data (Barclay 1987: 73–93).

let yourselves be circumcised,' he writes, 'Christ will be of no value to you at all… You who are trying to be justified by the law have been alienated from Christ; you have fallen away from grace' (Gal. 5:2, 4). Paul is incredibly, uncomfortably bold here. And yet, within a chapter, he's making lists of dos and don'ts and telling his readers to fulfil 'the law of Christ' (Gal. 6:2).

How can this be?[13] This is the point at which several commentators divide the audience in Galatia in two. In the first part of the letter Paul deals with legalists susceptible to the ministry of law-observant Jews; in the second part he deals with libertines turning his original proclamation of grace into a mandate to live as they please.[14] Others favour an even more drastic approach. Perhaps the difficulty here betrays the clumsy hand of an editor splicing together originally distinct texts intended for different situations, perhaps even for different audiences?[15]

Unitary readings have, of course, been explored, but even the best of them see signs of Pauline naivety here. His proclamation of the gospel among Gentiles like the Galatians without legal obligations, indeed without substantial ethical guidance of any kind – though charming – was hopelessly idealistic. And now the birds were coming home to roost. Thanks to the vacuum he bequeathed to his readers where the rigorous observances of their pagan religious affiliations used to stand, they were now being drawn towards Jewish Christianity which at least had something constructive to offer in their place. But the damage had already been done. Paul's 'law free' gospel had left moral anarchy in his wake. The transition he performs from warnings to ethics as we move through the letter shouldn't be attributed to policy on Paul's part but to frantic back-pedalling, steering his spiritual protégés away from Judaism and then backfilling urgently needed moral instruction as fast as his amanuensis could take it down.[16]

2.2 The Complexity of Paul's Stance Concerning Law

A second more subtle but equally troubling internal tension should also be noted here. Paul, as we've just seen, opposed law-observant Jewish Christians in Galatia, and he considered law-observance toxic for his readers. Law is associated with 'the present evil age' in the letter (Gal. 1:4) and with the past from which God called Paul himself by grace (Gal. 1:15; 4:4–5). Law is associated

---

13 Barclay provides a helpful summary of the extant interpretative options in his volume dedicated to the integration of Pauline polemic and paraenesis in Galatians, *Obeying the Truth* (see Barclay 1988: 9–23).

14 See, for example, Hardin: 2008; Kahl: 2009.

15 See, for example, O'Neill: 1972.

16 Barclay himself proposes a unitary reading of this type (see Barclay: 1988).

with a curse affecting all humanity, and it is powerless to affect our deliverance (Gal. 3:10–12). Law is a 'guardian' given charge over God's people until Christ's coming, a slavemaster to whom it would be madness to return (Gal. 3:23–4:7). It's associated with captivity, not freedom (Gal. 4:21–23), with the earthly and not the heavenly realm (Gal. 4:24–26). Indeed, it's hard to imagine how Paul could have been more negative about law in the letter if he'd spent a month of Sundays trying. And yet even in a composition containing such striking anti-legal elements, there are discordant notes.

The most obvious occurs in Paul's account of the Jerusalem meeting in Galatians 2:1–10 where, with Barnabas and Titus, he meets Peter, James and John, and the group agree not only on a common policy regarding circumcision but on a division of the task of evangelism throughout the known world, assigning leadership of the mission among Jews to Peter and leadership of the mission among Gentiles to Paul himself (Gal. 2:6–10). The striking detail to note here is that the men with whom Paul brokers this arrangement are not just fellow Christians, but *law-observant Jewish* Christians. For all the negative things he has to say about law before and after this, for all the dangers with which law-observance was clearly connected in his mind, these are men with whom Paul was plainly happy to be associated (while being careful, of course, not to acknowledge them as the *source* of his authority, cf. Gal. 1:1, 11–12, 18–20). He was glad to share the right hand of fellowship with them and he proactively disclosed his partnership with them, even in the midst of an argument designed, in the opinion of many commentators, to do nothing less than expose their way of life as a desecration of the gospel.

James's law-observant inclinations become painfully apparent in the section immediately following, when his representatives arrive in Antioch hoping to steer the church there in a direction more palatable to Jews in Jerusalem (Gal. 2:11–13). Peter, at least initially, seems to have pursued a different policy, falling in with the established Antiochian practice of eating with Gentiles. But not even this should be read as an indication that he had abandoned law-observance altogether. That the law required abstinence from certain foods is well known, and it's easy to assume that it also proscribed eating with Gentiles. But this is not, in fact, the case.[17] When table fellowship with Gentiles was forsworn among Jews, it was a pragmatic step designed to avoid situations where breaches of the food laws *might* occur.[18] But it wasn't an article of the law itself.

---

17 David Rudolph offers a penetrating analysis of the issues surrounding table fellowship with Gentiles in the Jewish diaspora of the period (see Rudolph: 2011).

18 Rudolph 2011: 120–130, 155–159.

When Peter ate with Gentile Christians in Antioch, he might have eaten different food, or the Gentiles with him might have eaten kosher food. Both of these strategies are abundantly attested in other law-observant Jewish contexts.[19] Not even the Antioch Incident, then, *actually demonstrates* an abandonment of law-observance on Peter's part – or Paul's for that matter. What it demonstrates is that Jewish Christian leaders at this early stage in the church's growth were still working out the implications of the gospel for their former practices and not always coming to the same conclusions.

And the same observation is reinforced when we look more broadly. Cooperation with, and indeed deference to, law-observant Jewish Christians is evident in 1 Corinthians, in Paul's acknowledgment of Peter as a worthy leader in the church (1 Cor. 3:21–23) and his description of himself as 'the least of the apostles' (1 Cor. 15:9). Acts famously records the circumcision of Timothy at Paul's own hands, perhaps within a few months of the composition of Galatians and probably in a very similar geographical location (Acts 16:1–3). Paul faces the accusation that he tells Jews 'not to circumcise their children or live according to [their] customs' during his final recorded visit to Jerusalem in Acts 21:21 and, on most conventional exegeses, we expect him to plead guilty as charged. But he doesn't. On the contrary, he defends himself against this misrepresentation of his practice, performing the legal purification rites expected for himself and his Gentile companions and hastening to the temple to make arrangements for the necessary sacrifices (Acts 21:26).[20] In Acts 18:18 he takes a Nazirite vow. In 2 Corinthians 11:24 he submits to synagogue discipline. Any coherent reading of Galatians in its larger scriptural context has to take these seemingly incongruous observations into account.

2.3 The Extremity of Paul's Warnings

A third tension also looms into focus, namely, the *extremity* of Paul's warnings about law-observance in the lives of his readers. This is clearly more than a matter of mere preference – the Galatians' very salvation is at stake. We've already noted the climactic expressions of his disquiet in Galatians 5:2, 4 where he directly equates circumcision with apostasy. But the same extraordinary intensity of concern is evident throughout the letter: in Galatians 1:6–7, where his readers' actions are described as 'deserting the one who called you to live in the grace of Christ' and 'turning to a different gospel – which is really no

---

19 Consider, for example, Ptolemy's reception of the Jewish elders in Alexandria, as recorded by Josephus (Ant. 12.94–97)

20 See Thiessen 2016: 164–167.

gospel at all'; in Galatians 3:1–4, where he condemns his readers' behaviour as folly, attributing it to bewitchment, and wrestles with the possibility that their apparent progress along the journey of discipleship may all have been in vain; and in Galatians 4:11, where the theme of wasted effort is resumed, and Paul expresses his fear that his audience may not in fact be converts at all.

All of this is comprehensible if we adopt a reading in which law itself is a bad thing in the New Covenant era which Paul and his fellow apostles had been charged with announcing. But as soon as we entertain the idea that, for Paul, law is *not* a threat to the gospel in all situations, the extremity of his language starts to feel very uncomfortable. If, as James Dunn has so influentially argued, the problem with law in Galatians is *really* that it's being misapplied as a system of 'boundary markers' by disruptive Jewish Christians – if Jewish festivals and circumcision are being misused as litmus tests for authentic membership in the community – then why does Paul give his readers such a hard time about it?[21] 'Why is Paul so opposed to Gentile circumcision?' writes Paula Fredriksen. 'What was so terrible about Gentile circumcision that it even undid the benefit of Christ?'[22]

In subsequent chapters, we'll grapple with a whole range of attempts to smooth out this apparent inconsistency. Perhaps Gentile law-observance was self-defeating in Paul's eyes – if God had ordained a completely separate path to effect their integration into his family, and the Jewish path was neither appropriate nor achievable for them? Perhaps Gentile law-observance disturbed Paul because it indicated a lack of appreciation for all that Christ had achieved on their behalf? But even here we have to wonder at the strength of Paul's reaction. For a Gentile Christian to embrace circumcision and submit themselves to the Jewish law might show a lack of understanding of all Christ had achieved, but did it really merit the verdict that he was *no longer of any value* to those who did so (Gal. 5:2)?

2.4 The Apparent Incoherence of Paul's Regression Language

Challenging though these tensions are to readings of the letter that many of us will have received as watertight specimens of responsible exegesis, none of them prepares us for the crowning tension of all. Whatever else is going on in the background, no serious scholar doubts that the Galatians were being urged

---

21 Dunn 2006b: 352; Dunn 2008: 8, 9, 12, 17, 23–28.
22 Fredriksen 2017: 106–107.

to submit to circumcision and Jewish legal observances. And yet, throughout the letter, Paul's diagnosis of the problem is that his readers are going back to their *pagan* past.

This explanatory strategy reaches its climax in Galatians 4:8–11:

> *Formerly, when you did not know God, you were slaves to those who by nature are not gods. But now that you know God – or rather are known by God – how is it that you are turning back to those weak and miserable stoicheia?[23] Do you wish to be enslaved by them all over again? You are observing special days and months and seasons and years! I fear for you, that somehow I have wasted my efforts on you.*

The 'special days and months and seasons and years' here refer, at least super-ficially, to the Jewish Sabbaths and festivals being imposed on the Galatians by Paul's opponents. But the reference to beings 'who by nature are not gods' looks back to their past experience as pagans. Somehow embracing Jewish law was stirring up and reanimating that past – even to the point where their knowledge of God was in doubt. In the Greek text, Paul uses words referring to the resumption of a previously familiar pattern of action four times in verse 9 alone.[24] But this is only the tip of the regressive iceberg.

In Galatians 3:23–29 and 4:1–7, Paul's argument turns on the folly of going back to an inferior religious paradigm with which his readers have prior expe-rience. In Galatians 4:21–31, the famous Hagar and Sarah allegory resumes the same idea – why would you want to go back to a mode of interaction with God marked by slavery when freedom has now been announced? In Galatians 5:1, Paul's familiar phraseology makes perfect sense in context, until we ask our-selves why he feels it necessary to insert the word 'again':

> *It is for freedom that Christ has set us free. Stand firm, then, and do not let yourselves be burdened* again *by a yoke of slavery.*

Even in his retelling of the Antioch Incident, the problem with Peter's behav-iour is expressed in regressive terms. Peter has rebuilt the very things that he destroyed, and it is *this* that identifies him as a lawbreaker (Gal. 2:18).

---

23 Paul's use of the notoriously fluid term *stoicheia* (literally 'elements' – but elements of what?) will be analysed in detail in Chapter 9. Until that point in the argument, I retain the original Greek.

24 See Martin 2020: 117–120.

3. The Problem With the Problem in Galatia

The problem with the problem in Galatia, therefore, is the difficulty of articulating a single, believable account of the crisis that accommodates all the data. Readers throughout history have registered and wrestled with the tensions and contextual lacunae surveyed above. But holding them together has proved far more difficult. In the next two chapters, we'll consider in detail the major options for a unified reading of the letter, noting as we go that the seeming incoherence of Paul's statements about regression is the least well-integrated tension of them all. In the remainder of the book, we'll discover how significant an omission that is if we really want to understand its message.

2

A Jewish Problem

Introduction

From John Chrysostom's fourth-century commentary on Galatians forward to the present day, attempts to produce a holistic account of the crisis that prompted Paul to write have assumed, for the most part, that the underlying problem was *a problem with Judaism*. The famously golden-mouthed pastor saw a direct connection between Paul's text and the situation in his home city of Syrian Antioch where – at least according to his vivid description of events – members of his church were routinely being drawn away to the attractions and amenities on offer at local Jewish synagogues (Adv. Jud. 1.1.5; 1.2.7; 1.3.4–5 etc.). Chrysostom launched his powerful counter-offensive from the battlements of Galatians, telling Christians tempted to embrace Jewish rites that they were 'sick with the Galatians disease' (Adv. Jud. 2.2.3). Any and all encouragements to participate in Jewish religious ceremonies were wholly toxic in Chrysostom's view, binding Christians to a community singled out in scripture for its obstinacy, clinging to laws that had long since been abrogated (Adv. Jud. 1.2.3).[1]

Jumping forward to the sixteenth century, Martin Luther's analogous move from his contemporary context to the text Paul wrote reinforced Chrysostom's interpretation of the Galatian crisis. This time the Judaizing agenda of Paul's Jewish opponents was positioned as a cypher for the excesses of medieval Catholicism.[2] The famous Pauline antithesis of 'Works of the Law' and 'Faith'

---

1 Chrysostom's hostility to Jews and Judaism, of course, has important precursors in the preceding centuries during which the Christian church emerged from, and ultimately came to distinguish itself against, the world of Jewish thought and practice. The late first- or early second-century *Epistle of Barnabas* provides a striking advance indication of the direction of travel (e.g. Barn. 2:4–5; 4:6–14; 14:1–5) but even half a century later, Justin Martyr was still clearly able to entertain the possibility of a viable, distinctively Jewish, response to the message of Jesus (Dial. 46–47). See also Bockmuehl 2006: 191–193.

2 'By reading the phrase as a rejection of works-righteousness the Reformers erroneously project back onto Paul the controversies of their own place and time: The degeneracy of Catholicism that offered forgiveness of sins by the buying of indulgences mirrored for Luther the degeneracy of a Judaism that taught justification by works' (Chester 2017: 324). See also Sanders 1977: 57. Luther's perceived parallel between medieval Catholicism and first-century Judaism is explored more fully in Chapter 13.

appealed to Luther not only as a description of the relationship between divine demands and divine promises in the larger Bible story but of the relationship between the structures he sought to throw down and the structures he sought to create in their place.[3] When Paul taught justification by faith without deeds of the law, he was contradicting Jews who believed 'the Law ought to be kept and Gentiles ought to be circumcised *or else they could not be saved*' (Comm. Gal. 2.1, emphasis mine). When Paul saw the light (literally) and abandoned his 'previous way of life in Judaism' (Gal. 1:13), what he left behind was a slavish observance of the Mosaic law not dissimilar to Luther's own early strivings to implement Catholic dogma (Comm. Gal. 1.14).

Later thinkers in the Reformed tradition would query revisit Luther's broadly negative take on law in the Christian life, but his reading of Galatians – with Judaism positioned squarely as the source of the problem – stuck.[4] Pastoral applications sought contemporary analogies for the Jewish observances that Paul positioned so clearly as dangerous alternatives to faith. Ministers urged their congregants to careful, critical, spiritual reflection – hunting down and eliminating forms of self-assurance based on church attendance, disciplined daily devotions, diligence in giving and all other perceived sources of 'merit'. 'All this is to be avoided,' says the apostle read this way, 'lest we lose our connection to Christ' (Gal. 5:2, 4) – courting, in the process, the very danger he seeks to avoid, but now with *the ruthless elimination of works* established as the false foundation of confidence before God.

1 The Old Perspective on Paul

Over time, Luther's distinctive take on the underlying problem in Galatia found its place within a larger framework of conclusions about Pauline theology commonly referred to today as 'The Old Perspective' on Paul. Judaism was – or at least it had *become* – a religion of works. And the Pauline message of justification by faith was its polar opposite: a unilateral declaration of acquittal for sinful men and women in God's court, appropriated by faith in Christ, irrespective of their moral achievements. Union with Christ was the mechanism within which that declaration was to be understood: when Jesus died, we died *with* him, our thanklessness and guilt was exposed and punished *in* him; and when he rose, *he himself* emerged as the living source of our own

---

3 Chester 2017: 118.

4 On the diverse trajectories within early reformation treatments of law in Paul, see Chester 2017: 118–121.

new life. Our sin was credited to him, his righteousness was credited to us. Much more could be said here, but already in these swift strokes we see the outlines of classic Reformed soteriology.

1.1 The Old Perspective Under Scrutiny

In recent years, this entire paradigm has been challenged by searching questions aimed at what at least purports to be its foundation: the idea that Judaism – or at least Judaism as Paul knew it in the first century – was a religion of works. The watershed moment – although not without important (mainly Jewish) precursors – came with the publication of E.P. Sanders' 1977 book, *Paul and Palestinian Judaism*. Sanders brought needed nuance to the suggestion that Judaism was 'legalistic' with a probing analysis of what 'Judaism' actually meant in the first-century context. *Which* Judaism are we talking about when we say that Judaism was legalistic in Paul's mind? For many of Sanders' readers, the realization that there was more than one option to choose from was new news.[5]

By far the most significant aspect of his argument, however, was the challenge he posed to the accuracy of the suggestion itself. Was there evidence to support the assertion that first-century Jews *of any description* believed they were justified before God and accepted in his sight on the basis of their obedience to the law? Sanders' massive survey of Second Temple Jewish texts, bringing previously inaccessible documents into the mainstream conversation about Paul for the first time, concluded emphatically in the negative. Sanders argued that Jewish authors across the board assumed the priority of divine action in drawing human beings into a relationship with himself. God was the prime mover. God was the covenant proposer. God moved towards Israel not because they were the greatest or the most numerous nation but 'because [he] loved [them]' (Deut. 7:7–8).[6] And from these observations Sanders drew out his now-famous conclusion that Judaism, as Paul knew it, was in fact a religion of grace.[7]

In the subsequent debate, Sanders' proposals have been subjected to critique from every conceivable angle. Is it true to the texts he cites to argue that works played no part in the Jewish concept of acceptance with God?[8] And is his wide-ranging selection of sources wide enough to justify the claim of

---

5 Sanders 1977: 422–423.
6 Barclay 2015: 152.
7 Sanders 1977: 426–427.
8 e.g. Gathercole 2002: 136–139.

complete coverage?[9] Is the distinction he draws between the role of works in 'getting in' and the role of works in 'staying in' a covenant relationship with God sustainable, and should the role of works in final judgment be included as a vital additional consideration?[10] Is his whole analysis, based as it is on discerning a distinctively Jewish 'pattern of religion', dependent on an anachronistic imposition of modern Western ideas to which real first-century Judaism simply fails to conform?[11] This diverse range of questions has generated an even more diverse range of answers.

In the last few years, John Barclay's contribution to the debate has proved particularly valuable, testing the claim that Judaism was 'gracious' against his own insightful analysis of gift-giving in the ancient world. Barclay finds that, wherever gift language is used in ancient texts, it's assumed that *the gift giver* is the party who takes the initiative. But beyond this he finds a whole variety of expectations about the worthiness of gift recipients and the extent of their obligations to respond. Just because Judaism was gracious in the sense that God was the prime mover in establishing the Jews as his special people, there's no necessary reason to believe it was gracious in the sense Paul has in mind when he describes the revolutionary new reality of incorporation into God's family by faith in Christ, irrespective of each individual's suitability for blessing.[12]

But despite the sprawling nature of the ensuing debate and widespread ongoing disagreements about the consequences of Sanders' work, the central thesis of his book has proved remarkably resilient. Very few scholars working on Paul today believe Judaism in the first century was inherently, programmatically wedded to the kind of 'works righteousness' that used to serve as the foil for 'salvation by grace' in less adequately informed examples of New Testament exegesis. Sanders set off a bomb amid the established axioms of Pauline theology, and the crater is still with us to this day.[13] If justification by faith and not by the works of the law (Gal. 2:15–16) doesn't contrast Christian and *Jewish* visions of acceptance with God, *what does it contrast*? Scholars have rushed to the scene of the explosion, some trying to put everything back nicely as it was, and others building novel structures where their more familiar-looking

---

9 e.g. Gathercole 2002: 139–142.

10 Gathercole 2002: 37–194; Wright 2009: 159–168.

11 Barclay 2015: 152–153.

12 Barclay 2015: 151–158.

13 'The general Christian view of Judaism, or of some part of it, as a religion of legalistic works-righteousness goes on, unhindered by the fact that it has been sharply – one would have thought, devastatingly – criticized by scholars who have known the material far better than any of its proponents. One of the intentions of the present chapter, to put the matter clearly, is to destroy that view' (Sanders 1977: 59).

predecessors used to stand. Consensus on the right way forward, however, remains elusive.

1.2 The Old Perspective in Galatians

Turning from wide-ranging attempts to identify the anchor points of Pauline theology as a whole to the narrower orbit of Galatians, it turns out there have always been reasons *in the text* to doubt the neat solutions offered by the Old Perspective.

We've already noted the difficulties facing rigid, anti-legal renderings of Paul's thought in his encounters with the Jerusalem apostles and with Peter in Antioch in Galatians 2:1–14. The problems continue as we follow his logic forward. In Galatians 2:15–16, the grammar of the underlying Greek text is complex, and early manuscripts vary on the question of whether Paul introduces the second verse as a contrast to the first or in continuity with it:

Contrast:

We ourselves are Jews by birth and not Gentile sinners; yet we know *that a person is justified not by the works of the law but through faith in Jesus Christ...*[14] (Gal. 2:15–16)

Continuity:

We who are Jews by birth and not sinful Gentiles know that a person is not justified by the works of the law, but by faith in Jesus Christ...[15] (Gal. 2:15–16)

Stephen Carlson's comprehensive study of the evidence finds the text-critical arguments for and against the inclusion of the single particle *de* (but/yet) that makes all the difference here too close to call.[16] But in the context of the letter as a whole, the latter 'continuity' reading seems far more likely. Of course, as relationships between the emergent church and the Jewish community deteriorated from the latter half of the first century onwards, it would have been tempting for manuscript copyists to 'help' Paul affirm that believing Jews were justified by faith *despite* their religious heritage. But the actual argument of the letter is that justification by faith is a *very* Jewish idea – an idea epitomized, in

---

14 NRSV; see also Wright 2009: 95.
15 NIV; see also de Boer 2011: 141.
16 Carlson 2015: 154–157.

fact, by the father of Judaism, Abraham himself, in whom the norms of God's covenant relationship with his people were established (Gal. 3:7–9).[17]

Galatians 3:10–14 is notoriously dense, and this isn't the place to summarize – still less to attempt to resolve – its interpretative mysteries.[18] As this book progresses, I hope to add at least a few intriguing new ingredients to the exegetical mix and to sketch their potential significance for Old and New Perspectives on the passage. But I draw attention to it here simply because, whatever else we make of it, this text too supports the continuity reading of Galatians 2:15–16.

The point emerges as soon as we notice the close linguistic parallels between Galatians 2:15–16 and 3:11 where Paul develops his thoughts about 'the curse of the law' with a citation from one of his favourite Old Testament texts, Habakkuk 2:4: 'Clearly, no-one who relies on the law is justified before God, because "the righteous will live by faith"' (Gal. 3:11). Grammatically, there's some doubt about whether the first or the second term in this sentence is actually the premise, not to mention whether the faith Paul commends is an attribute of the believer or the object of their belief.[19] But whichever route we plot through this interpretative minefield, it's certain that, for Paul, there is no orthodox Jewish way to talk about justification that makes law-observance the practical means to obtain it.

What Paul is saying in Galatians 2:15–16, therefore, is that, far from locking the people who fell within its boundaries into a life of slavish legalism, Judaism as Paul and Peter knew it was built on the assumption of justification by faith *before Jesus ever arrived*. Sure, there were Jews who'd lost their moorings in this fundamental truth – witness the self-righteous Scribes and Pharisees of the gospels. But, for Paul, this wasn't a distinctively Jewish trait. Quite the opposite. Abraham knew it, every one of his true descendants knew it, Jews by birth knew – and had always known – that a person was not justified by the works of the law. Self-righteousness was an aberration for Jews. The people for whom it made sense were 'sinful Gentiles'.

---

17 So also Mark Elliott: '[P]agan sinners might mistakenly think that the Torah is a mechanism for justification, but Jews know better than to make that category mistake' (Elliott 2014: 144). When the 'contrast' reading is preferred, translators naturally also prefer to maintain contrast as the verse continues. So, Hays: 'We ourselves are Jews by birth and not Gentile sinners, *yet*, knowing that a person is justified not by the works of the law but through the faith of Jesus Christ, *even we* have trusted in Christ Jesus' (Hays 2015: 1067). However, there is nothing in the Greek text to suggest that the expression, *kai hēmeis* – rendered here as 'even we' – should carry adversative force other than the prior decision to include the disputed particle *de* at the start of the verse.

18 So Gombis 2007: 81.

19 On the problem of identifying the premise here, see Wakefield 2003: 207–214. On the meaning of faith, see Morgan 2015: 276. See also Wright 2021: 200–202.

The Old Perspective reading of the text is also heavily dependent on attributing a particular set of beliefs and motives to the 'Agitators' who were famously causing all the trouble in Galatia. Undoubtedly these Agitators *existed* – Paul exposes them immediately after his truncated introduction:

Evidently some people are throwing you into confusion and are trying to pervert the gospel of Christ. (Gal. 1:7)

They reappear on several other occasions as the letter develops: in Chapter 4, as those who are zealous to win the Galatians over to themselves and alienate them from Paul; in Chapter 5, as those who Paul caustically wishes 'would go the whole way and emasculate themselves'; and in Chapter 6, as those who wish to 'impress people by means of the flesh' and 'avoid [persecution] for the cross of Christ'.

But as we also saw in the previous chapter, none of this justifies the far more detailed descriptions of the people involved on which Old Perspective interpretations of the letter are typically based. That the Agitators were Jews, or at the very least converts to Judaism, seems certain given their enthusiasm for circumcision and several other key components of the Jewish law. And the majority of scholars envisage them emphasizing the example of Abraham – after all, he was a Gentile convert too and was circumcised. But the jump from there to the Agitators as representatives of a coherent legalistic movement consciously distorting the gospel by imposing a layer of mandatory works in addition to faith in Christ is pure speculation as far as the text of Galatians is concerned.[20]

John Barclay, once again, injects a helpful dose of realism into the discussion here. Mirror reading – reconstructing the circumstances and motives of a letter's recipients from the one half of the correspondence we actually possess – is a necessary but perilous process with potential to illuminate, but also to lend false plausibility to fanciful reconstructions. Barclay's use of Galatians as a test case for an evidence-based approach continues to rein in more far-fetched claims about the various characters the letter alludes to.[21]

---

20 On the Influencers as representatives of a coherent Jewish/Jewish Christian opposition to Paul, see Baur 1845: 253. Campbell argues that the same group of opponents threatened the Gentile Christian communities in Galatia, Philippi and Rome (Campbell 2014: 142; see also Gager 2015: 25–28). For a contemporary restatement of the idea that the Influencers represent a Pharisaic faction in the Jerusalem Church, see Tomson 2017: 234–259.

21 Barclay 1987: 73–93.

Paula Fredriksen's contribution is also helpful here, suggesting that the depth of Paul's outrage in Galatians perhaps indicates *proximity* more than it indicates *distance* between his own theological stance and that of the Agitators. Certainly, these people perceived themselves to be Christ-followers as Paul was, whatever the dissimilarities in the consequences they envisaged for Gentile converts. 'Given Paul's strident opening emphasis on his "zeal for the tradition of my fathers", his conjuring his own past persecutions of the ekklesia, and his insistence on his own excellence in *Ioudaïsmos*,' Fredriksen writes, 'I suspect that these opponents, like the ones mentioned in Philippians 3:2 and in 2 Corinthians 11, were virtually clones of himself: Jewish apostles of the Christ movement who were taking the gospel of the crucified and returning messiah to pagans.'[22]

But not even Fredriksen tackles the elephant in the room here: the underlying assumption that the problem Paul perceived among his Galatian readers *was the same problem* he perceived among the people influencing them. Every major commentary I'm aware of makes this same move: the Galatians were being reprimanded for legalistic works righteousness, *therefore the Agitators must have taught* legalistic works righteousness; the Galatians were being warned against embracing circumcision as a necessary mark of inclusion in the believing community, *therefore the Agitators must have taught* circumcision as a necessary mark of inclusion in the believing community. But this is hopelessly unrealistic. One of the most common experiences in any attempt to communicate unfamiliar religious ideas to new audiences is the observation that the response is influenced not only by what is said, but also by the audience's preconceived ideas about religion and what religion does.

Even if we concur, then, with the Old Perspective analysis that, in Paul's opinion, the Galatians were using circumcision and other Jewish legal observances in an attempt to impress God and bind him to bless them in some way, can we say with any confidence that this is what the Agitators *intended*? Of course not. History furnishes abundant examples of well-meaning preachers and missionaries who unwittingly stirred up similar sentiments among their hearers without the least suspicion of what they were doing, let alone any deliberate intention to do so.[23] Galatians simply doesn't allow us to draw

---

22 Fredriksen 2017: 81.

23 Reflecting on the Christianization of Gaul in the fourth century, Charles Taylor describes just one such example, concluding that local converts 'must have seen the new religion in terms of those categories of sacred power that they were already familiar with... it is obvious that the meaning of the new rites for them would be different from the correct, canonical meaning held by the clerical missionaries', Taylor 2007: 63.

conclusions about the motives of the Agitators beyond what Paul actually tells us, and even this material needs to be handled with extreme care given the highly charged polemic in which he's engaged.

2 The New Perspective on Paul

How, then, does the New Perspective fare as an alternative response to the challenge of making sense of *all* the available data?

Any attempt to answer this question compactly risks oversimplification, perhaps even more than it did in the case of the Old Perspective. Although it's possible to group modern analyses of Paul into a small number of relatively coherent schools of thought – followers of Dunn, followers of Wright, apocalyptic Paul, Paul within Judaism and so forth – nobody doubts we're living in an era of *multiple* New Perspectives, not just one, with ingredients that overlap and interpenetrate to different degrees depending on exactly who one chooses to read.[24]

In this section, we'll limit our attention to a few dominant early voices – forerunners of Sanders and first responders to Sanders, who wrestle with, among many other issues, a single foundational question: 'If legalism wasn't the problem with Judaism in Paul, *what was?*'

In the work of Krister Stendahl, the problem with Judaism was a product of Paul's theological creativity *after* his encounter with the risen Jesus. The apostle himself had not been anxiously striving to observe the law as a means to secure acceptance with God beforehand, and it was only later, faced with the great 'solution' of Jesus' death and resurrection, that he reclassified his former experience of life under the law as a 'plight' from which deliverance was required.[25]

In the work of James Dunn and Tom Wright, despite numerous differences in their treatment of the implications, the problem with Judaism is handled in a similar manner: Jews were not trying to earn their way to heaven by works – Jews simply didn't think about works (or about heaven) like this. No, the problem with Judaism was that circumcision and other distinctively Jewish

---

24 Westerholm's summary marking the twenty-fifth anniversary of the New Perspective provides a good illustration of the problem, and things have become more, not less, complex in the intervening years. Westerholm 2001: 1–38.

25 Stendahl 1963: 199–215. See also Pitre et al. 2019: 31.

practices were being used to communicate inclusion in the covenant community, and their absence was being used to communicate exclusion.[26]

In the work of J. Louis Martyn, the central issue is not so much a misunderstanding of the purpose of the law (was it a boundary marker?) as a misreading of the eschatological clock. Paul was animated by the onset of the new age that overturned every system and every norm, introducing an entirely different religious calculus. God, in Christ, had done what human beings could not do. God had brought the future hopes of Israel crashing into the present, leaving Jewish legal observances high and dry as relics of a now-redundant past.[27]

2.1 New Perspectives Under Scrutiny

With this range of new emphases has come a range of new questions.

Following Sanders, as we've already seen, most scholars today think it doubtful that first-century Jews of any type saw works as a way to *initiate* a relationship with God. The question is hard to adjudicate because it hardly ever arises – all good Jews believed membership of the covenant was a privilege of birth, not a consequence of their own good deeds. But even in the case of Gentile converts to Judaism, there's little evidence to suggest that good works formed the basis of their confidence that God had accepted them in the first place.

Sanders acknowledged a vital role for works in Jewish sources, of course – a role he framed in terms of 'staying in' a covenant relationship with God, not 'getting into' it in the first place – and this distinction has attracted criticism, not least on the basis that it's inherently unstable. However much we strive to banish works from the realm of 'getting in', their significance for 'staying in' seems to allow the very thing we're setting out to deny. If works of the law are *necessary* to express our identity as covenant members, failure to perform them surely disqualifies us, and the problem with Judaism becomes the problem of dependence on grace *plus* works, even if it isn't 'legalism' in quite the same way the Reformers imagined.

The role of works has also been considered from the perspective of final judgment. Regardless of how a person enters the covenant and the part their works play in maintaining that position, the question of how their life will ultimately be assessed in God's court is evidently connected to works in Second Temple Jewish literature. Elective grace and a determinative function

---

26 Amid a wealth of material articulating their distinctive approaches, note in particular Dunn 2008: 99–120 and Wright 2013: 851–879.

27 Martyn: 1997.

for works are *combined* in all the key texts, undermining Sanders' claim that works play no part in Jewish 'soteriology'.[28] But this still offers little help in explaining the contrast between faith and works in Paul, because Paul too clearly believes in the importance of works in final judgment.[29] We're forced to appeal to the possibility that 'transformation by Christ and the Spirit' has some sanctifying effect on *a believer's confidence* in works that eludes unbelieving alternatives.[30]

Another way to approach the first responders' question – 'If legalism wasn't the problem with Judaism in Paul, *what was*?' – is to challenge the applicability and/or relevance of the evidence used to make the judgment. Despite the range of voices from the Second Temple Jewish world highlighted by Sanders (Hillelites, Shammaites, Qumran Covenanters, etc.) his challenge to traditional models of Pauline exegesis depends on the existence of a common denominator – a single, generic, Jewish 'pattern of religion' that can be labelled 'gracious' to counter traditional allegations of legalism. But even if this denominator *really was* common, should Sanders' appeal to the larger Jewish literary context be accepted as a control for understanding Paul? Should Paul not rather be understood *on his own terms*? And if Paul's own text demands a diagnosis of legalism among his opponents, should this interpretation not carry the day, whatever evidence to the contrary is found in non-canonical texts.[31]

Superficially appealing though this approach might seem, however, its flaws are obvious. Wright highlights the false underlying claim to objectivity, asking where the 'diagnosis of legalism' comes from in the first place and pointing to the controlling role external citations play in determining the meaning of biblical words in all serious exegesis, especially when their use in the New Testament is infrequent or obscure.[32] Even within the bounds of scripture, appeals to the context in which the key passages are situated produce both validators and falsifiers for the traditional position depending on how the texts are read.[33] We have no option, then, but to engage with external evidence. Traditional readings will be augmented if they're right and undermined only if they're wrong.

---

28 Gathercole 2002: 135.

29 e.g. Rom. 8:13; 14:10–12; 1 Cor. 3:12–15; 6:9; Gal. 5:19–21; Eph. 6:8.

30 Gathercole 2002: 249.

31 John Piper ushers us along this path with his warnings about the use of first-century sources and 'conceptual frameworks' in New Testament interpretation. His remarks cautioning against neglect of the Christian exegetical tradition through the centuries, however, are well made. See Piper 2008: 33–38.

32 Wright 2009: 30–33.

33 Wright 2009: 33–34.

John Barclay's response is more sophisticated. The tension between Paul and the wider world of Jewish thought lay not so much in his belief in the *priority* of divine grace as in its *incongruity*.[34] Paul believed God did more than merely take the initiative to bless the worthy, he took the initiative to bless *the unworthy too*. And yes, of course, this brought obligations with it to respond to God with gratitude and obedience, but these obligations in no way undermined the graciousness of the gift. Barclay sees no reason to deny the significance of works of the law as boundary markers in Jewish society, or to doubt Paul's desire to keep that kind of thinking out of his churches. But this is not the only way, or even the best way, to explain the tension between justification by faith and by works in passages like Galatians 2. For Barclay, it's enough to see a lingering belief in Jewish observances as qualifiers for blessing standing in antithesis to the Pauline emphasis on incongruous grace.[35]

Martyn's approach has inspired and intermingled with many other readings, helping to restore the norms and priorities of Jewish apocalyptic to the centre of the discussion.[36] But his emphasis on the radical newness of the gospel comes at the cost of a balancing emphasis on continuity from the Old Testament to the New that is no less important in Paul's letters. Galatians itself is structured around two profound excursions into the Abrahamic narrative seeking – and, in Paul's view, finding – significant precursors of the present in Israel's past. With justification by faith and works framed as a contrast between two biblical eras, the overarching theological picture strays uncomfortably close to Marcionism.[37] If the accursedness of the law and the blessedness of the gospel imply divine detachment from the former even as they disclose divine engagement with the latter, Paul's positive remarks about law elsewhere become difficult to explain. One wonders how Martyn's Paul would respond if accused, as Luke's Paul is accused in Acts 21:21, of discouraging

---

34 'It would be a mistake to regard the incongruity of grace as ubiquitous in Judaism, but equally wrong to consider this notion uniquely Pauline,' Barclay 2015: 565.

35 'What Paul denies here [in Gal. 2:15–16] is that Torah observance makes a person a fitting beneficiary of divine gift, since no-one is (or will be) considered righteous on that basis,' Barclay 2015: 378.

36 Martyn's treatment of the apocalyptic theme in Paul comes to its fullest fruition in his ground breaking commentary on Galatians; see Martyn 1997.

37 Wright notes and exposes the fragility of the claim common to many well-known apocalyptic readings of Galatians that, for Paul, the God of the gospel necessarily stands at a distance from the Mosaic Law (see Martyn 1997: 354, 364–370; de Boer 2011: 226–232; Pitre et al. 2019: 77–82). His reference to angelic involvement in the giving of the law in Galatians 3:19 can only be brought into alignment with a larger narrative unifying life under the law with the experience of Gentiles living under hostile spiritual powers at the cost of significant violence to the larger Jewish tradition, Wright 2013: 871–872, 876–877.

Jewish Christians from circumcising their children?[38] Surely not with the flat denial and immediate, public, legally observant acts in the temple that we observe in the canonical text (Acts 21:26).

2.2 New Perspectives in Galatians

Narrowing our focus on Galatians once again, the quest for a new Jewish problem to replace the allegation of legalism that characterized the Old Perspective may actually be leading us *away* from the text.

Introducing his analysis of 'the works of the law' from Galatians 2:15–16 in the article which many credit with launching the entire era of Pauline scholarship in which we still live, James Dunn argued that

> *'works of the law' are nowhere understood here, either by [Paul's] Jewish interlocutors or by Paul himself, as works which earn God's favour, as merit-amassing observances. They are rather seen as* badges: *they are simply what membership of the covenant people involves, what mark out Jews as God's people; given precisely for that reason, they serve to demonstrate covenant status.*[39]

If Sanders is to be believed, this analysis is indeed accurate. Neither Jews in general nor Paul in particular believed that the Mosaic law was a system designed to engineer divine acceptance.

But is that really what Paul is trying to say in the passage from Galatians Dunn cites? If we're right to perceive continuity in Paul's thought from Galatians 2:15 to 16 – if he thinks that Jews *naturally* embrace the logic of justification by faith because they've been raised with it from their mothers' knees (or at least they should've been) – then Paul shows no concern whatsoever here about the meaning of 'works of the law' for 'his Jewish interlocutors' or even for himself, either as meritorious deeds, or boundary markers, or anything else. It's *Gentiles*, not Jews, who have the problem processing justification by faith in Galatians 2 and the antithetical relationship that Paul famously describes between faith and works there can only be truly understood in that context.

Stepping back just one verse to Galatians 2:14, we reach the start line for Tom Wright's distinctive interpretation of the letter. Framed by Peter's memorable withdrawal from table fellowship with Gentiles in Antioch, the key question for Wright is this: 'Is it right for Jewish Christians and Gentile Christians

---

38 Thiessen 2016: 164–167.
39 Dunn 2008: 111.

25

to eat together?[40] Everything that follows therefore has to do with *ethnic identity*. The works of the law are all about 'living like a Jew' and separating oneself from 'Gentile sinners'. 'They are not, in other words, the moral "good works" which the Reformation tradition loves to hate.'[41] From here, Wright tells us that 'the lawcourt metaphor behind the language of justification, and of the status "righteous" which someone has when the court has found in their favour, has given way to the clear sense of membership of God's people'. And this might be true if the exegetical foundation in Galatians 2:14 was firm.[42] But what Paul tells us here is that Jews eating or not eating with Gentiles is *not* actually the key question in his argument but merely a window onto something even more problematic – the fact that Jewish Christians can unwittingly *force* their Gentile brothers and sisters to follow their customs. This is the link between the dispute in Antioch and the situation now brewing among his Galatian correspondents. Membership of God's people and the behavioural badges appropriate to it are clearly topics of vital interest to Paul, but they may not hold the keys to understanding justification by faith in this context.

The first responders to Sanders also struggle to account for the severity of Paul's warnings in Galatians. A sidelong glance at 1 and 2 Corinthians provides some helpful perspective here: in Corinth we have a church with factions, with gross immorality, with an overheated interest in spiritual gifts, with socio-economic discrimination at the Lord's Supper; and yet even here Paul finds something to say in the thanksgiving sections with which his letters customarily begin. But in Galatians, uniquely, he can't think of anything to be thankful for.[43] The crisis he perceives calls out from him some of the harshest words in the New Testament. Twice he wishes that advocates of alternative gospels to his own will be accursed (Gal. 1:8–9). He accuses his readers of deserting the good news they received (Gal. 1:6). He calls them 'fools', he calls them 'bewitched' (Gal. 3:1), he wonders whether all the efforts he has expended on them have been wasted (Gal. 4:11). In Galatians 5:2 he warns them that, if they let themselves be circumcised, 'Christ will be of no value to [them] at all.' And, in case that wasn't blunt enough, he then elaborates:

> You who are trying to be justified by the law have been alienated from Christ; you have fallen away from grace. (Gal. 5:4)

---

40 Wright 2009: 94. See also Wright 2013: 854.
41 Wright 2009: 96. See also Wright 2013: 858–859.
42 Wright 2009: 100–101.
43 See Weima 2016: 80–89.

How are these verses to be understood if the fundamental problem in Galatia is inappropriate acceptance of Jewish boundary markers like circumcision? Sure, we can excuse a measure of frustration on Paul's part on the basis that this involved embracing structures whose primary purpose was *preparatory* to Christ's coming (Gal. 3:15–4:7).[44] But he's still content for *Jewish* Christians to continue with these practices, indeed, he's content to continue with them *himself* to judge by his submission to Jewish conventions elsewhere (2 Cor. 11:24; Acts 15:3 etc.).[45] Presumably, participation in legal observances had become for him an opportunity to recognize and celebrate their once-mysterious-but-now-unveiled object, Christ himself. So why not also for Gentiles? If there was no *fundamental danger* in such actions, if they didn't directly affect one's standing with God, it's hard to make sense of his evident conviction that they were bringing his readers to the very brink of apostasy.[46] Shouldn't Paul, instead, have been *encouraged* by the extent of their commitment? Volunteering for circumcision, after all, was no small undertaking in the first century without either anaesthetics or antibiotics if things went wrong. If justification by faith in Galatians is all about divergent but nonetheless earnest visions of how to show yourself to be a member of God's people, Paul's response seems more than a little disproportionate.

---

44 Wright 2013: 863–879. Wright positions voluntary submission to the Torah after Christ's coming as an implicit denial that he had, in fact, come (Wright 2013: 862–863).

45 Even Luther recognizes Paul's willingness to allow Jewish observances to continue among Jewish Christians, 'for the time being... provided they do so from a right motive' (Comm. Gal. 2.2).

46 Wright tackles the problem by downplaying the severity of the warnings: '[Paul] is writing about *discipline*, not about the eternal salvation of those against whose teaching he is warning. "Salvation" as such is never mentioned in this letter...' (Wright 2013: 1135). This may be true as far as the Agitators go, but it is difficult to sustain for the Galatians themselves in Galatians 5:2 and 4 where he warns them that they stand on the brink of alienation from Christ.

3
A Gentile Problem

Introduction

Already, in the previous chapter, we've seen both the longevity and the intrinsic instability of the idea that Galatians was written to deal with a *Jewish* problem. In the Old Perspective the problem was Jewish *legalism*, in the New Perspective it was Jewish *ethnocentricity*, but neither avoided the conclusion that it was a problem *with Jews*, and we ought to think carefully before attributing this attitude to Paul. Did he really believe that Jews were intrinsically more prone to self-righteousness than other races, or more inclined to insist on conformity to their distinctive patterns of behaviour? He certainly could have done. But the alternatives ought also to be fully examined.

Paul says all kinds of harsh and critical things about circumcision and observing the Jewish calendar in Galatians, but his willingness to divide the work of gospel proclamation throughout the ancient world with law-observant Jewish Christians like Peter, James and John should caution us against plugging the interpretative gap too hastily with stereotypes. In Galatians 2:15–16, we saw that the people who were the most prone to stumble over justification by faith were not Jews at all but Gentiles – exactly the kind of people Paul was writing to. How, then, might our interpretation of Paul's text alter if the underlying problem was not so much a problem with *Jews* and *Jewish traditions* as it was a problem with *Gentiles* and the way they received them?

1 Gentile Political Identity

Several interesting interpretative experiments of this type have begun with an attempt to situate Paul's readers in their Roman imperial context.

Certainly, Paul lived in a period witnessing an astonishing expansion of imperial influence, particularly through the medium of the cult of the emperor himself. More than thirty imperial cult temples were established in Asia Minor

28

alone before the end of the first century.[1] Augustus's birthday was adopted as 'New Year's Day' across large parts of the region, and cities that failed to celebrate his cult festivals were fined.[2] Construction of shrines to traditional deities also continued apace, of course, and the growth of the imperial cult can be attributed at least as much to local civic administrations currying favour with their Roman overlords as it can to the kind of popular connection to the emperor as a god that was evident in other common forms of religious devotion.[3] But there's little doubt that imperial power in general, and the increasing visibility of the emperor cult in particular, would have cast a long shadow over all the viable locations that have been proposed for the Galatian churches.

Combining these observations with a balancing awareness of the widespread nature of the Jewish diaspora in the period, Bruce Winter invites us to imagine the popular reaction to the emergence of Pauline church communities, which – to outsiders at least – must have borne all the classic hallmarks of a Jewish sect (cf. Acts 18:12–16). Despite the fact that pagan worship was woven into the infrastructure of society at the most basic level – touching social transactions from buying food to formalizing contracts – Jews survived and thrived, Winter tells us, thanks to their status as an officially sanctioned religion, or *Religio Licita*. Jewish prayers *on behalf of* the emperor were accepted in lieu of prayers that addressed him directly. Jews were excused participation in pagan games and cults.[4] But all of this would have been profoundly upset when churches like those we read about in Galatians started attracting Gentiles and encouraging them to withdraw from the infrastructure of pagan religion, effectively availing themselves of *Jewish* privileges, but without becoming Jewish proselytes and marking that transition with the rite of circumcision.

How would local Jewish communities have reacted? Winter is surely right to imagine a response of fear and alarm. No sensible Jew would have wanted these renegade 'Jesus people' disturbing the delicate equilibrium of their relationship with Rome, worked out and carefully cultivated over decades of

1   Price 1984: 249–274.

2   Hardin 2008: 44–46.

3   On the construction of shrines to traditional deities, see Price 1984: 162–165, 169. On the question of the true 'popularity' of emperor worship, see Price 1984: 117–120; Clauss 1999: 339, 419; Pleket 1965: 347. Despite Pliny the Younger's obvious enthusiasm for the cult of his childhood friend, the Emperor Trajan, it's interesting that he assures the emperor he is praying *on his behalf,* not *to him* on behalf of others (e.g. Let. 10.35, 51, 100).

4   Winter 1994: 133. Winter argues that, if Gentile believers underwent the rite of circumcision, 'Galatian Christians as a whole would have a recognized legal entity that was distinctly Jewish… they would not be required to give divine honours in the imperial temples in the province of Galatia' (Winter 2015: 241). See also Winter 2015: 244–249; Gill 2017: 82.

sometimes uneasy coexistence with their pagan neighbours. However extensive the expulsion of Jews from Rome under Claudius actually was in practice (Acts 18:2, see also Suetonius Claud. 25.4), it demonstrates at least the fragility of the settlement that Jews were seeking to preserve, and the potential for catastrophic consequences when things went wrong.[5]

With this reconstruction of the background in our minds, how does the problem in Galatia look? Paul still warns his readers vehemently against circumcision but not so much because he has a problem with Jewish law. His warnings are motivated by his awareness that circumcision for his readers is *a political tactic* – it's a way to avoid persecution from civic and imperial authorities, and to help the Jews who are influencing them avoid it too (Gal. 6:12). Paul is fearful that he's wasted his time with the Galatians because staying out of trouble is clearly more important to them than faithfulness to the gospel, although quite why the situation requires such an in-depth, theologically grounded response remains a mystery.[6]

Justin Hardin picks up the baton here with both a critique and an extension of Winter's thesis. Questions have rightly been raised about whether the Jews in the Roman world in fact enjoyed *Religio Licita* status at all. The evidence rather points in the opposite direction. Jews had no *formal* constitutional protections under Roman law and were forced to defend their historic privileges on an ad hoc basis.[7] But even without formal protection, Hardin claims diaspora Jews were a 'normalized group' in the kinds of cities Paul was writing to. Jews had found acceptance in their host communities as positive contributors to society despite their religious quirks. The problem with Pauline church plants was that *they broke this norm* by inviting and even commanding *Gentiles* to withdraw from the regular routines of pagan worship. Circumcision was a way for them to repair it.

But even this modified version of Winter's thesis leaves loose ends both within and beyond the confines of the letter. For Winter and Hardin, the reading depends on recognizing circumcision as a kind of 'passport' to

---

5   On the difficulties of dating and accurately characterizing this 'expulsion', see Murphy-O'Connor 2012: 9–15.

6   Brigitte Kahl expands on Winter's thesis arguing that ethnic Galatians were considered paradigmatic opponents of Roman power, and that asserting membership of the Abrahamic family without circumcision – which she also takes to be the officially sanctioned mark of inclusion – would have been considered an act of insurrection against the Roman state. See Kahl: 2009.

7   Rajak 1985: 20; Trebilco 1991: 8–12; Hardin 2008: 102–103. See also Martin 2020: 90, 143–147.

immunity from obligations to local cults for Gentiles.[8] But there's no evidence to suggest it was anything of the kind. If Graeco-Roman authors of the period are anything to go by, circumcision was viewed with the highest distaste – more likely to aggravate than ameliorate disquiet about the activities of Gentile converts.[9] Neither is there any certainty that Gentiles like the Galatians would have been accepted as converts in local *Jewish* communities. As we'll see shortly, positivity about Gentile proselytes is far from uniformly attested in Second Temple Jewish texts – there's a reason why Philo felt the need to *urge* his fellow Jews to welcome them as equals (*Virtues* 102). And proselytes to Jewish *Christianity* would have been even less certain of their status. For real security among Jews, circumcision alone would not have been sufficient. Gentile Christians would have had to renounce Christ as God.[10]

Hardin openly acknowledges that his reconstruction also leaves Paul addressing two distinct audiences in Galatians – talking one part of his readership down from the ledge of circumcision, while at the same time rebuking others for returning to the pagan cults from which they'd only recently been converted.[11] But before we fracture the letter into two separate halves like this, we should at least explore reconstructions that allow it to be read as a whole.

2 Gentile Theological Identity

If the problem in Galatia was really a Gentile problem, perhaps it gravitated less around their political identity than around their theological identity? This possibility can be explored from multiple angles.

In recent years, scholars have sought to reconstruct the underlying situation in Galatia by studying more closely the kinds of religious tradition Paul's readers might have been exposed to before he met them. Might these past experiences go some way to explaining their susceptibility to the Agitators' demand for circumcision, not to mention the contours of Paul's response to it? We'll return to these suggestions in Chapter 6. In this chapter, however, I want

---

8   See also Kahl 2009: 210.
9   See, for example, Juvenal Sat. 14.96–106; Horace Sat. 1.4.139–43; 1.9.67–70; Seneca Civ. 6:11; Tacitus Hist. 5.4–5. See also Elliott 2003: 234–236.
10 Lane Fox 2005: 482.
11 Martin 2020: 92–93.

to concentrate on an alternative point of view that has generated significant interest as an alternative to both Old and longer-standing New Perspectives on Paul in recent years – the idea that the problem in Galatia was all about Gentile theological identity *looked at through Jewish eyes.*

2.1 The Radical New Perspective on Paul

Under the terms of the Old Perspective, Paul is not read, and should not be read, as a Jew because he's a Christian. He's a convert from the former to the latter, and Galatians is one of the prime texts used to prove the point. In the previous chapter we noted Martin Luther's sense of empathy with Paul in Galatians 1 when he describes his renunciation of his past life in Judaism and his acceptance of new life in Christ (Comm. Gal. 1.14). But is a 'renunciation of his past life in Judaism' really the right way to talk about the consequences of Paul's experience on the road to Damascus?[12]

Krister Stendahl proved his farsightedness here again with his provocative suggestion that the language of 'conversion' perhaps describes Paul's experience less accurately than the language of 'commissioning' or '[prophetic] call'.[13] The point is obvious in Galatians itself as soon as we notice the tradition Paul is drawing on when he reflects on what happened to him:

> But when God, who set me apart from my mother's womb and called me by his grace, was pleased to reveal his Son in me so that I might preach him among the Gentiles, my immediate response was not to consult any human being... (Gal. 1:15–16)

This is the familiar vernacular of Old Testament prophetic appointments. Take the calling of Jeremiah, for example:

> The word of the Lord came to me, saying,
> 'Before I formed you in the womb I knew you,
> before you were born I set you apart;
> I appointed you as a prophet to the nations.' (Jer. 1:4–5)

Or the familiar words of the second servant song in Isaiah, noting again the prenatal commission to take God's word *to the nations*:

---

12 For an excellent summary of this discussion see Wright 2013: 1417–1426. See also Dunn 2006b: 346–354.

13 Stendahl 1976: 7–23.

Listen to me, you islands;
hear this, you distant nations:
Before I was born the Lord called me;
from my mother's womb he has spoken my name. (Isa. 49:1)

These are not descriptions of conversion from Judaism to something else –
these passages describe the process by which God sets aside particular individuals to announce his purposes *in* Israel, confronting and even declaring
judgment *upon* Israel where necessary, but not leaving Israel, or proclaiming
Israel in any way obsolete.

The point is reinforced when we note the anachronism involved in the traditional 'conversion' account of Paul's experience. What would Paul have
converted *to*? He certainly didn't convert *to Christianity*. Christianity didn't
exist as an unambiguously separate entity even when he wrote Galatians.[14]
Paul seems to have come to see himself as the herald of a pivotal development *within* Israel's story – the coming of the long-expected Jewish Messiah –
with consequences for Jews and Gentiles envisaged in the Hebrew scriptures.
Indeed, it was the very messianic expectations contained within those scriptures that seem to have convinced him that this great change of eras had come
about. The anticipated age of resurrection had, somehow, unaccountably begun in the actual, historical events of the first Easter.[15]

The danger of anachronism also looms over talk of conversion *from* Judaism. Judaism as Paul knew it wasn't a religion in the sense that we understand
religion today – gravitating around articles of faith which, in turn, generate
consequences for life and worship. Judaism was an ethnic identity. Judaism
was a national story. It's hard to imagine circumstances in which Paul *could*
have ceased to identify himself as a Jew even if he'd wished to. And that certainly doesn't seem to be the case on the evidence of Galatians.

Taking Paul as a Jew, then, albeit a very unusual Jew who believed that the
eschaton was actually unfolding before his eyes, we can begin to probe the
question, 'What did Paul think of Gentiles *theologically*?'

Returning to Galatians 2:15, the first clue lies in the passing comment he
makes about Gentiles in contrast to Jews. Paul reminds Peter that it's Gentiles who have a problem grasping the concept of justification by faith. But he
doesn't just say 'Gentiles', he says '*sinful* Gentiles'; and that reveals something

---

14 See Eisenbaum 2009: 135–136.
15 See Wright 2013: 1043–1265.

of his mindset.[16] Jews in the first century quite typically referred to Gentiles as 'sinners'.[17] Following Jeremiah and Isaiah, they equated Gentile religion with idolatry, scolding Gentiles for forming their own objects of devotion instead of worshipping the God who forms everything including his devotees.[18] Pagan worship was considered an inversion of the natural created order (Rom. 1:18–32), consigning its practitioners to the same nothingness that ultimately stood behind their idols (Isa. 44:9).[19]

But Jewish visions of the spiritual future for Gentiles were not, for this reason, uniformly pessimistic. Sanders, it's true, found the rabbis comparatively disinterested in the question of who might or might not be 'saved' beyond the boundaries of Judaism.[20] But in the diaspora, where the question was more pressing, more accommodating views seem to have been common, built largely around the Old Testament prophetic expectation of a final ingathering of the nations.[21]

Would Gentiles be included as converts to Judaism or as Gentiles in their own right in the eschatological age? There are certainly texts that endorse the latter view, as Paul himself seems to do in concord with the other apostles at the Jerusalem Council in Acts 15.[22] Would Gentiles be expected to embrace the Mosaic law or something different? Once again, there are texts that affirm the latter, expecting nothing more from righteous Gentiles than conformity to the 'Noachide commandments' – a body of ethical principles derived from pre-Sinaitic texts which also seem to have influenced the apostles when they drew up the Jerusalem Decree (Acts 15:24–29).[23] If Paul believed

---

16 Martyn 1997: 248; see also Dunn 2008: 230–235.

17 On the connection between wickedness and disassociation from God's law, see Ps. 1:1–5; 37:34–36; Sir 41.8. For the specific identification of Gentiles as sinners, see Ps. 9:5, 15–17; Tob. 13.6; Jub. 23.23–24; Pss Sol 2.1–2 (Dunn 1993: 132–133). On the identification of Gentiles as sinners in wider Second Temple literature, see T. Jud. 23.2; T. Dan. 5.8; T. Naph. 3.3–4.1. Sanders' analysis of the book of Jubilees overstates its negative assessment of Gentile behaviour and yet still helpfully identifies both positive commands given to Israel that they might not be like the Gentiles (Jub. 2.19; 3.31) and negative commands targeting behaviour characteristic of Gentiles that they are to avoid (Jub. 1.9; 11.16; 20.6–7; Sanders 1977: 374–375).

18 Jer. 10:2–5; Isa. 44:2, 9, 10, 12, 21, 24. See also T. Naph. 3.3–5; Jub. 20.6–7.

19 See Wis. 14.12–14, 23–27; T. Reub. 4.6; T. Naph. 3.3–4.1; Jub. 20.6–7; 1QS 4.5–9; 4Q271 fr.2; Diog. 2.5. The view that Gentile religion could be framed as part of a legitimate quest for God evident in the Letter to Aristeas (Let. Aris. 16) is conspicuous by its absence in the vast majority of Second Temple sources. See Donaldson 2007: 493–498.

20 Sanders 1977: 207, 211.

21 Donaldson 2007: 469–505.

22 See Bockmuehl 2003: 145. See also Isa. 25:6–10.

23 Jub. 7.20 provides something very close to a summary of the Noachide commandments: '[Noah] bore witness to his sons that they might do justice, and cover the shame of their flesh, and bless the one who created them, and honour father and mother, and each one love his neighbour and preserve themselves from fornication and pollution and from all injustice.' Jub. 7.23–24 prohibits bloodshed; Jub. 7.28–33 prohibits the consumption of blood. See Bockmuehl 2003: 145–173; Wyschogrod 2004: 190–193.

the eschaton had actually *commenced* with the resurrection of Jesus and if his thoughts about Gentiles in any way mirrored this larger network of Jewish expectations, then his passion for including Gentiles in his new communities and his hostility to the idea that they should submit themselves to laws intended *for Jews* perhaps begin to make more sense.

Enter, then, the self-styled 'Radical New Perspective on Paul' or the 'Paul Within Judaism School' which turns this set of insights into a programmatic reading of Pauline theology in its entirety.[24] Working on the assumption that everything Paul says about law across his entire output is directed towards Gentiles and has nothing directly to say about Jews at all, scholars of the Radical New Perspective present Paul not only as a Jewish thinker but as a law-observant Jew throughout his ministry.[25]

Doesn't Paul undermine this by eating with Gentiles, and '[living] like a Gentile, (Gal. 2:14), and becoming 'like one not having the law' to those 'not having the law' (1 Cor. 9:21)? 'Not so,' says the Radical New Perspective. Sure, Paul adopted a less strict form of Jewish practice than he had done beforehand in his life as a Pharisee, but not one that was unrecognizably Jewish.[26] He dined with Gentiles, but that doesn't mean he ate Gentile food. He declared all foods clean *for his Gentile readers* (Rom. 14:14), but that doesn't mean he availed *himself* of the opportunity to eat them. Paul didn't perceive any ongoing obligation to observe the Jewish law for Gentiles, quite the reverse. But perhaps he did perceive an ongoing obligation to observe the Jewish law for Jews? Indeed, this might provide a solution to the great puzzle of Galatians 5:3, where Paul tells his readers that if any of them allow themselves to be circumcised, they will be required to obey the entire law.[27]

Just like the New Perspective, it shouldn't surprise us to find divergent opinions within the ranks of its 'Radical' stepchild. Building on the suggestion that Paul acknowledged different sets of legal obligations for Jews and Gentiles, some scholars have attempted to redraw Paul as an apostle preaching Jesus to the Gentiles because only the Gentiles *need* Jesus. In this reconstruction of his thought, obedience to the Mosaic law suffices for Jews to participate in

---

24 Introducing the Radical New Perspective, see Eisenbaum 2009. See also Gaston 1979; Gager 1985; Thiessen 2016; Fredriksen 2017; Nanos et al. 2015.

25 'Paul's audience is made up of Gentiles, so everything he says about law applies to Gentiles, unless specified otherwise,' Eisenbaum 2009: 216.

26 Rudolph 2011: 125–130; Rudolph 2016: 155–159.

27 Martin 2020: 196. Thiessen makes a similar point although he limits the scope of Paul's remarks in Galatians 5:3 to the law of circumcision. See Thiessen 2016: 74–75.

the eschatological age.[28] But here the necessity to overlook glaring contradictions in the text becomes too much to stomach.[29] How could Paul have written Romans 9:1–5 – where he tells us that, to him, his fellow Jews are a source of 'great and unceasing anguish' and that '[he] could wish [himself] cursed and cut off from Christ for the sake of his people' – if, in fact, he felt confident about their spiritual situation and believed Christ unnecessary either for him or them? The suggestion also fails to grapple with the parallel between the Mosaic law and the Noachide Commandments. If indeed the former forms the substance of God's saving plan for Jews and the latter for Gentiles, Jesus is unnecessary *in both cases*.

Setting aside these extremes, however, the Radical New Perspective does at least provide us with a framework for interpreting the letter holistically. How can Paul say such negative things about the law and yet still share the right hand of fellowship with law-observant Jewish Christians like James in Galatians 2:9? The answer is that law is just fine for ethnic Jews. The law is still what it always was: appropriate for Jews, perhaps even binding for Jews, and Paul acknowledges that reality in the lives of his fellow apostles as he does in his own. The problem with law is just that it isn't fine *for Gentiles*.

2.2 Gentiles and the Law

But *why* isn't law fine for Gentiles? Why did Paul take such vehement issue with Gentile Jesus-believers keeping the Jewish law if he still thought it was appropriate for Jews? Clearly, he didn't think Gentiles *had to* keep it. But it's a long stride from there to the idea that keeping the law is *actively dangerous* for Gentiles – a conclusion that's impossible to avoid in Galatians. Obviously, Paul was frustrated with the individuals who were forcing this issue to the surface in the Galatian churches. But his denunciation of their activities in no way necessitates an equivalent denunciation of the Galatians' response, especially if the negative effects of their ministry were more inadvertent than intentional, as they were in Peter's case at Antioch (Gal. 2:14). If the Galatian Christians wanted to convert to Judaism and 'identify' (to use contemporary terminology) as Jewish Christians, *why shouldn't they*? Why shouldn't they enter God's kingdom as *Jewish* Christ-followers in just the same way Paul and his fellow apostles hoped to do?

---

28 See Eisenbaum 2009: 240–249. See also Gaston 1979: 48–71.

29 'Any suggestion that the Jewish people could simply continue as they were without any transformation, that the One God would vindicate them as they stood, came face to face with the fact of the crucified Messiah,' Wright 2013: 1417.

One way to respond to this question is to return to the topic of conversion and ask how Paul would have felt about *Gentiles converting to Judaism*. Taking the whole arrival of Jesus out of the equation for a moment and thinking simply about the phenomenon of Gentile proselytes from a Jewish perspective, there's a real diversity of opinion among modern scholars about the extent to which converts would have been integrated into Jewish communities in the first century and the proactivity with which they were or were not sought.[30] To be sure, Philo urges his Jewish readers to extend a warm welcome to Gentiles who had '[abandoned] their kinsfolk by blood, their country, their customs and the temples and images of their gods, and the tributes and honours paid to them' (Virt. 102). And several well-known Jewish texts elevate converts as examples of faith (the biblical stories of Rahab, and Ruth; the apocryphal story of *Joseph and Asenath*, to name just a few). But doubt remains about whether Gentile proselytes or their descendants ever attained equality with born Jews *in all respects*, and it's possible that Paul's argument signals his awareness of this fact.[31] Perhaps he feared his readers wouldn't find the welcome they hoped for among Christian Jews even if they embraced circumcision and the other traditional norms of Jewish life? Perhaps they'd be better off staying as they were?

For most interpreters, however, this is too slender a thread to bear the weight of Paul's dire warnings in Galatians, and attention turns instead to approaches derived from his distinctive eschatology. We've already noted the apostle's changed perspective on *eschatological time*. Jesus' arrival had unexpectedly propelled God's people into the resurrection era, triggering the long-anticipated ingathering of the nations and allowing Gentiles to be saved *as Gentiles*. Might this explain his reluctance to allow his converts in Galatia to keep the Jewish law? Circumcision and all the other paraphernalia of proselyte conversion might have been appropriate once upon a time *before God's Christ appeared*. But now, for Paul, seemingly it was not. Now conversion to Judaism ignored and devalued the glorious new way God had made for Gentiles to be

---

30 The two poles of the debate, with their attendant bibliographies, are well represented in Feldman 1993 and Goodman 1994. On the question of whether active outreach was needed to attract converts, see Donaldson 2007: 492, 512. See also Delling 1987: 80; Wyschogrod 2004: 190–193.

31 See Cohen 1999: 308–309f. See also Schürer 2014, vol. 3i: 174–175; Feldman 1993: 339–341; Goodman 1994: 63. 'Numerous passages in Philo and in rabbinic literature praise the proselyte and enjoin upon Jews the equitable treatment of those who have entered their midst... But none of these passages demonstrates that the proselyte achieved real equality with the native born' (Cohen 1999, 161).

accepted in their own right.[32] Now it turned back the clock to an era that, for God's people, had been decisively consigned to the past.

This brings us much closer to a solution, with an argument that coheres much more closely with the text of Galatians. But we still don't have all the pieces. However *inadvisable* conversion to Jewish Christianity might have been for Paul's readers on this basis, however unnecessarily difficult it would have made their lives, we *still* can't justify the strength of his warnings. Remember, Paul doesn't merely chide his readers for their failure to correctly read the times, he tries to snatch them from the very jaws of apostasy (Gal. 5:2, 4). Paul obviously believed there was hope in Christ for ethnic Jews. He himself was an ethnic Jew. But that makes it hard to rationalize his response to the Galatians when they're tempted to 'become' ethnic Jews through proselyte conversion. He portrays their behaviour as absolutely incompatible with faith and salvation.

Something more radical is required, then, to explain Paul's language – something perhaps like Matthew Thiessen's recent reworking of the letter which positions Paul not so much as a typical Jew but as an extremist on the question of conversion.[33] Pointing to *the Book of Jubilees* as a precedent, Thiessen suggests Paul believed Gentile conversion was simply *impossible*. In *Jubilees*, Judaism is 'inherent, genealogical, and impermeable to penetration by non-Jews'.[34] Circumcision in particular is reserved for ethnic Jews alone. Legitimate circumcisions are performed on the eighth day after birth *with no exceptions*, and any deviation from this norm involves unfaithfulness to God's covenant even in the attempt to obtain entry into it.

Does this bring our search for a holistic reading of Galatians to a conclusion? It certainly offers a potential explanation for the severity of Paul's warnings. Paul perceives his readers to be teetering on the brink of a catastrophic spiritual mistake, and naming that mistake has won Thiessen some influential supporters.[35] But his thesis is fragile nonetheless. Anyone wanting to take Acts seriously as a canonical text will immediately see the conflict with Paul's circumcision of Timothy in Acts 16:1–3, and the marginal position of Jubilees within Jewish thinking about Gentiles is only amplified by Old Testament

32 'Christ is the sacrifice for all those sins that have accumulated on all those Gentiles. For Gentiles to take up Torah observance now would be an act of faithlessness. It would be to deny the grace that God has extended to the Gentiles' Eisenbaum 2009: 224. 'To embrace Torah as your badge of identity is to say, "I don't believe that the Messiah has broken though the barrier, has rescued us from the present evil age, has died as the faithful Israelite,"' Wright 2009: 116. See also Wyschogrod 2004: 188–201.
33 Thiessen 2016: 73–101.
34 Thiessen 2016: 100. See Jub. 15.25–26, 30–32a.
35 See Fredriksen 2017: 129–130.

examples of legitimate adult circumcisions (e.g. Josh. 5:2–8).[36] If circumcision on the eighth day was indeed the immovable criterion turning the Galatians' new enthusiasm for Jewish law into a source of danger, it's strange that the letter stubbornly omits to mention it (cf. Phil. 3:5). But the most troubling part of all is Thiessen's failure to explain how all of this constitutes a return to the Galatians' spiritual past. Ironically his interpretation of Galatians brings us back to a *Jewish* problem, the problem, once again, of who does and who doesn't enjoy membership in the Jewish community. This is the solution Old and New Perspectives alike ultimately offer us. But in the letter itself, time and again, Paul connects the problem to his readers' prior religious experience *as pagans*.

---

36 See Donaldson 2007: 510 n.3.

Part II
GOING BACKWARDS
IN GALATIA

4

A Disconcerting Diagnosis

Introduction

In our work so far on the Old, New and Radical New Perspectives on Paul and the different ways they handle the underlying problem in Galatia, we've studiously avoided the perplexing topic of regression. Now the time has come to give it some detailed attention. Why, when Paul gives himself the opportunity to name the issue – to explain what it is about getting circumcised that makes it such a dangerous enterprise for his readers, does he describe it in terms of going back to something they've done *before*? And why does he do it *so consistently* throughout the letter?

Explorations aimed here seem destined at first only to complicate an interpretative task already beset by intractable problems. If commentaries are anything to go by – and they should be: since the turn of the twentieth century, commentaries on Galatians have been published at the rate of about one every eleven months – scholars over the years have felt very little appetite for opening this can of worms. But this is not the right solution. As our story unfolds, we'll discover that regression holds a central place in Paul's argument for a reason. The apparent incoherence of this motif can be explained and, in the process, bring coherence to a host of other interpretative challenges.

1 Troubling Logic

Circumcision is the central issue in Galatians. Yes, it was part of a larger package of Jewish behavioural norms that Paul's readers were being urged to adopt – sacred days are explicitly mentioned in Galatians 4:8–11, the question of diet comes up by implication in Galatians 2:11–14, Paul summarizes the entire situation under the rubric of reliance on 'the works [plural] of the law' (Gal. 2:16; 3:2, 5, 10). But within this package, circumcision is particularly prominent.

Circumcision and uncircumcision are mentioned *sixteen times* in the letter as a whole, often in the context of apparently imminent danger (e.g. Gal. 5:2–4).[1]

Why was this such a big deal? In all probability – and in keeping with Jewish norms attested abundantly elsewhere – circumcision was being presented to the Galatians as the crowning step in a process of proselyte conversion.[2] Paul's opponents weren't trying to stop the Galatians believing in Jesus, of course; they were encouraging them to bring their faith in Jesus within the established boundaries of Jewish covenant identity. They considered this a minimum requirement for a legitimate expression of allegiance to the Jewish Messiah. For Paul, however, it was a signal of complete capitulation to a counterfeit vision of the gospel (Gal. 1:6–9).

As we saw in the previous chapter, plausible explanations for this reaction abound: circumcision was redundant, circumcision was inappropriate, circumcision was risky from a medical perspective. If *the Book of Jubilees* is allowed to steer our reading, circumcision for Gentiles was self-defeating and illegal.[3] But what is the explanation Paul himself gives? Paul throws up his hands in horror in Galatians because circumcision involves being 'burdened *again* by a yoke of slavery' – a yoke of slavery with which his readers clearly have significant past experience (Gal. 5:1). Paul throws up his hands in horror in Galatians because they're 'turning back to [the] weak and miserable *stoicheia*' they were enslaved to before they knew God in the first place (Gal. 4:8–9).

As we'll see in the next section, Paul's response is at least consistent, recurring again and again in different forms throughout the letter. *But it doesn't make any sense.* Paul writes to an audience of recently converted Gentiles tempted to embrace Judaism, and he tells them they're going back to something *they have done before.* What is he thinking? Circumcision is something you can't 'go back' to *by definition.* As Augustine notes in his commentary on Galatians 4:8–9: 'When [Paul] says *turn back* he is certainly not saying that they are turning back to circumcision – they *had never been circumcised*' (Com. Gal. 33.3, emphasis mine). So, what in the world can Paul have meant when he squared up this congregation of Gentile Christ-followers and told

---

1 Circumcision/to circumcise (*peritomē/peritemnō*) Gal. 2:3, 7, 8, 9, 12; 5:2, 3, 6, 11; 6:12, 13; 15 (twice). Uncircumcision (*akrobustia*) Gal. 2:7; 5:6; 6:15.

2 On the significance of circumcision in Jewish proselyte conversion, see Donaldson 2007: 482–492; see also Cohen 1999: 156–162. The question of whether or not circumcision is required to sufficiently express Jewish identity takes centre stage in the conversion story of Izates of Adiabene (Josephus Ant. 20.38–48).

3 Thiessen 2016: 80–82, 100. See Jub. 15.25–26, 30–32a.

them that embracing this particular Jewish tradition involved reawakening their spiritual past?

As if the oddity of his diagnosis wasn't challenging enough, Paul deepens the mystery further by drawing *the whole wider landscape* of Jewish and pagan religious practices into an uncomfortably close relationship. It isn't just that he thinks circumcision might somehow lead his readers back to the norms of their religious past. He thinks circumcision and the legal observances associated with it in Galatia are *equivalent* to pagan worship in some sense, so that embracing them entails renouncing Christ (Gal. 5:2, 4).[4]

Follow along with the logic that brings him to the climactic expression of this diagnosis in Galatians 4:8–11:

In Galatians 3:23–29, Paul memorably describes the Jewish law using the image of a *paidagōgos* – a servant employed in Graeco-Roman households with particular responsibility for guiding the children to and from school and administering appropriate discipline en route.[5] 'We,' he says were 'held in custody' under this *paidagōgos*, 'locked up until the faith that was to come would be revealed'. And the 'we', of course, refers to Paul and his fellow Jews.[6] But notice where his argument is going. Having attained liberation from this arrangement through the coming of the Messiah, the 'we' in Paul's logic gives way to a 'you'. '*We Jews* have finally graduated beyond the oversight of the *paidagōgos, and you Gentiles* are also beneficiaries.' 'In Christ Jesus *you* are all children of God through faith,' he says (Gal. 3:26 emphasis mine) – before lifting their eyes to the privileges they now enjoy, pointing in particular to the privilege of baptism.

From there we come to Galatians 4:1–7, which parallels the previous section closely, sharing the same distinctive progression in the use of the pronouns.[7] Paul begins with an heir, living the life of a slave on account of his minority; and with the law as a 'guardian', charged with keeping the young man in check

---

4   See Deenick 2018: 188.

5   Wright 2021: 238.

6   The question of the significance of the pronouns here has been debated throughout the history of exegesis. Augustine downplayed the transition from 'we' to 'you' in both Galatians 3:23–29 and Galatians 4:1–7, understanding the former passage as applicable exclusively to Jews and the latter to Gentiles (Com. Gal. 29.4). Following Karl Dick, Scott Hafemann stresses the significance of shifts in pronoun usage for communicating the authority of the author and/or involving the reader (Dick: 1900; Hafemann 1990: 13). Contra Martyn, who disparages the possibility of discerning meaning in Paul's pronominal choices in Galatians, Dunn assigns first-person references in 3:23–4:7 to Jews (albeit with a 'transition in thought' in 4:3 that increasingly incorporates all those who trust in Christ) and second-person references to Paul's Gentile readers (see Martyn 1997: 334–336; Dunn 1993: 197–198, 212).

7   See Dunn 1993: 197–198, 212; Longenecker 1990: 164; Meiser 2007: 198. McCaulley is also struck by the close connection between 3:24–25 and 4:1–7 (McCaulley 2019: 177).

until the appointed day of his inheritance. Like the heir, says Paul, 'we were in slavery under the *stoicheia*,' the 'we' referring, once again, to Paul and his Jewish contemporaries. And that continues to be the case even as his simile of choice shifts from inheritance to adoption.[8] Like an adopted son, he says in Galatians 4:5, 'we' have entered into the full privileges of family membership. But Paul has not forgotten the trajectory of his argument even here. Just as we saw in Galatians 3:23–29, the consequences of these momentous developments for *the Gentiles* are expressed with a switch to 'you' pronouns in verses 6–7, tacking back from the image of the adopted son to the heir:

> *Because* you *are his sons, God sent the Spirit of his son into our hearts, the Spirit who calls out 'Abba, Father.' So* you *are no longer a slave, but God's child; and since* you *are his child, God has made* you *also an heir.* (Gal. 4:6–7 emphasis mine)

Much could be said in response to this intriguing description of blessings for *Gentiles* flowing out from the achievements of the *Jewish* Messiah. But the point I want to notice here is simply the conclusion Paul forces us to draw as we move forward into Galatians 4:8–11. We've already seen how these verses articulate the climactic description of the problem in Galatia: Paul's readers are in danger because they're returning to their past enslavement to pagan gods. But notice now that the words he uses *mirror* the words of the foregoing section. He talks about enslavement to the *stoicheia* when he wants to describe *both* the Galatians' former religious allegiances and *his own* past experiences under the Jewish law.[9]

It remains to be seen how a Jew like Paul could hope to avoid this enslavement when he engaged in Jewish practices even after embracing Jesus as the Jewish Messiah. We know from 1 Corinthians that he had no qualms about becoming 'like a Jew, to win the Jews' (1 Cor. 9:20). But in Galatians it's clear that this is not a move *his readers* can hope to emulate. In Galatians, circumcision is the trigger issue; circumcision is the point of no return in Paul's mind. But undergirding that assessment of the facts is a larger awareness that the whole way of life his readers want to adopt will be *for them* equivalent in some sense

---

8 Barclay is one of many scholars to note the awkward nature of this transition (see Barclay 2015: 408).

9 'Paul's point, evidently is that everyone (whether Jew or Gentile) was in the same boat prior to Christ and thus also that everyone (whether of Jewish or Gentile origin) benefits from Christ's redeeming work in the same way despite initial appearances to the contrary,' de Boer 2011: 259. 'What is astonishing is that Paul equates subjection to Torah with paganism,' Schreiner 2010: 278. See also Barclay 2015: 419–420; Keener 2019: 358; Moses 2014: 131; Hays 2000: 282; Martyn 1997: 393.

to their former way of life under the pagan gods. It's this former life to which Paul fears they're about to return.

2 Logic That's Integral to the Argument of the Letter

The strangeness of the allegation that, for Paul's Gentile readers, embracing Jewish law involved going back to their pagan past might perhaps have been mitigated to some degree if it was limited to the confines of Galatians 4:8–11. But, as we saw briefly in Chapter 1, nothing could be further from the truth. References to the imminent risk of returning and submitting once again to their former religious masters are peppered throughout the letter and touch on its most central themes.[10]

2.1 Prevalence

Pauline introductions often hint at ideas that will become important as his letters develop, and Galatians is no exception to this rule.[11] The conventional self-description of Galatians 1:1, 'Paul, an apostle', is expanded to tell us he was sent 'not from men nor by a man' – prefiguring his subsequent response to the Agitators who questioned his credentials.[12] And the conventional grace bene-diction in Galatians 1:3–5 is also nuanced to include a reference to the purpose of Christ's work.[13] He 'gave himself for our sins to rescue us from the present evil age'. Implication: 'as citizens of the new age, *don't go back* to the age from which you've just been rescued!'

After a lengthy autobiographical section dealing at greater length with the allegation that his gospel and his apostleship were in some way derived from, and inferior to, those of other men (cf. Gal. 1:11), Paul's account of the An-tioch Incident in Galatians 2:11–21 marks the beginning of the letter's sub-stantial engagement with the pastoral problems his opponents were causing. Peter's withdrawal from table fellowship with Gentiles – implicitly '[forcing] Gentiles to follow Jewish customs' (Gal. 2:14) – is as an example of how Jew-ish leaders shouldn't behave in mixed congregations. The requirement that

---

10 Susan Elliott provides a helpful summary of passages emphasizing regression (see Elliott 2003: 254–255).

11 The interpretative significance of context-specific modifications to standard epistolary formulae in Paul is comprehensively examined in Weima: 2016.

12 Weima 2016: 19–25.

13 Weima 2016: 44–50.

uncircumcised Gentiles keep their distance, and the failure of Jews to fully comprehend the consequences if they do, remain key points of contact between Antioch and Galatia throughout the discussion that follows.

But there's a further point of contact in Galatians 2:17–18. Does eating with sinners, as Peter did originally, involve Christ in their sin and even make him a sponsor of sin? No, says Paul, the opposite is the case. The thing that makes you a sinner is *rebuilding what you destroyed* when you first grasped the implications of Christ's coming. And this is a point Paul wants his present readers to hear.

The primary reference, of course, is to Peter. Peter has just flirted with precisely this kind of 'rebuilding'. In Acts 10, emboldened by a direct revelation from Jesus, Peter left his former scruples about fellowship with Gentiles behind and entered the household of Cornelius the Centurion. As the story continues, the church endorses his approach. Indeed, in Galatians 2:6–10 we may have, in sketch form at least, a Pauline recollection of the subsequent 'Jerusalem Council' where accepting Gentile believers without insistence on Jewish traditions became a matter of concerted policy.[14] In Galatians, rehearsing this event only serves to emphasize Peter's shocking volte-face in the very next passage. But his example has more than just historic value in the letter. It warns the Agitators (if we should include them in the audience) against going back on the church's collective decisions; and it warns the Galatians against *going back* to their own religious past.

In Galatians 3, the application to Paul's readers becomes less allusive and more direct; and regression, once again, stands at the centre of it. In Galatians 3:3, his logic contrasts old and new ways of doing things. The new way – the way associated with faith in Christ – is the way of the Spirit, the old way is the way of the flesh. And for Paul, his readers' behaviour is a return to the old. For all the venerability of circumcision, and despite the Abrahamic precedent to which the Agitators had in all probability turned for support judging by Paul's immediate Abrahamic counterpunch in Galatians 3:6–9,

---

14 The question of aligning the autobiographical material in Galatians with the version of events presented in Acts continues to provoke a range of responses from outright denials that Acts has anything determinative to tell us about Paul's biography (e.g. Campbell 2014: xv) through to detailed harmonizations (for an overview of the discussion, see Martin 2020: 19–23). Among attempts to harmonise the Pauline and Lukan sources, opinion is divided as to whether Galatians predates the Jerusalem Council and consequently makes no mention of it (e.g. Moo 2013: 8–18, 120–121) or antedates the meeting and includes a summary of the proceedings at Galatians 2:6–10 (e.g. Dunn 1993: 87–91). In my doctoral thesis I argue that, though the evidence is finely balanced, a convincing chronological case can be made for the latter option (see Martin 2020: 25–36).

the Galatians' present determination to embrace Judaism was a sign of regressive stupidity:

Are you so foolish? After beginning by means of the Spirit, are you now trying to finish by means of the flesh?

As the chapter develops, Paul linearizes the story of Israel from Abraham forward. After a respectful interval, law is added to covenant. But the law has a strictly time-limited function, watching over the people of God as they wait for their inheritance. Blessings for Jews entail blessings for Gentiles when it comes, as the pattern of pronouns in Galatians 3:23–29 and 4:1–7 reveals. But the overarching point is still regression. If we see the direction in which the story is moving – from infancy to maturity, from slave-like anticipation to inheritance – how could anyone willingly do anything so ridiculous as going back to where they'd been before?

The tight connection between the fate of Jews and Gentiles in these verses also hints at the full diagnosis when it comes in the next paragraph. Just as Gentile liberation from enslavement to idols depends on the coming of the Jewish Messiah, so returning to the Jewish status quo before his coming thrusts Gentiles back under the domination of idols. Paul sees an indissoluble link between Jewish practice in the present and his readers' situation as Gentiles in the past.

The regression theme comes to the boil in Galatians 4:8–11, where the Greek text stresses the danger of going backwards *four times* in the space of just fourteen words. In verse 9, the main verb *epistrephō* clearly expresses the idea of turning *back* with the addition of the preposition *epi* to the standard Greek expression for turning. But, not content with this, Paul bolsters the verb with an adverb, *palin* (meaning 'again'), and with an additional adverbial compound, *palin anōthen* (literally 'again from above'), which is used by other ancient authors to talk about making things according to a previously used pattern, performing calculations according to a previously used formula and assessing medical cases according to a previously used procedure, to name but a few examples.[15] Paul could not be clearer here that he's talking about the Galatians acting again in accordance with a pattern they already know.

And of course, the origin of that pattern couldn't be clearer. In Galatians 4:8, Paul points his readers to their past life as pagans, reminding them that they

---

15 See Wis. Sol. 19.6–7; Nichomachus of Gerasa, Int. Arit. I.22.2.24; Galen, Plac. Hip. Plat. 2.4.1.1–7; Sem. 4.566.8–9; and especially Hip. Aph. Comm. 17b.794.8. We use a similar phrase in English in musical contexts when we say, 'take it from the top'.

were slaves, literally to the 'not-gods' – a direct indication, once we've famil-
iarized ourselves with Paul's underlying Jewish presuppositions, that he perceived idolatry in his readers' backgrounds and perhaps even a devotion to the
Roman emperor that was ripe to be reawakened somehow through their close
encounter with Jewish law.

Paul returns to the Abrahamic narrative in Galatians 4:21–31 with his famous
allegorical interpretation of the Hagar and Sarah story, and once again regression
is the main point he has in mind. The two women represent two covenants. Hagar
is the covenant of Mount Sinai, law and slavery, the covenant associated in Paul's
mind with Jerusalem as he knew it at the point of writing. And Sarah, by contrast, is the covenant of freedom and the heavenly Jerusalem. Much more could
be said here too about Paul's covenant theology and the significance of the mountain imagery in a letter written to a region with a long tradition of worshipping
mother deities at mountain shrines.[16] But for all these interesting details, the primary point of application is unchanged. 'Therefore, brothers and sisters, we are
not children of the slave woman, but of the free woman' (Gal. 4:31). And we must
act like it. The biblical narrative on which Paul draws leaves no room for doubt
that the hope of Sarah's children categorically surpasses the hope of the children
of Hagar. 'The slave woman's son,' he says, citing Genesis 21:10, 'will never share
in the inheritance with the free woman's son' (Gal. 4:30). Nothing could be more
foolish or dangerous than returning from the one to the other. Hence the famous
statement of the believer's freedom that follows immediately afterwards.

*It is for freedom that Christ has set us free. Stand firm, then, and do not let
yourselves be burdened again by a yoke of slavery.* (Gal. 5:1)

We noted in Chapter 1 the oddity of the little word 'again' in this sentence.
But the point bears repeating. Paul isn't just talking here about some unfortu-
nate new development in the lives of the Galatians that's robbing them of the
freedom he wants them to enjoy in Christ. Paul is talking about a slavery of a
type akin to the slavery they've known in the past. The same point that we saw
drawn out in the movement from Galatians 3:23–4:7 through to 4:8–11 is repeated here. Embracing Jewish law – returning to Hagar, to Sinai, to slavery –
is actually returning to an experience his readers have experienced *before*. The
problem once again is regression.

---

16 On covenant theology, it is striking that, in Galatians 3, Paul refrains from describing the law as a
covenant, or even as a *codicil* to a pre-existent covenant (Gal. 3:15), but in Galatians 4:24, he describes
Hagar as the allegorical equivalent of a covenant. On the particular relevance of mountain mother
imagery in Asia Minor, see Elliott 1999: 661–683.

In Galatians 5:12 – 6:10, the practical implications of regression are exposed. This is no mere conceptual return to the logic of the old age that Paul has in his sights – a regression that only affects the realm of the mind. If the people Paul is writing to here are the same people he's writing to in Chapters 3 and 4, the move to embrace Jewish law is leading them back into quintessentially pagan *behaviour*.[17] Returning to the Spirit–flesh dichotomy we met for the first time in Chapter 3, Paul warns them that they cannot now live as they once did in the past. That past has been decisively ended in the lives of real believers: 'Those who belong to Christ Jesus have crucified the flesh with its passions and desires' (Gal. 5:24). From the beginning of the letter to the end, regression is the danger Paul wants his readers to see and to avoid.

2.2 Structure

But regression isn't just a frequently repeated motif in Galatians. It also plays a pivotal role in the *structure* of the letter. In the main body of the argument, running from Galatians 3:1 to 5:12, regression emerges both as a frame and as a focal point in Paul's argument.[18]

We've already noted the emphasis on *turning back* in the sections that introduce and conclude the central portion of the letter. In Galatians 3:3, the contrast between the Galatians' early faith and their more recent enthusiasm for the 'works of the law' makes the point. In Galatians 5:1, the curious 'again' in Paul's exhortation to stand firm against (re-)enslavement underlines it. But the significance of regression as a theme running through the heart of Paul's text only emerges when we notice the *similar function* these sections play in his larger argument. In each case, the accusation of regression forms *part of an exasperated outburst* from Paul.

In Galatians 3:1–5, condemnations of the Galatians' folly alternate with forceful rhetorical questions about their experience when he was last with them:

> *You foolish Galatians! Who has bewitched you? Before your very eyes Jesus Christ was clearly portrayed as crucified. I would like to learn just one*

---

17 The apparent disconnect between the vehement argument against circumcision and other associated 'works of the law' in Galatians 2–4, and the ethical commands of Galatians 5–6, has generated a host of alternative interpretative proposals. Barclay provides a helpful summary of the options in Barclay 1988: 9–23. We will return to the issue with an original suggestion derived from our work on regression in Chapter 11.

18 Structural outlines of various kinds have been proposed for Galatians, agreeing for the most part on the major movements from introductory formulae, to autobiography, to Antioch and from there to the theological core of the letter, followed by paranesis and the concluding exhortation. Betz famously discerns an argument constructed according to the norms of judicial rhetoric (see Betz: 1979). Dunn's less exegetically adventurous model accords broadly with the proposal set out in this chapter (see Dunn 1993: 21–22)

thing from you: Did you receive the Spirit by the works of the law, or by believing what you heard? Are you so foolish?... So again I ask, does God give you his Spirit and work miracles among you by the works of the law, or by your believing what you heard?' (Gal. 3:1–2)

Paul is seemingly unable to process the reality that these young believers, who had experienced such a great transformation through the agency of the Spirit, could now be committing themselves to a path that he equates with the old age of 'the flesh'.

Exasperation surfaces again in Galatians 5:1–12. 'Mark my words!' he tells his readers, 'if you let yourselves be circumcised, Christ will be of no value to you at all' (Gal. 5:2). 'You were running a good race. Who cut in on you to keep you from obeying the truth?' (Gal. 5:7) – whoever they were, Paul doesn't spare them a dose of his own memorably pungent advice (Gal. 5:12)! But the point to notice is that exasperation – driven by what Paul sees as regression to the Galatians' pagan past – characterizes the opening *and* the closing of the whole main body of the letter, framing it and holding the material together.

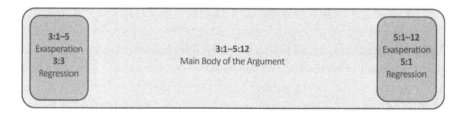

3:1–5 Exasperation	**3:1–5:12** Main Body of the Argument	**5:1–12** Exasperation
3:3 Regression		**5:1** Regression

Within this frame, careful structuring continues to be evident in the symmetrical positioning of Paul's two lengthy excurses into the Abrahamic narrative. Immediately after his opening expression of annoyance and immediately before its mirror image at the end, Paul leads his readers back into the Old Testament to explain what it means to be a true child of the promise. In Galatians 3:6–4:7, Abraham is deployed in a salvation historical argument, defining the relationship between covenant and law, and returning at the end to the identity of his descendants. In 4:21–31, Abraham returns in an allegorical argument, explaining present differences between those who do and those who don't accept Jesus as the Jewish Messiah. And at the centre of this structure, held between the arms of this larger Abrahamic story, we have exasperation and regression again, each raised to a point of climax.

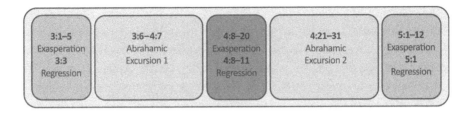

In Galatians 4:11, Paul expresses his fear that he has 'wasted [his] efforts' on his Galatian readers. In 4:12–16 he pleads with them, urging them to trust him now as they trusted him at first. In 4:17–18 he begs them to forsake the influence of their new teachers who are motivated more by a desire to convert them to their own opinions than by genuine concern for their welfare. And in 4:19–20 he concludes with one of the most poignant expressions of pastoral concern in the whole Bible, comparing himself to a woman in labour and longing that he might see them in person and change the tone in which he now feels it necessary to write.[19]

Exasperation, then, does more than just identify the frame of Paul's argument, it points to its centre – it identifies the perimeter, and it identifies the core. And there at the core we find not just a climactic expression of Paul's annoyance, but a climactic expression of its cause. If we want to know what the problem was in Galatia, the place to look is Galatians 4:8–11. The problem was the Galatians' imminent return, by means of embracing Jewish traditions, to the norms of their pagan past.

2.3 Significance

Might these observations help us overcome the sticking points in existing interpretations? Richard Hays' work on the narrative substructure of Galatians 3:1–4:11 suggests, perhaps, they might.[20]

Debates between Old, and New and Radical New Perspectives predictably focus on the perceived implications of their readings *for the content of Paul's gospel*. The gospel is the assertion of grace over *Jewish legalism* – God achieves what our works cannot, overcoming the curse of the law and justifying us on account of Christ's righteousness. The gospel is the assertion of grace over *Jewish nationalism* – God achieves what Israel could not, overcoming the curse of the law and opening the way for Gentile inclusion. The gospel

---

19 Dunn highlights the 'personal appeal' in Galatians 4:12–20 framed by Paul's two appeals to scripture, but he fails to draw out the parallels to the similarly impassioned entreaties of Galatians 3:1–5 and 5:1–12 (see Dunn 1993: 21–22).

20 Hays 2002: 163–207.

is the assertion of grace over *supersessionism* – God achieves a salvation for Gentiles that wasn't needed for Jews because they already possessed the law. None of these competing claims are even addressed, still less *resolved*, in the part of Galatians that our analysis has placed at its centre. Appeals to more familiar passages are typically made to force these 'right answers' to emerge – like Galatians 2:15–16, with its classic dichotomization of faith and works, or Galatians 3:10–14, where the curse of the law meets its match in the accomplishments of Christ. But according to Hays these texts are not so easily separated from the structural hub we've identified.

For Hays, as Paul tells and retells his gospel narrative, its characteristic elements are repeated under different names and each should inform our understanding of the others as we note their reappearance. Wherever he tells it, Paul's gospel story begins with an 'initial state of deprivation'.[21] In Galatians 3:10–14, it's life under the curse. In 3:23–29 it's imprisonment under the law. In 4:1–7, it's life under the *stoicheia*. And each of these articulations of the problem informs all the others.[22] We can't know what the curse of the law means until we've seriously considered the image of imprisonment. We can't know what imprisonment under the law means until we've seriously considered enslavement to the *stoicheia*. And enslavement to the *stoicheia*, as we've just seen, lies right at the very heart of Paul's description of regression.

Regression is treated as a minor issue, if at all, in most major exegeses of the letter – it's an example of rhetorical hyperbole, an eschatological sleight of hand, a gesture towards unspecified Jewish experiences lurking in the background. But if going backwards really occupies the central position sketched out for it above, none of this will do. We simply can't understand what Paul's gospel in Galatians means until we've understood why embracing Jewish law involved a return to his readers' pagan past.

---

21 Hays 2002: 201.

22 'The correspondence between [Gal. 3:23–29 and 4:3–7] reinforces the unavoidable identification between the Law and the *stoicheia tou kosmou* which is such a peculiar feature of Paul's thought in Galatians' (Hays 2002: 201). De Boer notes the semantic relationship between Christ's work of 'redemption' (*exagorazō*) in Galatians 3:13 and the enslavement language used in Galatians 4:3, 8–9, 25 (de Boer 2011: 210). See also Longenecker 1998: 91–95.

5
Going Backwards to a Jewish Past

Introduction

So, Paul's friends in Galatia are on the brink of accepting circumcision and Jewish festivals and other unspecified 'works of the law' that served to mark Jews out as Jews in the ancient world, and in response he tells them they're going back to something they've done before. Can't this be explained simply by appealing to their *prior experience of Judaism*? Acts, after all, makes it pretty clear that Paul's missionary endeavours in Asia Minor began in cities with synagogues and substantial populations of Godfearing Gentiles (e.g. Acts 13:16, 26, 48, 50; 14:1–2). And even if Galatians wasn't written to these locations but to cities further north, surely we can imagine him deploying similar tactics? In short, if Paul founded Gentile churches by starting with people who were already interested in the Jewish God, wouldn't 'going backwards' have been quite a good way – quite a *logical* way, in fact – to talk to them about embracing Jewish law?

It's often assumed that solutions like this tell us everything we need to know about the problematic prominence of regression in Galatians. But the reality isn't so simple. In this chapter, we'll expose the flaws in this logic by taking a journey back into Jewish life and experience in the period and in the place where Paul's readers actually lived.

1 Into the Past

Our starting point is the observation that *there certainly were* Jewish communities in Asia Minor at the time Paul wrote. They'd been there for at least 250 years. In 205 BC, the Seleucid king Antiochus III relocated a group of 2,000 Jewish families from Babylon to Lydia and Phrygia with extensive privileges and protections (Josephus Ant. 12.148–153).[1] By the latter half of the

---

1   Jews may have reached the region considerably earlier if we accept the suggestion that 'the exiles from Jerusalem in Sepharad' mentioned in Obadiah 20 were actually inhabitants of Sardis (see Allen 1976: 131). See also Littman 1916: 23–38; Lipinski 1973: 368–370; Van der Horst 2014: 144; Dupont-Sommer 1966: 112–117. Trebilco remains sceptical about the connection (Trebilco 1991: 38).

second century BC, 1 Maccabees tells us they were prospering and had spread out across a wide area (1 Macc. 15.15–24). By the latter half of the first century BC, they were sending extraordinary quantities of gold back to Jerusalem for the upkeep of the temple there (Cicero Flac. 68).

Exactly how extensive these diaspora communities were in Paul's day is a hotly debated topic. Some scholars reckon Jews accounted for 10% of the total population of the empire, perhaps even 20% in the east.[2] But even if we adopt a cautious approach to extrapolations like this, there's little doubt that Jews constituted a significant segment of society, and little reason to question the realism of a writer like Philo when he tells us that, at the time of the Alexandrian embassy to Caligula in AD 40, they were 'very numerous in every city [in] Asia and Syria' (Embassy 245).[3]

In Chapter 3 we glanced briefly at the life situation of diaspora Jews when we thought about Bruce Winter's suggestion that they enjoyed statutory protections under Roman law. Privileges were certainly granted to Jewish communities in Graeco-Roman cities from time to time, most notably under Julius Caesar, who exempted them from what were otherwise sweeping restrictions on private religious meetings in gratitude for the military help provided by the Jewish Ethnarch, John Hyrcanus II (Josephus Ant. 14.213). But not even Josephus' highly selective description of the situation amounts to evidence of established constitutional rights for Jews, or masks the reality that their relationships with their pagan neighbours were sometimes tense.[4] Jews were frequently required to petition local governments, sometimes even the Roman Senate, for ongoing permission to practise their unusual brand of monotheistic worship. Josephus dwells on the appeals that were successful, but we also know of several that weren't (e.g. War. 2.285–292, 306).[5]

In Asia Minor specifically, these exchanges reveal the presence of substantial Jewish communities in many of the largest cities. We have Jews in Ephesus (Ant. 14.226), Sardis (Ant. 14.260), Laodicea (Ant. 14.241–243), Miletus (Ant. 14.244–246), Pergamum (Ant. 14.247–255) and Halicarnassus (Ant. 256–258).

---

2 Feldman 1993: 92. Feldman's figures are drawn from analyses conducted by Salo Baron, who leans heavily on a questionably reliable twelfth-century Syrian account of a census taken by the emperor Claudius in AD 48 (Baron 2007: 381–400) and Adolf von Harnack (Harnack 1962: 1–8). For a similarly maximalist use of the underlying data, see Wilson 1995: 21.

3 Writing a century earlier, the Greek geographer, philosopher and historian Strabo comes to a similar conclusion: 'This people has already made its way into every city, and it is not easy to find a place in the inhabited world which has not received this nation and in which it has not made its power felt' (cited in Josephus Ant. 14.115).

4 As Barclay notes, Josephus's testimony 'is anecdotal and partial (in both senses of the word)' (Barclay 1996: 260 et passim). For a parallel debate about the usefulness of Josephus as a witness to Hellenistic politics, see Schwartz 2004: 47–61.

5 See Rajak 1985: 31.

Together with Laodicea and Pergamum, Cicero mentions Apamea and Ad-ramyttium as regional hubs for the collection of the temple tax (Flac. 68). And some of this data can be reinforced archaeologically. In 1962 a massive syna-gogue was discovered in Sardis.[6] Originally constructed as the southern wing of a public gymnasium complex in the second century AD, the building was taken over by local Jews and accommodated a thousand people in comfort in its fourth-century heyday.[7] Coins minted in Apamea in the late second and early third centuries depicting Noah and his wife in a box-like ark or '*Kibōtos*,' recognizable throughout the region as the city's distinctive commercial 'logo', reveal the presence of Jews with sufficient influence to shape the design of key civic symbols.[8] If the peculiarly Phrygian retelling of the biblical flood story in the *Sibylline Oracles* is anything to go by, Jews had been making their pres-ence felt in the surrounding region for more than 300 years.[9]

Noah Coins
Apamea, Early Second Century A.D. Public Domain

Plot these cities on a map and the results show Jewish settlements concen-trated in the southern and western portions of Asia Minor in large cities with easy access to the coast. To date, archaeology has yielded barely any evidence of Jewish life in the northern cities of Pessinus and Ankara, which have some-times been suggested as possible locations for the Galatian churches, and no evidence of synagogues at all.[10] In the southern cities, however, documentary and material evidence largely corroborates the picture provided by Acts. These

---

6   For a brief summary of the history of the Sardis synagogue, see Kraabel 1992e: 270–273.

7   See Seager 1972: 425–435. See also Kraabel 1992c: 226–228, 230; Kraabel 1992d: 242–248; Trebilco 1991: 40–43.

8   See Trebilco 1991: 86–95. See also Schürer 2014, vol. 3i: 29; Van der Horst 2014: 149; Lightfoot 2007: 367–370; Trebilco 1991: 92–93. *Kibōtos* is first attested as a nickname for Apamea shortly before the turn of the era (Strabo Geog. 12.8.13).

9   See Charlesworth 2009, vol. 1: 331–332.

10 See Breytenbach 1996: 127–133, 144–148.

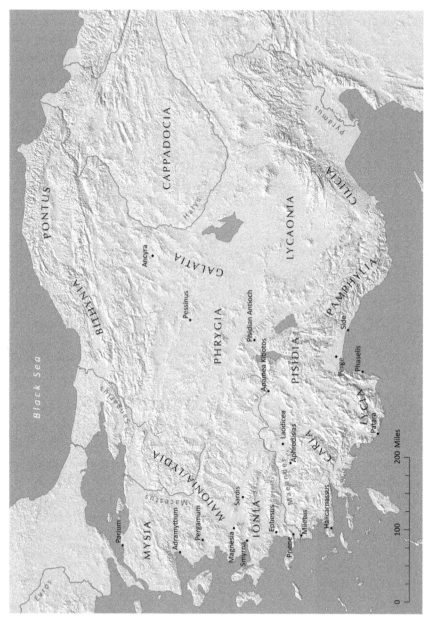

Map 1 Jewish Background: Select Sites

58

were places with synagogues to preach in and, if they existed, Godfearing Gentiles to evangelize.[11]

2 Godfearers in Asia Minor

But did Godfearers actually exist? Like all other parts of the Acts account, the stories of Paul meeting Gentiles with pre-existent affinities to local Jewish synagogues have been exposed to searching criticism over the years. The idea that Jewish communities in the first century played host to a substantial class of Gentile affiliates – attracted to the timeless solemnity of the Mosaic law, participating in the Jewish sabbath and then returning to the rites and rhythms of pagan life for the rest of the week – is viewed by many as fanciful nonsense. Forty years ago, the noted Jewish archaeologist Thomas Kraabel declared that Godfearers had simply 'disappeared'.[12]

In part, this judgment reflected a welcome reframing of the debate after generations of unwarranted negativity about Jewish life and culture in the Roman world. Biblical scholars had grown used to anachronistic portraits of diaspora Judaism as a syncretistic 'religion', and of diaspora Jews as subservient, socially and intellectually backward, conscious of their 'foreignness' and desperate to attract sympathizers and sponsors by any means possible.[13] Kraabel redrew the picture along radically different lines. Diaspora Jews were confident and self-possessed, stepping forward to meet Gentile culture and contribute without compromise. And there is evidence to support this view.

We've already noted the administrative lengths to which Jewish leaders went to secure exemptions from the broader expectation of participation in pagan worship. Literary and epigraphic evidence suggests they were just as energetic in maintaining their own forms of devotion amid the prevailing norms of Gentile culture. A third-century AD inscription from Hierapolis records the last will and testament of a Jew named Publius Aelius Glykon, in which he urges his former colleagues in the local guild of purple dyers and carpet weavers to decorate his family tomb with wreaths in perpetuity on the great Jewish festivals of Passover and Pentecost.[14] In the second century, *The*

---

11 Van der Horst 1990: 170; Van der Horst 2014: 150; Wilson 1995: 26. Mitchell develops Epiphanius's reference to the conversion of Lydia in Acts 16:13–15 (Pan. 80.1.5) as part of his argument that Paul deliberately targeted Godfearers in his evangelistic endeavours (Mitchell 1999a: 93, 115).

12 Kraabel 1992b: 119–130.

13 Kraabel 1992a: 6–11.

14 IJO: no. 196. See also Van der Horst 2008: 286. On the importance of purple-dying industry in ancient Hierapolis, see Strabo, Geog. 13.4.14.

Epistle to Diognetus's stylish description of dogged diaspora commitment to traditional Jewish festivals – not to mention dietary laws, sabbaths and circumcision – presents us with a similar vision (Diog. 4.1–5).[15]

In time, Jewish distinctiveness also expressed itself in contrast to Christianity, mirroring concurrent developments in Christian life and thought. Jews in Smyrna in the second century AD are very clear about the differences between themselves and their Christian neighbours in the martyrdom account of the local bishop, Polycarp, even if it comes at the expense of collaborating with the pagan authorities – or so the Christian author of the account alleges (Mart. Pol. 12.2; 13.1; 17.2–18.1).[16] Something similar could be said of the situation in contemporary Sardis according to the few works of the city's fiery preacher–bishop, Melito, that remain to us.[17] Trypho, the eponymous Jewish debating partner in Justin Martyr's famous mid-second-century *Dialogue* lingers on distinctiveness as a key area in which Jews excel over their Christian neighbours, charging Christians with hypocrisy because they 'claim to be pious and believe [themselves] to be different from... others [but they] do not segregate [themselves] from them nor do [they] observe a manner of life different from that of the Gentiles, for [they] do not keep the feasts or sabbaths, nor do [they] practice the rite of circumcision' (Dial. 10.3).

Jewish distinctiveness can also be observed in relief in the opinions of contemporary Greek and Roman historians. Strabo notes the peculiar Jewish practice of aniconic worship (Geog. 16.2.35–7). Marcus Terentius Varro does the same (Augustine Civ. 4.31). Epictetus is familiar with Jewish food laws and with the distinctive features that mark out authentic Jewish converts (Disc. 1.11.12–13; 1.22.4; 2.9.19–20). And in each case distinctiveness breeds respect. But even where it breeds contempt, the resilience of diaspora Jews to assimilation is no less evident. Horace sees Jewish distinctiveness as a basis for playful mockery, Seneca sees it as a basis for vituperative abuse.[18] Tacitus is no less abrasive:

The Jews are extremely loyal toward one another, and always ready to show compassion, but toward every other people they feel only hate and enmity.

---

15 Martin 2020: 157.

16 See McCreedy 2005: 154–155.

17 Notice, in particular, Melito's excoriating treatment of Jewish responsibility for Jesus' execution (Per. Pas. 72, 81, 91–92), culminating in their arraignment before the nations on the charge of regicide (Per. Pas. 94), in contrast to his broadly excusing remarks about the Romans (Per. Pas. 92).

18 Horace Sat. 1.5.96–104; 1.9.60–78. As part of his broader distaste for eastern religious influences in the Roman world, Seneca considered the Jewish Sabbath a pretext for idleness and its popularity an indication of the low ebb to which Rome had descended (Civ. 6.11).

> *They sit apart at meals, and... abstain from intercourse with foreign women... They adopted circumcision to distinguish themselves from other peoples by this difference. Those who are converted to their ways follow the same practice, and the earliest lesson they receive is to despise the gods, to disown their country, and to regard their parents, children, and brothers as of little account... They regard as impious those who make from perishable materials representations of gods in man's image; that supreme and eternal being is to them incapable of representation and without end. Therefore they set up no statues in their cities, still less in their temples; this flattery is not paid their kings, nor this honour given to the Caesars.* (Hist. 5:5)

But for all this emphasis on self-possession and distinctiveness, there is still abundant evidence of Jewish *engagement* with Gentile host cultures.

Jewish apologetic literature may itself be a manifestation of this phenomenon. Texts like Josephus's *Against Apion* and *The Letter of Aristeas* are ostensibly addressed to Gentiles with the goal of persuading them to embrace the Jewish way of life. But even if this is unrealistic, they clearly demonstrate a familiarity with the wider pagan environment sufficient to discern where the external criticisms of Judaism lay as well as a capacity to '[highlight] the aspects... which were most acceptable to cultured Gentiles'.[19]

The Noah coins of Apamea narrate a similar willingness to make connections with the surrounding context. Jews are certainly seen stepping forward into creative collaboration with their pagan neighbours here, but the result is compromise *on both sides*.[20] Jewish influence is evident in the name of the hero the coins depict, but the choice of the story has as much to do with the popularity of flood myths in contemporary Phrygian folklore as it does with widespread local familiarity with the Hebrew Bible, and it's striking that the secondary image of Noah and his wife on the coins – giving thanks for their deliverance – portrays them with their hands raised in a gesture that is typically Hellenistic.[21]

The synagogue in Sardis offers only frustratingly late evidence for Jewish interactions with Gentiles in Asia Minor, but it's suggestive, nonetheless, to note that the congregation that met there heard scripture read sabbath by sabbath from a table standing on legs decorated with massive Roman eagles grasping

---

19 Collins 2000: 15. See also Delling 1987: 29; Collins 2000: 14, 271; Donaldson 2007: 6–7; Schürer 2014, vol. 3i: 153–155.

20 Trebilco 1991: 86–95. See also Van der Horst 2014: 149. In dissent, see Schürer 2014, vol. 3i: 30.

21 Trebilco 1991: 87.

the fasces, and flanked by equally massive stone lions characteristic of Lydian art and architecture.[22] Coins recovered from the building confirm that Jews commissioned and laid the synagogue's vast and intricate mosaic floor in the fourth century AD with floral and animal patterns on the contemporary pagan model.[23] Inscriptions on the wall commemorate nine (possibly ten) Jewish city councillors.[24]

Kraabel, who was himself actively involved in the excavations, interpreted all of this as symptomatic of Jewish self-confidence – their religious identity was so robust not even high levels of pagan social engagement could shake it.[25] But the assertion stretches credence. A more natural reading of the evidence from Sardis suggests that Jewish life in the city was far from unaffected by Gentile influence or involvement.[26] And this leads us directly to the question of Godfearers.

The inscriptions at Sardis include several references to individuals described as *theosebēs* (God-venerators) – a term interpreted as a reference to Godfearers in traditional scholarship but reimagined as a commemoration of Jewish donors by Kraabel.[27] *Theosebēs* is not used in Acts which prefers the literalistic description *hoi phoboumenoi ton theon* (ones who fear God) when it describes Cornelius the Roman centurion and Paul's Gentile audience in the synagogue in Pisidian Antioch. The reference to *hai sebomenai gynaikes* (women who venerate) in Acts 13:50 is an interesting exception, but the whole Lukan account of Godfearing Gentiles was dismissed nonetheless by Kraabel as Christian propaganda. Similar examples in contemporary inscriptions were also waved away as part of his larger effort to rehabilitate diaspora Judaism from the slights of former generations of scholars. Kraabel didn't see it as a compliment to imagine that Jews welcomed Gentiles into their communities on their own terms.

But the plausibility of at least this part of Kraabel's reconstruction suffered a devastating blow even before it could gain any significant momentum with the publication, in 1987, of a third- or fourth-century AD Jewish inscription discovered in Aphrodisias, just a few miles west of Laodicea.[28] The text, carved into

---

22 See Kraabel 1992d: 245–247; Trebilco 1991: 42. See also Hanfmann et al. 1983: figs. 256–258.

23 See Kraabel 1992d: 245.

24 See IJO: nos. 62, 72, 77–78, 85–87, 92, 95, 98.

25 Kraabel 1992e: 279–284.

26 See Martin 2020: 174.

27 IJO: nos. 67–68, 83, 123, 125, 132. On the interpretation of *theosbēs* see Kraabel 1992b: 119–130.

28 Reynolds et al.: 1987 = IJO: no. 14. See also Collins 2000: 267; Van der Horst 1990: 169; Feldman 1993: 70; Levinskaya 1996: 70–80.

the surface of a massive marble pillar, lists on one side the eighteen members of a group called the *dekania* (literally 'the ten' – presumably the group had ten members to begin with). Thirteen are born Jews (with Jewish names), three (with adopted Jewish names) are described as *prosēlytos* (proselytes) and two (with Greek names) are described as *theosebēs*. On the other side, the names of 125 'donors' are listed together with their occupations. Sixty-eight are born Jews (with Jewish names), three are *prosēlytos* (with Jewish names) and fifty-four are *theosebēs* (with Gentile names). Among the *theosebēs* we find individuals engaged in some very typically Gentile lines of work: 'boxers', 'athletes' and 'sellers/producers of mincemeat'. Clearly, we have Gentiles involved in the life of the Jewish community as Gentiles here on a massive scale. This is now viewed as decisive evidence that Godfearers did indeed exist.[29]

3 The Godfearing Lifestyle

Godfearers, then, are an admissible ingredient as we seek to reconstruct the background of Galatians, as commentators through the centuries have generally assumed.[30] Paul's readers *might* have been familiar with the Torah before he met them. They *might* have heard it read every week if they'd participated in the life of local synagogues. And this *might* go some way to explaining the detailed familiarity with the Abraham story that Paul seems able to assume as he writes, not to mention his wider use of Old Testament allusions.[31]

But before we jump to any premature conclusions, let's ask ourselves first what the Godfearing lifestyle might have actually involved in a place like this.

In the kinds of cities Paul was writing to, we have very little evidence of Jewish communities at all and only the hints provided by Acts to tell us about the activities of Godfearers in the region.[32] The Aphrodisias inscription is hugely significant, but it draws us far away from the Galatian churches in place and time. So, is there any other data we can call upon to fill in the gaps?

---

29 Trebilco 1991: 152–155.

30 'Paul drew his pagans from that penumbra of already-interested outsiders, the "god-fearers"' (Fredriksen 2017: 126). See also Munck 1959: 132. Even if Paul's readers were not themselves former Godfearers, Barclay argues that the attractions of synagogue worship were widely recogniszed in the Jewish diaspora of the first century and that 'by beginning to observe the law... the Galatians were following a path which many of their contemporaries would have understood' (Barclay 1988: 69).

31 Nanos argues that the Galatians' competence to grasp Paul's Jewish argument was a fruit of his own ministry among them (Nanos 2002: 76–77). Dunn attributes it to the ministry of the Agitators (Dunn 1993: 9–11).

32 The synagogue in Iconium seems to have incorporated Gentile sympathisers, even if Luke doesn't identify them specifically as he does in his portrait of life in Pisidian Antioch in Acts 14:1–7.

The prime extrabiblical example of Godfearing behaviour in first-century Asia Minor is that of a wealthy Roman noblewoman known to us through multiple epigraphic sources as Julia Severa. Julia Severa was a priestess of the imperial cult in Acmonia, about 100 miles west of Pisidian Antioch. She was also the mother of a future Roman Senator and was known for her service as a magistrate in the AD 50s and 60s alongside the high-ranking Roman immigrant Servinius Capito.[33] In a second-century inscription commemorating the renovation of the local synagogue, Julia Severa emerges as its original benefactress. Not only was she responsible for its construction but she also endowed it with a golden shield – 'so excellent', we're told, '[was] her attitude and her benevolence and zeal for [the institution]'.[34]

Following the collapse of Kraabel's 'disappearance' hypothesis, scholars have increasingly located Julia Severa on a spectrum that includes the kinds of Godfearing behaviours that interest us here.[35] It's impossible to tell how typical she was of the larger phenomenon. But it's striking nonetheless that Jews in Acmonia were willing to publicly acknowledge their indebtedness to this pagan lady. And it's striking too that her involvement in their synagogue clearly didn't come at the cost of renouncing her obligations to pagan gods. In this instance at least, the Godfearer lifestyle was compatible with participation in the worship of the emperor. Indeed, it was compatible with officiating at his rites.[36]

Neither is Julia Severa a lone example of her type. The proximity of Luke's reference to 'Godfearing women of high standing' in Pisidian Antioch in Acts 13:50 is particularly enticing. So is a third-century AD inscription from Tralles in Caria commemorating another wealthy noblewoman, Claudia Capitolina, who funded the construction of a platform and an inlaid staircase in her local synagogue, and who is explicitly described as a *theosebēs*.[37] In each case we get the impression that synagogues in the region were open to interested Gentiles who were given the freedom to weave elements of Jewish worship into

---

33 Schürer 2014, vol. 3i: 30–31; Donaldson 2007: 464; Van der Horst 2014: 148; Trebilco 1991: 58–60. Recent excavations have also revealed Julia Severa's involvement in the establishment of the imperial cult in Perge (Bru et al. 2016: 65–82).

34 IJO: no. 168.

35 Kraabel 1992a: 12; Kraabel 1992b: 119–130; cf. Cohen 1999: 147. See also Overman 1992: 150 and Donaldson 2007: 465–466.

36 'Apparently [Jews in Acmonia] were prepared to honor a Gentile who demonstrated support and appreciation for the Jewish community in such a public way without either expecting that she demonstrate exclusive loyalty to the God of Israel or feeling that their own identity was somehow compromised or threatened in the process' (Donaldson 2007: 466). See also Goodman 1994: 55.

37 IJO: no. 27. See also Van der Horst 1990: 177; Trebilco 1991: 157–158.

the larger fabric of their personal devotions. On the fifth row of seats in the theatre at Miletus, it's still possible to see a late second- or early third-century inscription indicating separate reservations for Jews and Godfearers.[38] Clearly the distinction was readily comprehensible in Milesian culture at the time, and both groups were regularly engaged in this aspect of city life.[39]

Switching to literary evidence, the early second-century letters of Ignatius of Antioch also bring us closer to Galatia in time and space than the Aphrodisias inscription and hint at the presence and activities of Godfearers in the period.[40] In his letters to the churches in Magnesia and Philadelphia, Ignatius is troubled by the extent to which Jews are influencing his Christian correspondents, and especially the role played by *Gentile* apologists for Judaism – who may have been Godfearers, proselytes or a mixture of the two (Mag. 10.3; Phld. 6.1).

Though distant from the life and circumstances of Asia Minor, the Roman poet Juvenal provides a glimpse of Godfearing behaviour in his famous description of a Jewish 'conversion' worked out over a period of two generations (Sat. 14.96–106). The father in this entertaining vignette is interested in Judaism to the extent that he 'reveres the Sabbath' and abstains from pork. But the larger world of his devotions is unaffected. He doesn't embrace circumcision or submit to the law of Moses. It's only in the subsequent account of his son's experience that we encounter the transition from Godfearer to proselyte.

Epictetus assumes that marginal 'pagan-Jews' were so familiar to his readers that he uses them as an illustration of his larger thesis that men and women are only truly satisfied when their beliefs and practice are consistent (Disc. 2.9.19–20). The third-century Christian Latin writer Commodian paints a similar picture, condemning Godfearers as 'duplicitous people' who attend the synagogue but then 'go outside again [searching] for pagan temples' (Instr. 1.24.11–14; 1.37; translation mine).

Few have embraced Stephen Mitchell's suggestion that Godfearers stand behind the extraordinarily large number of inscriptions dedicated to *Theos Hypsistos* ('the highest God') that have been recovered from Asia Minor in this

---

38 IJO: no. 37.

39 Note Christian Marek's helpful survey of the interpretative options for this text (Marek 2018: 133–134). See also Trebilco 1991: 159–162.

40 See Weijenborg: 1969; Joly: 1979; Hübner 1997: 44–72; Ehrman 2003, vol. 1: 209–213; Foster 2012: 3392–3395.

period.[41] His proposal – that Godfearers, used to combining elements of paganism and Judaism, collaborated with hellenized Jews to create a distinctive *Theos Hypsistos* cult – has faltered for lack of evidence. The inscriptions are probably generic, representing a variety of cults and expressing devotion to a variety of gods.[42] But the fact that Mitchell's thesis could have even been seriously entertained only underlines the emerging consensus on Godfearing behaviour. Gentiles who had formerly participated in the life of local synagogues but who had not for that reason ceased simultaneous participation in pagan rites could very plausibly have been a significant factor in the constitution of early Pauline churches.

All this, then, brings us to the key question we're seeking to resolve in this chapter: if the believers Paul was writing to were Godfearers in the past, if they were the kind of people we read about in Acts 13–14 – Gentiles who were already established members of synagogue communities before he met them, who heard his message about the coming of the Jewish Messiah and who responded with faith – can *that* explain why he describes their newfound interest in Jewish law as *going back* to something they had done before? There are two ways to approach this.

4 Regression to a Godfearing Past

The first option sees Paul's criticism of the Galatians as a literalistic description of returning to the same kind of religious lifestyle they'd engaged in before he met them.[43] As Godfearing members of local Jewish communities before his arrival in the region, they had the freedom to participate in the life of the synagogue as much or as little as they wanted with no sense of obligation to change the larger pattern of their devotion to pagan gods. Interest in the God of Israel – perhaps even some measure of commitment to the God of Israel – was just one component in a larger portfolio of religious affiliation, and there was nothing particularly unusual about that. The example of the pagan priestess Julia Severa makes the point.

Paul's readers lived in a pluralistic culture where it was normal to worship a variety of gods, and very few households shared exactly the same set of sacred

---

41 Mitchell justifies his equation of Hypsistarians and Godfearers by comparing the physical settings in which their respective acts of worship may have taken place and the descriptions of each offered by Epiphanius and Gregory of Nazianzus, and Cyril and Juvenal respectively (Mitchell 1999a: 92–95, 120).

42 See Marek 2018: 144.

43 Martin 2020: 177–179.

allegiances. Some components were expected, of course – if not officially, then through the medium of social pressure.[44] We saw earlier in the lengthy quote from Tacitus how disgusted he felt about Jewish proselytes renouncing the Graeco-Roman pantheon as a whole; in the next chapter we'll see something of the weight of disapproval experienced by people who failed to participate in time-honoured local cults.[45] But Godfearers were spared these difficulties. Godfearers could show up at the synagogue on a Saturday (perhaps attracting some mild abuse for laziness – the idea of a weekly sabbath had yet to take hold across society more widely – but nothing worse) and then carry on with their lives as normal on a Sunday, paying their respects to the emperor at his temple, participating in communal rituals seeking blessings on harvests and battles, honouring the household gods venerated by their parents and grandparents and so forth.

Could something similar have been replicated *in a church*? Imagine Paul's Galatian readers participating in the life of the Christian community whenever they gathered – eating, hearing, worshipping together – and then returning to normal pagan life immediately afterwards. Some residue of this deeply ingrained attitude to religious allegiances seems to have been lurking in the background amid all the other problems in Corinth. Might the same thing have been true among the believers in Galatia? We can certainly see how it would have solved a host of pressing practical problems in their relationship to larger society. And we can also see it solving some pressing interpretative problems in Paul's text. How is it that he can describe embracing Jewish law as returning to paganism? That's the key question this book sets out to answer. And *here is* an answer, or so it seems. The Galatians were reverting to the model of religious participation they had practised in the synagogue in the past. With the Agitators' encouragement, they were sharing in the life of the Christian community, but without renouncing the religious norms of the surrounding culture.

But there are obvious problems with this. For a start, we ought to be careful about the unstated leap we're making here from 'former Godfearers as a potential *component* of Paul's audience' to 'former Godfearers as his *exclusive* target'. James Dunn goes further than most when he argues that, the earlier in

---

44 According to the Historia Augusta's biography of Marcus Aurelius, in the late second century, those with sufficient financial means were expected to keep images of the emperor in their homes or be 'deemed guilty of sacrilege' (Hist. Aug. 4.18.5). But there is no evidence of a general *obligation* to participate in local imperial cult activities until the reign of Decius in the third century (see Marek et al. 2016: 536).

45 See, for example, Beichtinschriften: no. 108.

the story of Gentile outreach we go, the more likely it is that former Godfear-ers were the largest group in all the little churches Paul planted.[46] But it would be a brave interpretation of Galatians indeed to assume they accounted for the entire audience; and that's what we're flirting with here. Paul's argument about regression in Galatians isn't targeted at a subset of his readership or restricted to a tightly circumscribed subsection of the text. It stands at the very core of the letter and is repeated throughout. The question we need to ask ourselves here is not 'can we think of an explanation for Paul's regression language that might work for *some* of his readers?' but 'can we think of an explanation that justifies him throwing the kitchen sink *at all of them*?'

The real problem with interpretations founded on the idea that the Gala-tians were returning to pre-established Godfearing norms, however, is that they don't match up with the facts as we know them. Amid the many frustrat-ing lacunae in the data about the Agitators in Galatia, one area of certainty does at least stand out – the newcomers were urging Paul's Gentile converts *to get circumcised*.[47] And that just doesn't fit with the suggestion that they were simultaneously encouraging the Galatians to adopt a new church-based ver-sion of the behaviour that had characterized their lives as Godfearers in dias-pora synagogues in the past. There is simply no evidence in Galatians to sup-port the idea that the Agitators thought like this – that Gentiles could and should embrace Christ as one god among many, as a part, and as no more than a part, of some larger suite of pagan religious affiliations. The Agitators seem rather to have been encouraging Paul's readers to follow Christ by be-coming proselyte Jews, with circumcision positioned as the crowning step in the process.[48]

Without any need to speculate about the Agitators' hopes and methods, however, the Galatians' readiness to embrace circumcision alone should crush the idea that they were returning to their former lifestyle as Godfearers if that is indeed what they had been. The whole rationale of Godfearing behaviour was the avoidance of exclusive commitment. Godfearers were people who ex-pressed devotion to the God of Israel *without getting circumcised*. If the be-lievers in Galatia were returning to the norms they had learned as Godfear-ers in the past, it was a move *away from* the social angularity of the exclusive Christian commitment Paul had urged them to adopt *and back to* the familiar

---

46 'A high proportion of the earliest converts, perhaps all of them in the early days, would have been proselytes and Godfearers' (Dunn 2006a: 165–166).

47 See Barclay 1987: 88.

48 See Chapter 3, pp. 37–38.

pluralistic behaviour of their past. But that has nothing to do with circumcision. Circumcision was a move in the opposite direction. Circumcision was an expression of exclusive commitment. Circumcision involved an *increase* in social angularity.

5 Regression *in the General Direction* of Judaism

How else, then, might we think about the possibility that the Galatians were returning to a past that was already familiar to them thanks to their prior involvement in local Jewish synagogues? If Paul *wasn't* accusing them of becoming Godfearers again, might he at least have been accusing them of regressing *in the general direction* of Judaism? Might his accusation amount to little more, in fact, than the observation that his readers had been enthusiastic about Judaism in the past and now they were doing it again?[49]

This approach has the great advantage that it accommodates *the direction of movement* clearly indicated by the Galatians' interest in circumcision – they were looking for more commitment, not less commitment; more exclusivity, not less exclusivity. This emphasis is lost if we imagine Paul accusing his readers of embracing a lifestyle that matched point for point their former behaviour as Godfearers. But not if we imagine him simply noting the continuity between their prior enthusiasm for all things Jewish and their new enthusiasm for circumcision and 'the works of the law'. If they'd willingly attached themselves to local synagogues in the past, why shouldn't Paul have described their new readiness to embrace Jewish practices as a form of regression in the present? We can certainly see the similarity between the influences that would have shaped their experience as Godfearers and the influences they were now tempted to embrace. But, once again, this explanation breaks down when we try to line it up against the letter Paul actually writes.

In the previous section we saw how the suggestion that Paul's readers were returning to a Godfearing past explained very effectively his concern that they were going back to their former pagan norms (Gal. 4:8–11) but struggled to accommodate the parallel reality that they also wanted to get circumcised. Now we have the opposite problem. Now we have an explanation that accommodates their desire to get circumcised – circumcision is a step back into the orbit of the synagogue, back into the network of connections that marked them

---

49 Martin 2020: 179–182.

out as Godfearers in the past – but it offers us no help at all with the allegation that they're returning *to paganism*. We can't fall back now on the idea that they were being encouraged to live as Christ-followers on the sabbath and as pagans for the rest of the week. Now we have Galatians who are even more determined to express exclusive commitment to God than they were when Paul left them, expressing their hope in the Jewish Messiah by embracing the traditional signs of inclusion in the covenant. To make *this* compatible with going back to paganism, we have to imagine a Paul so changed in the process of embracing Christ as Lord that, for him, circumcision and Sabbaths and food laws had not only passed their sell-by date (Gal. 3:23; 4:2), they had become active evils in and of themselves, means through which devotion was expressed to the not-gods, not to the God who is (Gal. 4:8).

And this, as we've already seen, is an untenable position. Paul certainly draws devotion to the Jewish law and devotion to the pagan gods into close proximity in Galatians 4:1–11. But he doesn't make devotion to the Jewish law an evil in its own right. He is *too positive* about the law in Galatians and elsewhere to sustain that reading. Paul is the apostle who shares the work of gospel proclamation with law-observant Jewish Christians like Peter, James and John, and who chooses this letter as the place to make that point *explicit* (Gal. 2:9–10). Paul is the apostle who seems to have been quite relaxed about the law in Jewish contexts because Jews by nature, like himself and Peter, already knew it posed no threat to faith as the foundation of justification (Gal. 2:15–16). Can we really imagine the same Paul painting Jewish legal observances as an exercise in the exaltation of idols?

If we accept the basic characterization of the Agitators favoured by the New Perspective, the problem gets worse. At least if we believe the Agitators were active advocates for 'works righteousness' as former generations of scholars argued, we can see a rationale for Paul's dire warnings about going back to Judaism. Even if we can't explain why he equates Jewish observances with paganism, we can see why he was getting so worked up. Understood this way, going back to Judaism undermines the gospel of grace. But if the Agitators were actually more concerned about covenant identity and the signs that accompany it, it's hard to see the basis for his severity.

If his readers wanted *more* commitment, if they wanted to express the exclusivity of their devotion *more* decisively – even if they were misguided as to the *necessity* of the thing – this was surely something Paul could have worked with. Paul himself was not afraid to trumpet his freedom as a follower of Christ to act like a Jew among Jews and like a Gentile among Gentiles when he needed to (1 Cor. 9:19–23). Could he not have embraced enthusiastic Gentiles wanting to become more Jewish on the same basis? And if not, could he not at least have coached them towards a more appropriate expression of their zeal? Even if the Galatians were being persuaded to embrace circumcision as a *necessary accompaniment* to trust in Christ, surely a refutation of the point would have been quite adequate without the alarmist remarks about apostasy (Gal. 5:2, 4)?

The problem in Galatia, then, isn't just that Paul's readers were embracing patterns of behaviour that were familiar to them on account of their prior exposure to the life of local Jewish synagogues. It's possible, indeed likely, that many of them had such prior exposure, and this can and should play a central role in our conceptualization of the background. But, on its own, it doesn't adequately explain the contours of Paul's response. The problem in Galatia was that embracing Jewish patterns of behaviour was leading Paul's readers back into *pagan* modes of thought and practice. Perhaps, then, a shift of focus from the Jewish background to the pagan religious background of the letter holds greater potential for a satisfying interpretation of the whole?

6
Going Backwards to a Gentile Past

Introduction

What would it have looked like in practice for the Galatians to revert to their pagan past? Paul clearly thought this was what his readers were doing, but the claim is difficult to penetrate given that – on the surface at least – they were trying to become more Jewish.

Paul himself, as we saw in Chapter 3, had his own distinctively Jewish take on pagan religion, and this must be allowed a determinative role in any respectable account of the regression problem. Whatever the Galatians' former religious practices *actually* involved, it should weigh heavily with us that, in Paul's mind, they equated to idolatry – inverting the distinction between the creator and the creature, with gods made in the image of man, not man in the image of God.

But his intimate familiarity with religious realities on the ground in Galatia must also be taken into account if we want to move forward here with confidence. Galatians is bulging with evidence of Paul's awareness of his readers' spiritual background. The letter's emphasis on curses and cursing mirrors the prevalence of curse inscriptions in the archaeological legacy of the region (Gal. 1:8, 9; 3:10, 13).[1] The reference to 'bewitchment' in Galatians 3:1 may also be an ironic nod to the Galatians' pagan past if the few spells and incantations that remain to us from Asia Minor after the systematic suppressions of subsequent centuries point to the presence of a popular phenomenon like that attested in contemporary North Africa.[2] In Paul's allegorical retelling of the Hagar and Sarah story in Galatians 4:21–31, it's striking that he pictures the two mothers as mountains given the prevalence of mountain mother worship among his

---

1 Arnold 2005: 447.

2 Arnold 2005: 446–447. Arnold is probably right to reject Elliott's suggestion that the verb Paul chooses here deliberately echoes beliefs about 'the evil eye' associated with devotion to the local mother goddess, Cybele (see Elliott 2003: 335–338). McCaulley is perhaps on firmer ground when he notes the use of the same verb to describe the experience of falling under the covenant curses in Deut. 28:53–61, although the application to the Agitators' motives is speculative (see McCaulley 2019: 103–104). Arnold highlights the allegation of witchcraft in Beichtinschriften: no. 69. On the suppression of magical texts see Acts 19:19 and Suetonius, Aug. 31:1. See also Betz 1986: xli–xliv.

readers – devotion to the mountain goddess Cybele and her cyphers Matar, Meter, Angdistis, and Artemis had dominated the religious landscape of the region for more than a thousand years.[3] In Galatians 3:1 again, the unusual reference to 'publicly exhibiting' Christ as crucified is strikingly similar in both its wording and its underlying ethos to the public confessions of guilt familiar from contemporary religious monuments, as are Paul's remarks about being 'caught in a sin' in Galatians 6:1–5.[4]

In a letter where going back to paganism is such a central element of the argument, then, and where the author is clearly capable of integrating detailed knowledge of local pagan norms into his text, a balanced, fact-based understanding of the background is vitally important if we want to think Paul's thoughts after him. In this chapter our goal is to familiarize ourselves with this background as far as the data allows and, in the light of it, to start putting the pieces of Paul's seemingly opaque, but in fact pastorally brilliant, diagnosis of the problem in Galatia together.

Waiting in the wings here, we also have some specific proposals for the regression problem to consider driven by specific reconstructions of the Galatians' religious past.

Influenced both by the assumptions of the Old Perspective and by fresh insights into first-century folk religion gleaned from a group of inscriptions known as the Lydian-Phrygian Confession Stelae, Clinton Arnold sees legalism and fear in the Galatians' prior experience of the gods as the explanation for their imminent capitulation to the demands of the Agitators.[5] Paul's liberating message of grace had won their hearts initially, but now the scales were falling from their eyes: it was all 'too good to be true'.[6] The Galatians were finally reading the small print of the contract pledging their devotion to the God of Israel and realizing that circumcision and other 'works' were necessary to secure and/or maintain their status as children of Abraham. But at least this all sounded familiar. The Galatians had faced similar demands under pagan gods in the past and were apt, as a result, to accept them again.

Taking a very different tack through the evidence, Susan Elliott focuses on mother-goddess worship in Galatia, lingering in particular on the tradition affirmed, especially among Latin writers, that the mountain shrines of Cybele were staffed by *Galli* – a cadre of eunuch priests who castrated themselves in

---

3   See Elliott 1999: 661–683.
4   See Beichtinschriften: nos. 15 and 59. See also Arnold 2005: 448–449.
5   See Arnold 2005: 429–449.
6   Arnold 2005: 445.

ecstatic initiation rites.[7] If Paul's reworking of the Hagar and Sarah story hints at the folly of returning to worship associated with any earthly mountain, perhaps his polemic against circumcision hints at similar ghosts from their pagan religious past? Might a desire for insider status and privileged access to the divine realm like that enjoyed by the *Galli* have driven the Galatians to embrace Jewish rites in general and circumcision in particular?

1 Setting Expectations

Unlike the situation we encountered in the previous chapter where our efforts to describe Jewish life in and around southern Galatia were limited by the *scarcity* of the evidence, our problem now is its *abundance*. Alongside a plethora of literary sources illuminating the fascinating religious history of Asia Minor, we can also appeal to an astonishing treasure trove of inscriptions dating especially from the second and third centuries when Galatia and its neighbouring provinces were swept by a positive craze for the memorialization of prayers, curses and epitaphs on plaques, votive tablets and grave markers.[8] Similar examples from the first century give us confidence that, while monument-making became particularly popular in subsequent decades, the sentiments the monuments express, and the underlying religious expectations they hint at, remained remarkably stable.

Texts and inscriptions, of course, are normally vulnerable to the criticism that they privilege the views of individuals with the means to write or to commission them – an educated and wealthy upper class with little in common with the kind of audience Paul seems to have been writing to in Galatia. But here, too, the data from Asia Minor breaks the mould, thanks to an accident of history that has preserved the voices of farmers and tradesmen as well as aristocrats and literary patrons. At Dokimeion, just 60 miles north-west of Pisidian Antioch, and at several other sites like it, the Romans found high-quality marble. Visit the Colosseum or the Pantheon today and you'll see the fruit of the quarries they developed and exploited there. Columns and sarcophagi were cut out and exported back to the imperial capital in vast numbers, and with that came a profusion of a by-product that priced ordinary men and women out of the inscription market in almost every other comparable context: sherds of durable, inscribable stone.[9]

---

7 See Elliott: 2003.

8 Drew-Bear et al. 1999: 31–33. See also Ameling 2009: 203–234; Mitchell 1999b: 419–433.

9 Strabo mentions the marble quarry at 'Docimaea' in Geog. 12.8.14. Products from the region are present in every major inscriptional catalogue. Drew-Bear et al.: 1999 is worthy of particular note due to its exclusive focus on Phrygian stelae.

The evidence in front of us, then, is rich and exciting but we need to exercise caution. None of this is going to tell us what the Galatians actually *thought*, any more than fantastically detailed archaeological documentation of our own era would tell historians of the future what *any of us* think as individuals or recover our individual stories. History simply doesn't work like that. The evidence will facilitate general discussion about the kinds of gods that were worshipped in the kinds of places Paul might have written to and the ways in which that devotion was expressed. It will let us talk about the evolution of religious practice over the centuries in the region and comment on areas of change and areas of stability. But it won't give us grounds for definitive statements about who the Galatians were or exactly what they did before Paul met them. For that we would need *a reply* from Galatia, and nothing of the kind is ever likely to be recovered. Remember, in the real world, we don't even know for certain where the Galatian churches *were*.

In the chapter ahead, then, our goal is more modest. We venture into the pagan religious background of Asia Minor now looking not for a conclusive picture of the life Paul's correspondents were returning to, but for *an envelope of options*, assigning relative probabilities to each. We're just as interested in religious practices and attitudes that were common to the whole region as we are in those that were unique to places where the Galatian churches could have feasibly been located. What we want is a sense for the realities on the ground, especially in the southern Galatian region where we know Paul was active both from Acts and from other extant letters. What we're looking for is a feel for the sights and sounds and smells of pagan religious life as the Galatians might have known it both as a means to exclude unbalanced reconstructions and as a source of inspiration for a better reading.

2 Into the Past

In the centuries prior to the New Testament era, the place Paul's Galatian converts would later call home was crisscrossed by violent winds of political, cultural and religious change, and adapting to them became something of a regional speciality.

As so often, geography provided the motive power for history here – Asia Minor was a bridge between east and west in the ancient world even more so than it is today. When the Hittite Empire collapsed in the second millennium BC, Balkan settlers moved east across the Hellespont, establishing the Phrygian empire in its place. Cimmerians and Lydians followed them, dominating the region until the westward expansion of the Persian empire

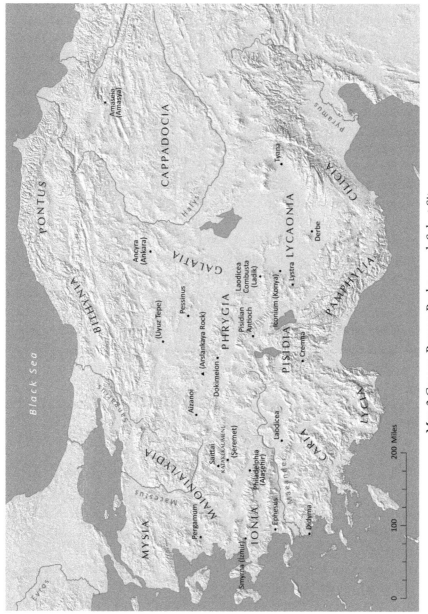

Map 2 Graeco-Roman Background: Select Sites

76

culminated in the fiery death of the fabled Lydian king, Croesus, in the sixth century BC.[10]

Cyrus the king of Persia declined to destroy the Lydian gods – Zeus, Artemis and Mēn. Instead he transformed them into living images of their Persian alter egos – Ahura Māzda, Anāhitā and Māh.[11] When the Greeks returned to power in subsequent centuries, they paid a similar compliment to the Persians' distinctive pyramidal model of government, incorporating their concept of the city state, or *polis*, within it.[12]

Contacts between east and west in Asia Minor played a significant role in the development of Greek and Persian literary and scientific culture.[13] But they also boiled over into war. Greek settlers recaptured coastal territories as fast as the Persians could claim them and used them as bases for colonizing lands as far away as Italy, Corsica and Spain.[14] When the Persian empire finally capitulated to Alexander and the young conqueror promptly died, the consequence in Asia Minor was just a new round in the long-established tussle between eastern and western influences. Seleucids east of the Taurus mountains and Attalids in Pergamum vied for power, with help and/or hinderance from various external forces including the Celtic settlers who later gave their name to the province of Galatia.[15]

Roman forces finally entered the region in earnest to settle this dispute in the second century BC, turning the needle of cultural dominance back towards the west. Initially exploited as a cash cow under the first and second Triumvirates, Asia Minor only began to fully realize its potential during the reign of Augustus.[16] Roman colonies were established at an unprecedented pace in Lycaonia – including Lystra and Iconium, and in Pisidia – including Pisidian Antioch.[17] Local dynasts were stripped of their powers and replaced with rulers who owed their privileges to Rome.[18] Gods were imported from the west,

---

10 Barnett 1975: 417–442; see also Marek et al. 2016: 94–96, 103–117. Cyrus' defeat of Croesus is memorably described by Herodotus (Hist. 1.85–93) although it is uncertain to what extent the account preserves an underlying historical reality.

11 Boyce 1975, vol. 2: 18, 143, 165 et passim, 220, 226–227, 229, 245–246, 257; see also Boyce et al. 1975, vol. 3: 254–308.

12 Marek et al. 2016: 179.

13 Marek et al. 2016: 133–138.

14 Ehrhardt: 1988.

15 On Seleucid and Attalid activities in Asia Minor, see Ma 1999: 53–105; and Hansen 1971: 14–165.

16 Sherwin-White 1984: 52–55, 80–92. On the exploitation of the region under the Triumvirs, see Cicero, Att. 109.2–3. See also Plutarch, Brut. 30.1–31.7 and Ant. 24.1–6. Marek et al. 2016: 313.

17 Mitchell et al. 1998: 5–14; Mitchell 1993a: 86–91; Levick 1967: 33–38, 68–91.

18 Marek et al. 2016: 313–326.

and the east following the steadily accelerating intellectual and commercial traffic through the region. But established traditions continued to prove resilient, even when practised under different names and using different images.

2.1 Literary Memories

What can we learn about the religious life of the region from the people who actually lived there?

Somewhere around the turn of the era, the Greek historian Strabo – who grew up in Amaseia just to the north-west of Galatia and knew the area intimately – arrived in Laodicea and recorded an amusing anecdote about the meandering habit of its famous local river which, at the time, was honoured as a god (Geog. 12.8.19). Tolls were payable at the temple of Maeander for crossing the river by ferry, providing him with a sizeable annual income. But fines could also be levied and deducted from his treasury when the river periodically washed away the projecting portions of the bank at each of its characteristic twists and turns, gradually eroding the value of the land holdings on either side. None of this, of course, points to symmetrical obligations between gods and humans – everybody knew that Maeander provided blessings that could not be repaid. But it does suggest accountability in both directions – with gods and people subject to common principles of reciprocity.

Moving forward a century, we meet another local resident, Dio Chrysostom, writing in Bithynia and addressing the same topic of reciprocity. Vows, he tells us, 'are made in the hope of receiving "boons" from the gods, and the greater the boons sought, the greater the variety of the vows made and the creativity applied in making them' (Disc. 38.44). Once again, there's no question of *symmetry* here. Dio talks about divine blessings in the language of 'boons', not wages. But it's still interesting that steps can be taken to make particularly desirable boons *more likely*. Later, in a passage dealing with a dispute between two local towns, he hints at the results that follow when hoped-for boons are received, highlighting the danger that *unrequited* favours rapidly turn into oppressive obligations (Disc. 40.3).

Moving from historical documentary to biography, the second-century *heroi logoi*, or 'sacred discourses' of Aelius Aristides introduce us to the strange and unfamiliar world of Asia Minor's healing cults. Aelius's description of his restless quest for personalized medical and vocational guidance runs like a roller coaster from overnight 'incubation' sessions in the shrine of Asclepius to the prescription of bizarre emetics and personal privations including riding through the snow to a local statue of Zeus and strictly avoiding fish sauce (Hier. Log. III.16–20, 34–6). Healing cults seem to have had no congregational dimension at all, focusing on individual needs in a similar way to the oracles that were also popular at the time (Hier. Log. IV.16).[19] The same emphasis on maximizing the chances of receiving divine favours that we saw in Dio, however, is also evident here. Aelius doesn't just deposit his thank offerings in Asclepius's temple, he positions them *under the right hand of the god's statue*, keeping his piety very much at the forefront of his attention (Hier. Log. IV.45–47).[20]

If the surviving letters of Apollonius are a reliable guide, this late first-century itinerant preacher and alleged wonder-worker from Tyana, 130 miles east of Iconium, struck a similar note, highlighting the importance of exacting ethical standards and physical privations in contemporary spirituality (e.g. Let. 43).[21] Apollonius was interested in cultivating positive relational equity with the gods – concluding that they favoured those who acquire wisdom and who 'do all the good in [their] power to humans who deserve it' (Let. 26).

2.2 Memories on Stone

For all the richness of these literary sources, however, inscriptions take us even closer to the action – now we can actually see and touch objects invested with significance by their dedicants in the place and in the period that interests us.

Funeral dedications represent a significant subset of the data in Asia Minor as elsewhere. In the latest edition of the great inscriptional catalogue of the region, *Monumenta Antiqua Asiae Minoris*, 249 of the 387 inscriptions listed fall within this class, illuminating the names and social positions of local worthies and reflecting on their legacies. Disinterest in the possibility of life after death – noted commonly in more abstract discussions of contemporary philosophy – is felt bluntly here, as inscription after inscription reflects the same sentiment: 'Be of good cheer, for no one is immortal.'[22] Doorstones represent a peculiarly local variation on the theme. These memorials – initially

---

19 Specialist oracles, like the famous institution at Didyma, were consulted by city assemblies far more frequently than they were by individuals. Oracular advice, however, still played a part in the popular piety of central Anatolia, as can be judged by the presence of at least nine dice oracles in the cities of the region (Horsley et al. 2000: 36; Nollé: 2007). See also I.Pisid.Cen.: nos. 5, 83, 159 and New Religious Texts from Lydia: nos. 3, 13, 53.

20 Alexia Petsalis-Diomidis argues that the *heroi logoi* is itself conceived as 'a votive thank offering requested by Asclepios' (Petsalis-Diomidis 2010: 129). While the composition of the work is certainly commanded and associated with thanks, however, there is no indication that Aristides pledged it to the god on the condition that particular prayers were answered, and he seems to have felt no obligation to complete the project either promptly or exhaustively (Hier. Log. II.1–4).

21 The sources and compositional circumstances of Philostratus' Life of Apollonius are so obscure that I omit it as a source for the purposes of historical analysis (Jones 2005, vol. 1: 1–13).

22 I.Pisid.Cen.: no. 133.

conceived as elaborately decorated, life-size doorways – gradually became simpler and smaller as their popularity increased and the vogue spread eastwards from the middle of the first century from Aizanoi in Lydia to Phrygia and Galatia.[23] Thank offerings are also well distributed throughout the region, reminding us – as do funeral dedications – that interactions with the gods were not always undertaken with the expectation of receiving blessings in return.[24]

Inscriptions were used to commemorate significant moments in public religious life – the founding of temples, the celebration of calendrical rites. A fascinating example from Philadelphia memorializes the occasion when, in response to a dream, a certain Dionysius repurposed a local shrine that had previously been dedicated exclusively to Angdistis as the new home of a private cult with altars to Zeus, Hestia and a whole series of other Greek deities.[25] This initiative is not presented as a *replacement* of the previous cult, but as an *extension* or *re-imagination* of it. The rules of the cult were still deposited with Angdistis, and she continued to be invoked as the guarantor of the members' strict code of moral conduct. The inscription itself also played a central role in their communal life, with participants required to come forward and *touch* it at their monthly and annual sacrifices, tangibly maintaining their connection to the pledges it contained.

By far the most interesting category of inscriptions in Asia Minor, however, are those that give us access to the hopes and aspirations of ordinary, living individuals. Here, the most common examples are votives – inscriptions, frequently augmented with relief carvings, memorializing what their dedicants believed to be the power of local gods to answer prayer.

An example from Ladık, roughly 25 miles north of Iconium, and dating between AD 41 and 138 illustrates the principal elements:

> For Meter Zizimene, in fulfilment of a vow: Alexandros, son of Alexandros, citizen of Dokimeion and of Claudiconium.[26]

The dedicant here is Alexandros, son of Alexandros, and the beneficiary is a local manifestation of the mother goddess Meter, identified by the addition of the local place name, Zizimene. The occasion of the dedication is the

---

23 Kelp 2013: 70–94.

24 E.g. New Religious Texts from Lydia: nos. 6, 19, 38, 39, 108. See also Hosios kai Dikaios: no. 1.

25 Barton and Horsley reproduce Sokolowski's edition of the text presented by Weinreich (Weinreich 1919: 4–6; LSAM: no. 20; Barton et al. 1981: 7–41).

26 MAMA XI: no. 255.

fulfilment of a vow, implying an earlier – probably public – declaration with conditional clauses: 'If/when Meter answers my prayer for some unspecified blessing, I Alexandros will raise a monument as a testimony to her power and faithfulness.'[27] The inscription itself is the monument he promised.

If the blessing sought is recovery from sickness, the inscription is often accompanied with a carving of the affected body part – arms, legs and eyes are the most common.[28] Prosperity and safety of family and friends, crops and animals are also dominant concerns.[29] Vows align with seasonal factors – a pledge to honour a local god made when seeds are sown in the spring is redeemed with a votive when the harvest arrives in the summer.[30] Some express intense personal intimacy – a craftsman dedicates his tools to the gods, a soldier his weapons, a mother an image of her child's injured limb.[31]

Votives also carry within them an awareness of the threat of reprisals for non-compliance in the human part of the 'votive contract'. An early second-century dice oracle from Cremna warns ominously: 'It will be better for you to repay the Daimon the vow which you have made, if you intend to accomplish what you care about.'[32] An inscription from Saittai, just north of Philadelphia, relates the disturbing story of the daughter of Syndonos, who disregarded her obligation to give an unnamed god the votive she had promised 'immediately' and was punished.[33]

In her work on the anatomical votives that are so prevalent, especially among the finds from Dokimeion, Justine Potts argues that carved body parts do more than merely *represent* the particular focus of their dedicants' prayers.[34] They're examples of *reification* – the ritual transfer of ownership of an item from the dedicant to the gods themselves, so that its restoration is now *in their interests*.[35] We can see something similar in votives focused on physical

---

27 'Votive inscriptions express the gratitude of worshippers who have been granted the fulfilment of a wish. When worshippers asked their gods for particular favours, the request was very often accompanied by a promise of giving something in return if the wish was fulfilled' (Rostad 2006: 92; see also Parker 2011: 120; Bergman 1987: 37; Burkert 1987: 69). 'A vow begins with a plea for *divine* action, followed by a conditional promise of the worshipper's response' (Cartledge 1992: 16).

28 E.g. Phrygian Votive Steles: nos. 11–69.

29 Barton et al. 1981: 27; Roller 1999: 329; Hosios kai Dikaios: nos. 5, 9, 15, 16.

30 Burkert 1987: 69.

31 Hosios kai Dikaios: nos. 8, 9; cf. Burkert 1987: 69–70.

32 I.Pisid.Cen.: no. 5, lines 28–29.

33 New Documents from Lydia: no. 55.

34 Potts 2017: 25–26.

35 'Our language of "representation" conspicuously fails in this regard, since in antiquity images held the promise of direct "presentation" – of superseding or effacing their purely representative function' (Squire 2009: 116; see also Platt 2011: 31–50).

property. A text from Maionia records the consecration of several golden objects lost by the dedicant to the divine mother,

> *so that [she] will track them down and bring everything to light and will punish the guilty in accordance with her power and in this way will not be made a laughingstock.*[36]

Physical location is also important for vows, just as we saw with the thank offering deposited by Aelius Aristides 'under the hand' of Asclepius. Votives were formed with protruding tenons on their bases that allowed them to be slotted into purpose-built shelves in local sanctuaries in proximity to – and, where possible, in the sightline of – the statues of their divine inhabitants. According to Walter Burkert, the challenge of accommodating them was one of the principal drivers for temple extensions in the ancient world.[37]

Votive Tablets With Mounting Tenons[38]
Ankara Museum of Anatolian Civilisations. Second and Third Centuries
A.D. Sketched by the Author

In the Cybele cult of the Phrygian imperial period, votive offerings were deposited in shafts bored into the rock behind images of the goddess, apparently in an attempt to keep the dedicants and their concerns at the top of her agenda.[39] In the early Christian era, the same practice was still being replicated at the Meter sanctuary in Aizanoi, where shafts located directly above the shrine seem to have been used for depositing votives, permanently memorializing the

---

36 SEG 28: no. 1568, published originally in Dunant 1978: 241–244, translation in Versnel 1991: 74. For further commentary on the text, see Roller 1999: 329; Chaniotis 2009: 126–128.

37 Burkert 1987: 94.

38 Phrygian Votive Steles: nos. 338, 64, 255, 337

39 Roller 1999: 98.

devotion of their dedicants and reducing the possibility that the goddess's reciprocal obligations might somehow slip her mind.[40]

Abundant though Asia Minor's votives are, however, nothing prepares us for
the wealth of detail provided by its so-called confession texts. Recovered for the
most part from the mountainous Katakekaumene region some 140 miles west of
Pisidian Antioch, these inscriptions document personal interactions with local
gods in extraordinary detail. Where votives typically express their underlying
raison d'être in a few brief words – sometimes with only a picture – confession
texts can run on for more than twenty lines. The longest has more than thirty.[41]

Confession texts reflect the belief that when things go wrong – when a child
gets sick, when property is stolen – the victim is experiencing divine retribu-
tion for some past sin that must be publicly acknowledged with a confession
inscription before the heavy hand of judgment can be removed. In a confession
recovered from a village just north of Philadelphia, a woman called Syntyche
describes the theft of a precious stone from her house by a local girl, Apphia.
Syntyche appealed to the moon god Mēn for justice and Apphia promptly died.
But after being asked by the girl's mother to keep the incident quiet, Syntyche
herself was punished for failing 'to make known and exalt the god', and the
stele represents the rectification of that fault.[42]

The texts reveal a host of behaviours capable of earning people places in the
gods' bad books: cutting wreathes in a sacred grove without permission, entering a local temple before the appointed time, examining the 'judgment seat'
of a god without proper ceremonial washing, entering a holy place in dirty
clothes, seizing a god's sacred doves or defiling a holy place without knowing
it. In one text the dedicant confesses to 'having sex with Gaia' in the local god's
sanctuary.[43] Angelos Chaniotis thinks the stelae were erected and read aloud
in public ceremonies – reminding us that the stones themselves preserve only
a fraction of a richer communal experience that is as irretrievably lost to us as
it would have been familiar to the people who were there.[44]

---

40 Roller 1999: 337–340. Van Straten notes the common practice of 'recharging' votive offerings with
fresh lamps or coins to remind the god of the dedicant's thankfulness and of their obligation to provide
ongoing aid (Van Straten 1981: 74). A second- or third-century AD inscription from a village just south
of Ancyra invokes *Hosios kai Dikaios* to avenge the theft of a woollen dress and two silver bracelets.
The dedicant, the son of Gellios, raises the stele not just as a form of remembrance but in confidence
that *the monument itself* will 'direct [the gods'] interest to this concrete case of injustice' (Hosios kai
Dikaios: no. 88, translation mine).

41 Beichtinschriften: no. 69.

42 Beichtinschriften: no. 59. Note the similar dynamics at work in a fragmentary text from Şeremet
(Beichtinschriften: no. 8).

43 Beichtinschriften: nos. 4, 19, 36, 43, 50, 110, 112.

44 Chaniotis 2009: 119–128. Cartledge argues that Hittite vows, like Babylonian and Jewish vows, were
typically made in conjunction with major feasts (Cartledge 1992: 101).

Should the confession texts be admitted as evidence for the pagan religious background of Galatians? Sceptics argue that public confession was restricted to the remote rural region where most of the stelae were discovered, and that their late second- and third-century dates rule them out of consideration.[45] Neither line of argument holds water.

Of the confession texts we know – 150, give or take a few – less than 60 can be dated with precision, and while it's true that most of them do indeed date back to the decades spanning the transition from the second to the third centuries, this shouldn't surprise us, given the surplus of inscriptions *of all types* from this period. Three examples can be conclusively dated to the first century, between five and seven more to the first quarter of the second century.[46] Neither is their geographical distribution as tightly circumscribed as some scholars suppose.[47] Justine Potts draws attention to similar confession plaques from southern Arabia. She also sees similar motives at work in the anatomical votives that are abundant throughout the region even when they don't explicitly mention sin and restitution.[48]

Complementing the recent publication of an early third-century confession from the village of Uyuz Tepe, 100 miles north of Pisidian Antioch, my own research identified a previously unrecognized confession text of a similar date in the survey report documenting Sir William Ramsay's discovery of the Mēn Temple just outside Pisidian Antioch in 1912.[49] The text confirms the presence of public confession as a religious practice in a region that Paul is known to have visited several times, as well as neatly illustrating the difficulties of deciphering texts inscribed on cheap stone sherds by inexperienced engravers with little experience of planning out the spacing of the letters and little interest, it seems, in the finer points of spelling![50]

---

45 John 2016: 180. See also Hardin 2008: 10.

46 For first-century texts, see Beichtinschriften: nos. 41 and 56 and New Religious Texts from Lydia: no. 188. For early second-century texts, see Beichtinschriften: nos. 52, 54, 57, 67, 78 and possibly also 39 and 44.

47 Potts 2017: 33. See also Ricl 1995: 68.

48 Levick 2013: 48–49; Potts 2017: 24. On ancient Arabian expiatory texts, see also Agostini 2012: 1–12. 'The dedicants of confession stelai and anatomical votives appear to have been part of the same material and intellectual world which suggests that the corpora were different epigraphic expressions of [a] common religious mentality' (Potts 2017: 42).

49 Hardie 1912: no. 65; CMRDM: no. 242.

50 Note how the inscription as a whole grossly transgresses the boundaries of the space prepared in this pre-cut tablet bearing the iconography of the moon god, Mēn. The engraver omits (and is then forced to insert in superscript) the final letter of the dedicant's name, Kyntis, as well as making numerous other mistakes including the spelling of the god's name and the formation of the key word *hamartanōn*. *Tekmoreuein* is probably a reference to a communal religious practice traditionally associated with the worship of mother goddesses in the region (see Blanco-Pérez 2016: 117–150).

Kyntis Mēni euchēn	Kuntis – a vow to Mēn. He
Hamartanōn tekmo-	sinned when he performed *tekmo-*
reusas meta gynai-	*reuein* with [his] wife
kos kai teknōn.	and children (translation mine).

Votive Dedication

Pisidian Antioch. Roman Imperial Period. Reproduced
courtesy of Cambridge University Press.

Curses and magical texts also form an important part of the inscriptional
evidence, providing further support for the thesis that local gods were widely
viewed as custodians of public justice. Grave inscriptions commonly invoke
the vengeance of the gods on would-be tomb-robbers, occasionally revealing Jewish influences, as in the case of a small number of inscriptions that
threaten miscreants with 'the curses written down in Deuteronomy'.[51] But
this shouldn't necessarily be seen as evidence for detailed familiarity with the
Jewish scriptures in the region. Curses and magical texts in general were apt
to plunder resources with reputations for otherworldly power irrespective of
their origin. The unutterable name of the Jewish God, Jewish angels and the
obscure backwards Jewish script fitted that profile perfectly, and they regularly
appear in curses and spells in all diaspora settings.[52]

In the spells that survive from the period, persuasive strategies include
pleading, assuring the god of one's best intentions, appealing to the god's better nature or to their vanity and reminding them of their good disposition

---

51 For the three explicit references to Deuteronomy, see IJO: nos. 173–174 from Acmonia, dated AD 248/9
and second/third century respectively, and IJO: no. 213 from Laodicea, dated second/third century.
For the probable references, see IJO: nos. 172, 179. See also Trebilco 1991: 62–63; Van der Horst 2014:
148.

52 An echo of the same phenomenon is still detectable today in the world's most cliched magical phrase,
Abracadabra, which owes its first two syllables to the original biblical patriarch.

on occasions in the past. Savants deploy various kinds of secret knowledge – pronouncing spells with specific physical or metrical forms, performing special magical gestures and exploiting propitious times for making their requests. They enlist the interests of the gods to their own causes by accusing their enemies of dishonouring them. They pull rank on conjured powers by impersonating more senior deities and cultivating relationships with them. They practise sympathetic magic akin to modern forms of voodoo. They invoke restless spirits. They attempt to coerce the gods by threatening them, by terrifying them, by depriving them of needed assets, by taking hostages and even by forms of physical constraint – in one case standing on the god's foot until they give the conjurer what they want![53]

But none of this should be taken as the norm for divine–human interactions more broadly. The religious legacy of Asia Minor confronts us with a range of practices ranging from open-ended thankfulness to outright attempts at manipulation. To read Galatians well against this background requires a balanced response to the data, working with elements that are common as far as possible and bracketing those which are marginal.

3 Regression in Galatia

Armed with a sense of the variety and the relative probability of the elements that might have formed part of Paul's readers' religious background, we can now return to the regression problem and to the specific solutions flagged at the beginning of this chapter.

Clinton Arnold points us to the confession texts as a source of insight into the underlying appeal of the Agitators' programme in Galatia. On the basis of their testimony, he tells us that the Galatians had a fundamentally 'nomistic orientation' before Paul met them, living in fear of the divine reprisals that would follow if they fell into any of the sometimes-minute ethical and ritual transgressions mentioned on the stelae.[54]

Arnold makes an important move here when he draws the confession texts and the letter to the Galatians into contact with one another. The underlying concept of the divine–human relationship brought to life for us so powerfully by the stelae very probably *was* shared to some degree by Paul's audience and should not be disparaged as a later, exclusively rural, phenomenon. Yes, there

---

53 For examples of physical compulsion, see PGM: IV 930–1114, XII 1–13. For a complete survey of the extant sources see Martin 2020: 68–71.

54 Arnold 2005: 446.

were distinctions between urban and rural religious practice in the region at the time, particularly when we think about degrees of commitment to the emperor cult.[55] But the trend to dichotomize these settings more or less absolutely is misguided.[56] Arnold is also right to encourage engagement with the Galatians' underlying religious motivations, despite the fact that these questions are notoriously difficult to penetrate when all we have to work with are ancient texts and stones.[57] By illuminating contemporary attitudes to divine commands and the consequences of failing to observe them, he gives us, perhaps, a glimpse at least of an impulse capable of propelling the Galatians to the drastic step of circumcision.

But the problem here is the limited range of the sources Arnold takes into consideration. The confession texts offer us a fascinating and illuminating insight into the question of the Galatians' past interaction with pagan gods.[58] But this is only one perspective on the larger world of religious experience in the region. Thanksgiving inscriptions, disconnected from any prior vows obliging them, present us with a very different take on local religious life.[59] So do the region's abundant funeral monuments which consistently omit to make the connection between death and punishment that the confessions would otherwise lead us to expect.[60] We can't simply *assume* Paul's readers were preoccupied with the concerns expressed in the confession texts *to the exclusion of this wider range of evidence.*

Arnold's thesis is also vulnerable to the problems we identified in Old Perspective readings more generally in Chapter 2. Even if the Galatians *were* obsessed with the minute observance of religious laws in their pagan past, and even if they saw costly acts of service as a means to cultivate divine favour, is there any basis for believing that *Paul's opponents in Galatia* were preaching a

---

55 Price 1984: 94.

56 See Martin 2020: 72–73. Wayne Meeks speaks for the majority when he characterizes villages in the first century as zones of cultural conservatism in contrast to cities which were moving rapidly 'in the direction of a common Greco-Roman culture' (Meeks 2003: 15). Classicist, Beate Dignas is more on target, however, when she argues that Hellenistic Asia Minor is better conceptualized as a single 'religious realm', and that 'all civic territories, included... a rural area whose religious life was more or less integrated into the life of the civic centre', Dignas 2002: 233; see also Lane Fox 2005: 42–45.

57 Potts 2017: 36.

58 Franz Seraph Steinleitner, who first classified the confession texts as a discrete phenomenon in the early twentieth century, read their testimony to interaction with the gods of ancient Anatolia within a master–slave framework (Steinleitner 1913: 76). Rostad argues that the asymmetric relationships that existed between patrons and clients in the period offer a stronger interpretative model but a sense of inescapable accountability is common to both (Rostad 2006: 100; see also Versnel 1981: 51).

59 For examples of spontaneous thanksgiving, see New Religious Texts from Lydia: nos. 6, 19, 38, 39, 108. See also Hosios kai Dikaios: no. 1.

60 See Rostad 2006: 97.

'gospel' with these same characteristics? In Galatians 2:15–16, remember, Paul looks Peter in the eye and tells him that people who are Jews by birth, and not sinful Gentiles, *know* there is nothing they can do to justify themselves before the God who made them. The assertion that the Agitators *didn't* know this – and that, in fact, they saw works as a way to do precisely what Paul says they couldn't – is a massive leap into the interpretative unknown.

Susan Elliott leads us in a different direction here with her work on the Cybele cult, arguing that circumcision itself had a substantial precursor in the region in the form of the ritual castration of the *Galli*. The suggestion is certainly ingenious and perhaps offers an insight into the famous barbed remark in Galatians 5:12 where Paul wishes the Agitators would go and do likewise. Elliott's thesis also leads her tentatively towards a move we shall embrace wholeheartedly in this book – breaking the link between what the Agitators *intended* in Galatia and the manner in which their ministry was *received*. In Elliott's view, the Galatians were attracted to circumcision because they understood the potency of similar acts of self-mutilation and the privileged status they conferred among the eunuch priests of Cybele, and they wanted the same thing themselves – hardly a motive the Agitators could have anticipated, let alone actively encouraged.[61]

But the problem once again here is that the range of sources is far too narrow. Arnold restricted us to a single source *type*. Elliott restricts us to a single religious cult, and within that, even further, to a peculiarly *Western* take on its activities. None of the evidence we reviewed in our tour of pagan religious data-points so far gave us *any hint* that eunuch priests and ecstatic initiation rites were a dominant feature of the landscape in Paul's time. The truth, in fact, seems to have been rather the opposite, especially in rural areas, where the emphasis fell on 'strict standards of justice and moral behaviour' and not on wild and ecstatic experiences.[62] One of the few contemporary inscriptions to even mention priests of the great mother describes a refreshingly ordinary father (clearly not a eunuch) and his son, both of whom served at the temple in Pessinus because it was a public honour, not because they were attracted to bloody acts of boundary-transgression.[63]

Roman writers, making pronouncements from a distance, emphasized what they considered unsavoury religious practices in Asia Minor, in part, as

---

61 'The Galatians are positively considering being circumcised, probably for mixed and not necessarily fully conscious or articulated reasons related to their Anatolian context as well as [for] the reasons those who advocate it give them,' Elliott 2003: 257.

62 See Levick 2013: 52. See also Mitchell 1993b: 43; Ricl 1992: 77.

63 See Devreker et al. 1984, vol. 1: 19–20, 221 nos. 17–18. See also Roller 1999: 342; John 2016: 124.

a propagandizing attempt to demonstrate the superiority of their own culture, and we should be very cautious about the quality of the evidence they provide.[64] But even if ritual self-castration existed outside the pages of contemporary anti-eastern polemic, it's hard to see how the 'appeal' of such a strange and socially alienating behaviour could justify the implication in Galatians that circumcision involved a return to paganism for *Paul's whole audience*, or provide a viable motive to embrace it for any but a few individuals on the very margins of the community. In Lynn Roller's careful diachronic study of Cybele worship in Asia Minor from the Hittite period forward, the striking thing is how local, time-honoured assumptions about the goddess and her attributes – her association with mountains and wild animals, her connectedness to personal devotion more than to 'the standard Roman program of procession, sacrifice, and games' – continually reasserted themselves, even when her name, clothing and posture changed.[65] If Paul's readers were still influenced by the long shadow of their former devotion to the divine mother, these more deep-seated elements of the experience are the ones we should expect to see coming back to the surface, not the imported – perhaps no more than the *projected* – behaviours on which Elliott's reconstruction depends.

4 Conclusions

Our journey back into the religious world of first-century Asia Minor has given us the tools we need to assess and critique two important reconstructions of the regression problem in Galatians. But are there any positive conclusions we can draw for our interpretation of the letter? I believe there are.

With Arnold and Elliott we ran into problems due to the artificial limitations they placed around the evidence. Arnold looked at only one source type – confession texts. Elliott looked at only one cult type – mother-goddess worship. But neither restriction helped us discern the true envelope of religious possibilities for Paul's audience. What we need is a three-dimensional approach, embracing all the source types, all the cult types, and monitoring the whole as it evolves and changes over time.

Under this more wide-ranging form of analysis, Anatolia emerges as a land where rapid superficial change conceals an underlying religious conservatism.

---

64 Juvenal's famous slam on eastern cultural imports provides a typical example of the genre: 'The Syrian Orontes has long since poured into the Tiber, bringing with it its lingo and its manners, its flutes and its slanting harp-strings; bringing too the timbrels of the breed and the trulls who are bidden ply their trade at the Circus' (Sat. III.62–65).

65 Roller 1999: 316.

This is the conclusion we drew in the context of mother-goddess worship, and the same thing is true as we watch other evolving religious trends, even when the devotees *perceived themselves* to be breaking the mould by, say, embracing religious innovations like the emperor cult or worshipping unfamiliar gods.[66]

Our data suggests that whatever cults they subscribed to before Paul's arrival, the Galatians would have assumed the gods were interested in their actions. The reaction may not always have been predictable, but there were always things one could do to cultivate, if not to actually secure, divine goodwill. Humans made vows to the gods, and they were bound to keep them with penalties attached. But the gods could also be 'incentivized' to act with varying degrees of forcefulness – through seasonal vows and festivals keeping vital cycles of blessing and thankfulness turning, through the tactical placement of reminders of personal piety in local temples, even through legal action in a public court if Strabo's reminiscences of the Maeander cult are to be believed.

We can assume the Galatians would have placed a high value on tangible and lasting expressions of devotion. Such things were commanded by their former gods to convert 'ephemeral [rituals] into perpetual [exempla]… for others', and as stakes in the ground, proving the existence of the divine–human relationship and commemorating its mutual obligations.[67] We can assume the Galatians expected the gods to favour the worthy – that's what they did in all the texts and inscriptions we've surveyed. And, if what we've learned about religious change in the region is anything to go by, we can also assume these assumptions would have been very hard to shift. Even if the Galatians embraced new religious convictions and allegiances, these were deep-seated habits, easily reanimated in contexts resembling those in which they first formed.

And perhaps that's exactly what happened in Galatia when the Agitators arrived? We don't have to imagine these teachers wishing for anything worse than an opportunity to guide Paul's readers into the same law-observant form of Jewish Christianity that he himself espoused in Jewish contexts. All we need is the realization that this new emphasis on keeping feasts, on the dos and don'ts of dietary purity and on circumcision – that oh-so tangible memorial of commitment to the God of Israel – was apt to reawaken their former religious expectations, whatever the Agitators actually intended.

---

66 Note especially the private cult inscription from Philadelphia (Barton et al. 1981: 7–41). See also Price 1984: 188–191.

67 Chaniotis 2009: 140.

7
Going Backwards to 'the Present Evil Age'

Introduction

One final area of investigation still demands our attention as we consider Paul's disconcerting diagnosis of regression in Galatians and the best scholarly attempts to make sense of it. Careful work in the letter's Jewish and pagan background has helped us shape and critique alternative hypotheses, to be sure. But might the *actual* explanation have more to do, in fact, with Paul's concept of the great change that Jesus' life, death and resurrection accomplished?

This change, of course, is far less obvious to us than it was to Paul thanks to our location in history. The coming of Christ is old news today. The radically different 'religious settlement' it created is the 'religious settlement' Christians have always known. And so it strikes us as unremarkable that a learned first-century Jewish teacher with convictions about a crucified and resurrected Messiah would spend his time travelling around encouraging Gentiles to share these convictions, assembling them into congregations and persuading them that without any of the conventional paraphernalia of conversion they'd become children of Abraham just as much as the Jews from whom his story derived. But this is a great mistake. Gentile congregations worshipping a Jewish Messiah as Gentiles were a complete novelty in the first century. When Galatians was written, the whole idea was probably less than a decade old – perhaps *much less* than a decade old – and the world of first-century Judaism was still barely beginning to process the shock. Within the period narrated by the New Testament documents, Jesus-believing Jews like Paul recognized that something had changed in the very fabric of history that necessitated a complete reconstitution of the way they thought about following God. When Paul wrote Galatians, that change was still stark and obvious and the question of how to behave in response was by no means settled, even among people who shared the same basic convictions.

What then *was* this great change? In short, as we saw in Chapter 3, it was the dawning of the eschatological age.

Paul, in common with many other Jewish writers of the period, looked forward to the day when God would set the world he had made to rights.[1] Beginning with Isaiah's remarkable vision of the new creation in which new heavens and a new earth would one day sweep away even the memory of the troubles and sorrows of this present life (Isa. 65:1–3), Jewish texts developed a rich and bold articulation of God's ultimate purposes for history, weaving all his redemptive acts together into one unified story. References to a coming 'Day of the Lord' increasingly looked beyond decisive acts of judgment and salvation in the present to a moment of final resolution in which God would establish a permanent new age of salvation. God, in the end, would reign in peace and justice. God's people would be vindicated after their years of oppression and exile. Death would be defeated, the curse would be ended.[2] In many texts, as we noted briefly in Chapter 3, the nations would be gathered in and find their place as servants of Israel's God. In many more, God's ultimate victory would be associated with the emergence of an ultimate Davidic king, (Isa 9.6f.; 11.1–10; Jer 23.5f.; Ezek. 34:23f.; 37:24f.; Mic. 5:2–4; Zech. 9:9f.).[3]

What sets Paul apart from his Jewish contemporaries entirely, however, is his conviction that, in some strange and unexpected sense, *this had already happened.* N.T. Wright is surely correct to locate the tipping point in Paul's encounter with Jesus on the Road to Damascus.[4] Prior to this moment, Paul, like his contemporaries, we assume, 'imagined that the great reversal, the great apocalyptic event, would take place all at once, inaugurating the kingdom of God with a flourish of trumpets, setting all wrongs to right, defeating evil once and for all, and ushering in the age to come'.[5] What he was confronted with instead, however, was the realization that the resurrection age had begun in the midst of normal human history *with one specific individual.*

Galatians is as good a place as any other to see the fruits of this seismic development in Paul's subsequent life and ministry. In the extended biographical introduction to his argument, he famously relates the events of his conversion/commissioning, dwelling on his meeting with the one he now acknowledges as Israel's long-expected, but up-till-this-point-concealed, Messiah – a revelation (literally, an 'apocalypse') that convinced him not just that preaching to Gentiles was a good idea, but that it was now a necessity of history: the eschaton

---

1   Richard Bauckham provides a masterful introduction to the world of Pauline eschatology in his IVP Bible Dictionary article. See Bauckham 1996: 336–339.

2   de Boer 2016: 53–54.

3   Bauckham 1996: 333.

4   Wright 1997: 35–37.

5   Wright 1997: 36.

had come and the nations *must* come in.[6] In his opening benediction, Paul reminds his readers of the purpose of Christ's death – '[he] gave himself for our sins *to rescue us from the present evil age*' (Gal. 1:4). And in his closing remarks, he returns to the same theme: what matters is neither circumcision nor uncircumcision *but new creation* (Gal. 6:15).

Clearly, in the letter, the work of new creation is a work in progress for God's people, even as it stands complete in Christ. Whatever else we learn from the ethical injunctions of Galatians 5 and 6 (a topic we will return to in Chapter 11), it's clear that his readers have to *live into* their new age identity, continually resisting the clutches of the old age. But the fact that, for Paul, something decisive had happened, that the future had come crashing into the present even while the present continued to some extent unaffected, is evident throughout the entire text. Paul doesn't just tell us he has come to a new view of the law in Galatians, he tells us that, in Christ, *he has died* to the law (Gal. 2:19–20), that the time has come, that the moment for Israel's inheritance has arrived (Gal. 4:2). He urges his readers to look up from 'the present city of Jerusalem' to 'the Jerusalem that is above' (Gal. 4:25–26).[7] The long imprisonment of God's people has ended with the revelation of the faith that was to come (Gal. 3:23).

Paul's message in Galatians is shaped by the realization that, in Christ, a way forward into the eschatological age had been opened for all who put their faith in him. Might Paul fear, therefore, that his readers were about to turn back the clock and *undo* this great change – or at least their own part in it – form the basis of his warnings about regression?

The answer to this question is unequivocally, 'Yes.' But to understand what this 'yes' really means, we have to probe a bit further.

1 Convergence and Divergence in the Apocalyptic Paul

Scholars in recent years have woven the kinds of insights we've just discussed in Galatians together with similar observations from Paul's other letters to conclude that eschatology is a dominant theme across the whole gamut of his theology.[8] Paul is read increasingly as an apocalyptic thinker – not as a writer

---

6   On the hidden Messiah theme, see Pitre et al. 2019: 88–93.

7   Paul's understanding of the state of 'the present city of Jerusalem' is discussed at greater length in Chapter 10.

8   For contrasting overviews of the present state of this interesting debate, see Blackwell et al.: 2016; Davies: 2016; Wright 2019: 133–134.

in the apocalyptic *genre* familiar to us from Revelation and Old Testament texts like Daniel, but as a writer preoccupied with apocalyptic *themes*.[9] The result is a widespread and welcome reaffirmation of new creation at the centre of Paul's thought, together with an awareness of the sharpness of the tension between the 'now' and the 'not yet' in the unfolding of this plan as Paul perceived it.[10] J. Louis Martyn's emphasis on correctly reading the time on Paul's eschatological clock, though developed in the context of Galatians, is similarly relevant to the whole.[11]

But there are also considerable differences in the way scholars put the picture together.

One key area of difference has to do with the extent to which Paul perceived continuity or discontinuity at the boundary between the world *as it was* prior to Christ's coming and the world *as it is* after he came. Popularizing and building on the work of Karl Barth, Ernst Käsemann is seen by many as a pioneer of discontinuity readings, although the point at which he saw the break was located relatively uncontroversially at Christ's *second* coming – splitting human history into two clearly contrasting realms, one of death and the other of life, one constituted under Adam and the other constituted under Christ.[12] Discontinuity has been given a sharper edge in contemporary discussions about Paul, however, by Käsemann's student, Martyn, whose vast and sophisticated commentary on Galatians moves the break point forward in time to Christ's *first* coming, without any diminution in its radical extent.[13] Martyn uses the language of 'invasion' to describe the cross and the parousia alike.[14] The death and resurrection of Christ is a radical, unprecedented irruption of God into human history, wresting control from the evil powers into whose hands men and women have fallen. This picture is modified and developed in subsequent helpful studies by Martinus de Boer and John Barclay, but never without a nagging sense of incongruity with the larger story Paul seems to want to tell – that the covenant under which God embraces Jews and Gentiles today *is the same covenant* under which he embraced Abraham (Gal. 3:6–29).[15]

---

9   For an illuminating discussion of the distinctions between 'apocalyptic', 'apocalypticism', and 'apocalyptic eschatology' see de Boer 2016: 48–50.

10 Wright 2013: 1143.

11 See Martyn 1997: 104–105.

12 See Blackwell et al. 2016: 7–12. See also Käsemann 1969: 108–137.

13 See Blackwell et al. 2016: 8, 10.

14 See Martyn 1997: 39, 105 etc.

15 See de Boer: 2011; Barclay: 2015.

Continuity is asserted *within* the apocalyptic paradigm by other writers. Richard Hays agrees with Martyn that the significance of Christ's coming was so vast and unexpected that it forced Paul to rework his understanding of the Old Testament story from the ground up. But his new picture of the whole – positioning Adam and Christ as parallel personalities in Romans and 1 Corinthians, and working forward from Abraham's faith to the faith of Christ's worldwide family in Romans and Galatians – was 'a rereading, not a repudiation' of what was already there.[16] N.T. Wright is similarly struck by the emphasis on continuity even as Paul struggles to process the shocking expansion/redefinition of the human problem implied by the manner of Christ's first coming.[17] God's vision for the 'rectification' of humanity may have dramatically outstripped Paul's expectations prior to his apocalyptic encounter with Jesus on the Damascus Road, but his subsequent description of it was still founded on a recognizably Jewish covenantal framework.[18]

Another key area of difference has to do with the significance of individual agency in Paul's apocalyptic vision. De Boer helpfully distinguishes two quite different perceptions of the human problem to set the context here, exemplified in different Jewish texts from the Second Temple period.[19] In 1 Enoch 1–36, the human problem is 'cosmological'. Evil angelic powers hold human beings captive and the only possible solution is cosmic war. Eschatology follows the pattern of Exodus here: God intervenes to liberate us from our state of bondage, acting unilaterally, defying this-worldly norms and expectations. Nothing humans can do or have experienced beforehand qualifies or prepares them for the scale and nature of the deliverance to be unveiled at the end. In 2 Baruch and 4 Ezra, by contrast, the human problem is 'forensic' – humanity itself is the problem and must look to itself for the solution. God doesn't have to wage a war of deliverance to achieve his purposes now, he need only convene the cosmic court to find and acquit the righteous, granting them a share in the world to come, even as the wicked are convicted and condemned.

Paul, of course, is no mere cypher for either pole in this in-house Jewish debate. But his interpreters can still be helpfully classified according to the framework it defines with Martyn emerging once again as an extreme voice, this time at the cosmological end of the spectrum. Paul's problem with the law

---

16 Hays 2014: 204.
17 Wright 2013: 749–750.
18 The language of 'rectification' is Martyn's preferred way of talking about the achievements of Christ (Martyn 1997: 39).
19 See de Boer 2016: 53–59.

in Galatians, in Martyn's view, has to do with its forensic expectations. Only a completely fresh start, a cosmological initiative taking human works completely off the table, can establish God's kingdom and win for Christ the victory he intends.[20] Martyn lingers long on references to humanity's enslavement in the letter. And at the key debating point between the Old and New Perspectives on the meaning of the famous faith and works dichotomy in Galatians 2:15–16, he emphasizes *Christ's* faithfulness, not *his followers'* faith, precisely because this faith, for Martyn, would involve a human contribution to a deliverance that God must work alone.[21]

Martyn is not unaware of the alternative viewpoint here, of course, that human choice itself – in Paul, as it is in the works of many of his Jewish contemporaries – is a sphere in which God's will can be authoritatively expressed.[22] But that idea is integrated far more successfully into the larger landscape of Paul's theology by other authors, particularly Wright.[23] Chester helpfully draws attention to the fact that even Calvin – who epitomizes the emphasis on God's sovereignty in salvation that Martyn seems determined to uphold – is unabashed to own this faith as the true possession of the individuals who express it.[24] Douglas Campbell mirrors Martyn in his presentation of a Paul who associates human initiative with the present evil age – an age whose norms Christ has decisively shattered.[25]

2 Apocalyptic Takes on Regression

Armed with a sense of the relationship between these competing visions of 'the apocalyptic Paul' and their respective pros and cons, do we now have a key capable of unlocking the significance of Paul's perplexing warnings about regression in Galatians? Four slightly different affirmative answers to this question now demand our attention, each with a slightly different take on the troublesome expression Paul uses to describe the enslavement common to

---

20 See Martyn 1997: 260–274.

21 Martyn 1997: 248–253.

22 'Thus when Paul speaks about placing one's trust in Christ, he is pointing to a deed that reflects not the freedom of the will, but rather God's freeing of the will,' Martyn 276.

23 See Wright 2009: 129–130. On the instability of the distinction between synergism and monergism in Christian thought, see Martin 2008: 162–176. Contra Dunn (e.g. Dunn 2008: 77–89), Paul does not appeal to the reality of the indwelling Spirit in Galatians to neutralize the importance of personal moral initiative. 'Although Paul clearly expects his converts in Galatia to be led by the Spirit, this does not prevent him from spelling out what it means to walk in the Spirit' (Barclay 1988: 229).

24 See Chester 2017: 332–337.

25 See Campbell 2009: 4, 254–255, 838–847.

his readers' – and his own – pre-Christian past: enslavement to the *stoicheia* (Gal. 4:3, 9).

2.1 J. Louis Martyn

Stoicheia – as we noted in Chapter 1 – is the Greek word for 'elements', and, just like its English equivalent, it's capable of a range of meanings. The standard Bauer Danker Greek lexicon lists two main possibilities: 'basic components of something' and 'transcendent powers'. The first is then divided into three subcategories: 'basic elements from which everything in the world is made' – usually the basic elements of classical cosmology, vis. earth, air, fire and water; 'heavenly bodies'; and 'fundamental principles'.[26] Since the latter half of the twentieth century, quantitative studies by Joseph Blinzler and others have increasingly been cited as a basis for believing that the meaning in Paul – especially when the word is combined with the genitive modifier *tou kosmou* (of the world/of the cosmos) as it is in Galatians 4:3 – is basic, material elements.[27]

Working from this start point, J. Louis Martyn argues that the believers in Galatia were element worshippers before Paul ever met them and that this explains Paul's curious allegation of regression.[28] Element worship, says Martyn, was a characteristic product of the old age that Christ's apocalypse was designed to sweep away. The dualities of earth and air, fire and water were central pillars of pagan cosmology, all of which were now destined to fall. And the same thing goes for the similar dualities of law-observant Judaism.[29] Jew and Gentile, sacred and profane, law and not law were features of the old age just as much as their pagan equivalents were in Martyn's mind. And this explains how embracing the former could result in a return to the latter. Jewish Christianity, for all its superficial distinctions from the Galatians' pagan past, was based on the same underlying dualistic structure, and was transcended by the coming of Christ in exactly the same way. Say 'yes' to Judaism, and you can't avoid returning to the presuppositions, if not the actual practices, of paganism. That's why enslavement to the law and enslavement to pagan gods are both described using *stoicheia* terminology.

But the problems here are immediately obvious.

First, we have the question of whether element worship is really a credible religious background for Paul's correspondents in Galatia. We saw nothing

---

26 Arndt et al. 2000: 946.
27 See Blinzler 1963; Schweizer 1988; Rusam 1992.
28 Martyn 1997: 396.
29 Martyn 1997: 402–406.

in the previous chapter to suggest that devotion to earth, air, fire and water as gods, or even as mere counterparts to the gods, is part of a realistic envelope of religious possibilities in the region. To the best of our knowledge, no trace of it remains in the inscriptions that survive. The closest connection we can make with confidence is Apuleius's allusive reference to the mother goddess in Pessinus as 'the mistress of all the elements' (Met. XI.5), but this observation comes from the middle of the second century. Philo of Alexandria, 150 years earlier, claims to be aware of element worship among the Gentiles in his orbit, but deity is only ascribed to the elements directly in a single text (Spec. Laws. 2.255).[30] Martyn turns to another Alexandrian document – the apocryphal *The Wisdom of Solomon* – for support, noting that it lists fire, air and water alongside the stars and 'the luminaries of the heavens' as objects of worship among '[those who are] ignorant of God' (Wis. 13.1–2). But despite locating this kind of thinking in the period in which Paul is writing, none of this amounts to local evidence that the elements were worshipped *in Galatia* in the first century, still less that this worship had anything to do with dualities.[31]

And what of the assumption that dualities are a feature of the old age only? Isn't Paul's own theology also full of *new age* dualities – grace and works, freedom and slavery, flesh and Spirit – even if we restrict our investigation to Galatians? Martyn himself acknowledges the importance of these new pairs of opposites in the gospel era, but only at the cost of substantially undermining his own attempt to resolve the regression problem.[32]

2.2 Martinus de Boer

Martyn's student, Martinus de Boer, has an alternative, if related, take on regression that challenges the limits of the conventional understanding of *stoicheia* – rehabilitating 'transcendent powers' and 'heavenly bodies' as interpretative possibilities. Working from the same data in *The Wisdom of Solomon* that inspired his teacher, de Boer sees a close connection between the activities of the elements and regular calendrical festivals.[33]

---

30 Like other Jewish writers, Philo occasionally asserts that worshipping pagan gods amounts to worshipping the elements – when the gods are properly interpreted, each with their own equivalent in the physical world (e.g. Contempl. 3–4).

31 David Winston assigns the composition of *The Wisdom of Solomon* to Alexandria during the reign of Gaius Caligula (AD 37–41; see Winston 2007: 20–25). Lester Grabbe prefers a date around 20 BC (Coogan et al. 2007: 69). Despite the substantial similarities between Wis. 12–15 and Romans 1:18–32, there is nothing to justify Sanday and Headlam's bold conclusion that 'at some time in his life St. Paul must have bestowed upon the Book of Wisdom a considerable amount of study' (Sanday et al. 1898: 51–52).

32 Martyn 1997: 100.

33 de Boer 2011: 252–261.

Reading Wis. 7.17–19 in the light of Wis. 13.1–2 – where the sun and the moon are included among the elements that pagans mistakenly worship – de Boer sees a role for the elements as gods in the regulation of seasonal events, orchestrating 'the beginning and end and middle of times, the alternations of the solstices and the changes of the seasons, [and] the cycles of the year'. Combining this with the tantalizing inclusion of calendrical observances in the very passage in Galatians where Paul's regression warnings reach their boiling point, de Boer believes he has come to a breakthrough. If Paul can summarize his concern for his readers by referring to their renewed interest in 'special days and months and seasons and years' (Gal. 4:10), perhaps a *common* pagan and Jewish interest in regular religious events underpins his diagnosis of regression?[34]

Jews and pagans alike depended on astronomical observations to correctly calculate the dates of their various festivals. *The Epistle to Diognetus* memorably chides Jews for '[celebrating] the new moon' and '[constantly observing] the stars and moon to keep track of months and days' (Diog. 4.1, 5). Paul, of course, says nothing explicit about astronomy in Galatians. But it's possible nonetheless that he'd come to perceive a dangerous proximity between Jewish Sabbaths and festivals and their pagan equivalents.[35] Perhaps he warned the Galatians about returning to their pagan past because their new enthusiasm for all things Jewish was committing them to similar kinds of seasonal activities? This, as we shall see, really could be *part* of the solution.

But it cannot be the whole solution, and not just because the evidence is so slender. Though Paul and the author of *The Wisdom of Solomon* clearly inhabited a shared milieu, this hardly proves that he would have followed the Wisdom Teacher's thought in every particular, or embraced the kinds of connections de Boer wants to make within his text. And even if he did, the scope of de Boer's solution is far too limited. It focuses on similarities between Judaism and paganism in calendrical matters, but this is not where the heart of the Galatian crisis really lies. Calendrical observances are *mentioned*, of course, as part of the Agitators' larger programme of encouraging Jewish practices among Paul's readers. But the central issue in the letter is circumcision. And for *this* to involve regression in Paul's mind, something much more comprehensive is required. Regression, remember, stands at the root of Paul's concern

---

34 Justin Hardin helpfully summarizes extant comments on the ambiguous nature of Paul's vocabulary in Galatians 4:10, arguing that he 'does not actually employ any Jewish terms', Hardin 2008: 120. Contra Hardin, Matthew Thiessen believes Paul is quoting Gen 1:14 LXX (See Thiessen 2016: 155–156).

35 The place of Sabbath observance in Pauline theology is disputed (see Weiss 1995: 137–153).

for his readers *throughout the text*, not just in Galatians 4:8–11. To explain it, we have to explain how it accounts for the entirety of the problem.

We might also ask ourselves, if de Boer's suggestion held good, why Paul responded with such evident alarm to the Galatians' fresh enthusiasm for calendrical rites. So Jewish and pagan festivals alike required observations of the stars to correctly assign their places in the year. So what? De Boer's explanation 'works' as a way to explain *at least a part* of the regression problem – it shows how Jewish rites might have resembled the Galatians' pagan past *in one specific respect*. But even here we're left asking, 'Why the extreme reaction?' 'Why would Paul condemn this as incompatible with faith in Christ?'

2.3 John Barclay

John Barclay may, in fact, have provided the original inspiration for de Boer's 'calendrical festivals' reading of regression in Galatians. He says something very similar in his own, still-influential, 1988 book *Obeying the Truth*, which made such a helpful contribution to the debate about the unity of the letter.[36] Barclay argued that regression was merely a rhetorical ploy in Paul's argument. He didn't intend it as a substantial allegation. His readers weren't really going back to paganism; they just needed waking up from their spiritual stupor and alerting to the seriousness of their actions: 'This is just as bad as going back to your pagan past, you idiots!' says Paul, or something like that. We're not supposed to imagine *he actually means it*.

In his later work, Barclay's treatment of the regression question has ranged more widely, dealing in larger, more abstract, categories. In *Paul and the Gift*, he acknowledges the statistically derived definitions of *stoicheia* that inform Martyn's and de Boer's attempts to interpret Paul's emphasis on the dangers of going backwards but immediately sidesteps their consequences. Rejecting enslavement to earth, air, fire and water as a plausible description of Paul's, or the Galatians', religious life before Christ, and even enslavement to heavenly bodies as points of orientation for Jewish and pagan religious festivals, he talks instead about slavery to '*the natural order of the cosmos* through alignment to its elemental, physical components' (emphasis mine).[37] Strongly associating

---

36 'It appears that the reason why Paul highlights the Galatians' calendar observance, out of all the manifold "works of the law", is because he sees here a point of direct comparison with their former pagan worship. Both pagan and Jewish worship involve observing certain sacred "days" and Paul deliberately chooses such general terms as "days," "months" and "seasons" in order to emphasise the similarities between these two forms of religion: *hence he can score a useful polemical point by describing their new Jewish practice as a regression into their former way of life*' (Barclay 1988: 63–64, emphasis mine).

37 Barclay 2015: 409.

himself with Martyn's 'discontinuity' reading of Pauline eschatology, Barclay sees the problem as a return to the elements or norms of the age before 'the Christ event' – norms that he associates in particular with estimates of personal worth.[38]

The argument here is that Christ has come and, in coming, has redefined everything we know about the worth of human individuals. Christ has offered blessings *to the unworthy* – unexpected, *incongruous*, blessings – unrelated to anything we can say or do to deserve them. And this radical initiative marks Christ's growing church out from everything that went before it. This is the heart of God's invasive apocalypse: it is human action effaced by divine action, human initiative by divine initiative.[39] And regression must be read through this lens. There simply isn't any need to justify Paul's language on the basis that Jews and Gentiles shared specific religious practices like annual festivals sequenced according to observations of the stars. It's similarity enough to observe their dissimilarity to the gospel. *Anything* other than Jesus is dependent on human concepts of worth – it's an 'old age' reality in Barclay's reconstruction of events, and embracing old age realities involves going backwards from the new.

Like de Boer's approach to the regression problem, Barclay's approach too includes components of the response I'm going to set out in the coming chapters. But it isn't free from problems. Barclay thinks Paul's logic depends on the *unconditionality* of God's gift to the world in Christ. Exchanging Christ for Judaism *or* paganism makes no difference. For Barclay, *both* are mired in the same set of reciprocal expectations that the gospel does away with, both depend on the recipients of divine gifts being *worthy* in some way to receive them. *But is that the point Paul is really trying to make?* In Galatians 2:15–16, Paul seemingly stresses *continuity* between his pre-Christ Jewish past and his post-Christ Jewish present in the specific area where Barclay finds himself asserting difference. And while his rendering of Paul's regressive logic *can in principle* accommodate an interpretative solution focused on the radical distinctiveness of God's grace to the unworthy in Christ, it hardly *necessitates* that solution. Making paganism and Judaism alike on the basis of their unlikeness to something that's unlike *everything* is really saying nothing. If Paul had

---

38 Barclay 2015: 391.

39 Barclay's emphasis on the utter alienness of Paul's gospel is indebted not only to Martyn's apocalyptic interpretation of Galatians but also to his interaction with the French Philosopher, Alain Badiou (Barclay 2015: 175–179; Barclay 2010a: 36–56; Barclay 2010b: 171–184).

no thoughts about worth at all and was simply lashing out at his readers for abandoning Christ altogether, Barclay's argument would work just as well.[40]

His explanation is also curiously silent on the fact that it is Jewish *Christianity* the Galatians are tempted to embrace here, not Judaism as it was *before Christ came*.[41] Jewish *Christianity* was a 'new age' reality; it certainly was in the case of Paul himself. But even if the Galatians were quitting the church and seeking acceptance in local synagogues to practise Christ-less Jewish worship, the alignment Barclay is striving to achieve here is poised on a precarious reconstruction of both the synagogue and the Galatians' religious background. In the synagogue it needs Jews with an atypically strong concept of human agency. It needs Jews who assigned positive conditionality to works, a conditionality not dissimilar to that envisaged under the Old Perspective if Barclay's portrait of the Agitators is to be believed.[42] And in the Galatians' religious past it needs pagan cults with an atypically *weak* concept of human agency. It needs pagans who saw human action merely as a condition for divine blessing, not as a way to actively incentivize it. But incentivization is what most of the data actually seems to envisage.

2.4 Brant Pitre, Michael Barber and John Kincaid

All of this then brings us to a final, controversial solution to the regression problem informed by an emphasis on apocalyptic themes in Paul.

In their recent book, *Paul, a New Covenant Jew*, Brant Pitre, Michael Barber and John Kincaid take *stoicheia* in Galatians as a reference to the angels and demons that so liberally populate 'cosmological' renderings of Jewish eschatology.[43] Their first move highlights the role of angels in Jewish life under the law. Paul mentions this himself in Galatians 3:19: 'the law was given through angels and entrusted to a mediator', and the same thought is preserved more widely across the New Testament and in other Second Temple Jewish texts.[44] Their next move notes that, in the same kinds of source, angels also play

---

40 This is the reconstruction of the crisis imaginatively developed by Troy Martin (see Martin 1995: 437–461).

41 The argument seems to imperil Barclay's own conclusion that the Agitators in Galatia are followers of Christ (see Barclay 2015: 334–335).

42 The Agitators saw 'the Jewish way of life as their definitive framework of value (righteousness)' Barclay 2015: 410.

43 Pitre et al. 2019: 73–82. In addition to the angelic appearances and demonic possession stories frequently recounted in the gospels, angels and demons are referenced explicitly on several occasions by Paul (Rom. 8:38; 1 Cor. 11:10; 2 Cor. 11:14) and implicitly under pseudonyms like principalities (*hai archai* – e.g. Rom. 8:38), powers (*hai dynameis* – e.g. 1 Cor. 15:24) and authorities (*hai exousiai* – e.g. Eph. 6:12).

44 Acts 7:37–38, 53; Heb. 2:2. See also Josephus *Ant.* 15.136.

important roles in pagan life and religion. Angels invisibly govern pagan kingdoms (Jub. 15.31); in 1 Corinthians 10:20, Paul tells us that 'the sacrifices of pagans are offered *to demons*'. Next, they note that, for Paul, at Christ's coming, the human relationship to these heavenly powers has been decisively *inverted*. God's people are no longer *under* law (Gal. 3:25; 4:7). God's people will sit in judgment *over* the angels (1 Cor. 6:3). And, with that, the situation in Galatia is elegantly explained: the Galatians were under angels in the past, if they submit to Jewish law they will be under angels again, and neither state is congruent with life in the new age.

Elegant though this solution seems, however, there are problems just below the surface once again.

Exegetically, I doubt that the bridge from Galatians 3:9 to 4:3 is really as secure as Pitre and his colleagues assume. Angels are clearly part of Paul's and his readers' shared conceptual world. When he throws down the gauntlet in 1:8 – 'If we or an angel from heaven should preach a gospel other than the one we preached to you, let them be under God's curse!' – there is clearly a common understanding of angels as authoritative and powerful beings who would never normally be disobeyed, and angels return to the argument with a similar function in Galatians 4:14. But if renewed submission to angels was really the crux of the letter – the underlying explanation for all of its warnings – it seems strange that Paul says nothing about being *under* angels in Galatians 3:19, and nothing explicit about angels at all in Galatians 4:3 or 9. Angels appear only to explain the law's inferior *origins* in the former case. And *stoicheia* can hardly be claimed as an obvious synonym for angels in the latter.

To the best of our knowledge there is only one *potentially* first-century text that definitively associates the *stoicheia* with angels. In *The Testament of Solomon*, the *stoicheia* appear in human form – bound hand and foot, announcing their names and asserting their proprietorial connection to the stars in the heavens (T. Sol. 8.1–4).[45] But the date of the text is very controversial, and D.C. Duling's assessment that it accurately reflects first-century Jewish thought seems generous at best. *The Book of Jubilees* associates angels with the physical elements (Jub. 2.2). 1 Enoch associates angels with the heavenly bodies that govern time and the seasons and, through them, the liturgical calendar of Israel (1 En. 82.7–8). But all of this is a fragile foundation for the view that submission to angels stands *at the heart* of Paul's logic in Galatians 4.

And even if the connection is allowed, we still have to ask how angels *function* in this interpretative model. Is Paul trying to tell us that the angels that

---

45 Pitre et al. 2019: 74.

gave the Jews their law were *wicked*?[46] That would explain, perhaps, the depth of his concern about the Galatians' religious progress and justify his assertion that they were going back to the same kind of slavery they had experienced in the past. But this is a counsel of despair for our larger understanding of Paul and the law, fully justifying the allegation of neo-Marcionism occasion-ally levelled at similar 'discontinuity' readings.[47] The discussion of angels in Galatians 3, remember, is simply designed to establish the mediated charac-ter of the law in contrast to the unmediated character of the gospel. It makes no claim whatsoever about their moral qualities. In every other text we know of where angelic mediation of the law is invoked, the angels are good angels, emissaries from God to humans obeying his command, not enslaving powers acting in violation of it.[48]

And if the angels who gave the Jewish law in Galatians 3:19 were *good* an-gels and Paul refers to them again in Galatians 4:3, we face a clash with the direction of his argument. Paul is not concerned with the mere practices his readers adopt. He tells us neither circumcision nor uncircumcision have any value *twice* before the letter is out (Gal. 5:6; 6:15). His concern is *their un-derlying spiritual orientation*, and if obeying the law involves submission to good angels, it's hard to see why that should bother him. Pitre would, I think, respond with the charge that, good or bad, life under angels is a mark of the old age. But Paul was clearly happy to continue such observances without the risk of returning to the old age himself. He would say, I presume, that he was 'no longer under the law' (Rom. 6:14), that he was free – as I will argue in Chapter 9 – to observe it or not as he chose. But why couldn't his Gentile read-ers say the same? Pitre and his colleagues fail to answer this important ques-tion. In the next chapter, however, we'll find that *Paul does not*.

---

46 Wright 2021: 231.
47 See for example, Wright 2013: 1481.
48 See Wright 1991: 158–162; Wright 2013: 871–872, 876–877. Wright 2021: 231–232.

8
Going Backwards in Corinth and Rome

Introduction

In the journey of discovery that led to the creation of this book, one of the most exhilarating, penny-dropping moments was the realization that Galatians is not the only place in Paul's letters where he deals with the perplexing topic of regression.

Reading the text in the light of the larger Jewish and pagan context of the region as we've done in the last few chapters, reading with an awareness of the time on Paul's eschatological clock, certainly informs and illuminates our understanding of the issues at stake. But all of it leaves us thirsting for clarification *from the actual actors in the drama.* What would *the Galatians* have said in response to Paul's warnings? The answer would doubtless be revealing if only we had access to their reply. And how would *Paul himself* have clarified his intentions? Most interpreters assume this question is similarly impenetrable. But the answer is not, in fact, the silence we expect.

In what kind of circumstances could the influence of mature believers have propelled immature believers back to their *pagan* past? In what kind of situation might Paul have condemned practices for some that he endorsed for others, including himself, as a threat to the very survival of their faith? At first glance these questions seem unpromisingly specific to Galatians. But answers provided by Paul himself are actually woven into a major – though sadly neglected – theme in his larger theology: his teaching about the weak and the strong.

1 The Weak and the Strong

Mention the weak and the strong and most of us will jump intuitively to the final chapters of Romans. In Romans 14–15, we picture Paul coming down the mountain after the extraordinary ascent of Chapters 1–11 brought us up through the clouds to some of the most dazzling peaks of Christian theology.

Everything that follows can feel like an afterthought. After the great indicatives of God's grace in Christ, we have the imperatives of living sacrificially, loving others, obeying the authorities and putting up with scrupulous brothers and sisters in our churches. This is the kind of thing Paul just feels he has to say to fledgling Jesus-communities to keep the wheels on while they contemplate the glory of the gospel, right? It isn't really the heart of the matter, right?

Wrong. These chapters are the destination that that breathtaking climb was actually designed to attain. And those throwaway (dare I say, patronizing?) comments about the scrupulous weak and the strong, and their duty to endure them, are nothing of the kind. The weak and the strong and the shape of their interaction is a picture of the gospel and an index of our comprehension of it for Paul.

Paul doesn't pigeonhole people in these chapters, labelling them according to their racial or religious background, positioning them as some kind of deadweight the community is obliged to carry. 'Weak' doesn't mean 'law-observant Jew' for Paul; 'strong' doesn't mean 'law-free Gentile'. Paul presents us with a rich and flexible wisdom principle here that cuts in multiple directions. Every believer is strong in some senses and weak in others – indeed, the very thing that *constitutes* strength in some situations can *constitute* weakness in others. Every believer is equipped to consider, but also needs the consideration of, others. Where there are different people with different backgrounds, with different strengths and different vulnerabilities – in every *real* congregation that has ever existed, in other words – this is the actual substance of Christian living. Without this, Romans 1–11 remains mere theory and the possibility of renewed relationship with God it holds out to us simply slips between our fingers. The new thing God is doing in his world through Christ, the new age his coming inaugurates, is only enacted to the extent that his people are enabled – even as they stand together on their core gospel convictions – to care for one another and love one another despite differences *in every other area*.

In this chapter we'll discover how all of this is relevant to our questions about regression. But the best place to start isn't Galatians *or* Romans but somewhere we can be surer of our footing in the underlying context – the first letter to the church in Corinth.

2 Weakness and Strength in Corinth

Corinth is the place, among all the other places Paul wrote to, where we have the clearest picture of the actual interaction between the author and his audience. True, as in every other case, we lack anything close to an independent statement from his readers. But we do know that the first half of 1 Corinthians was written in response to information received from Corinth via messengers 'from Chloe's household' (1 Cor. 1:11), and we also know that the second half was written in response to a letter the Corinthians had sent him themselves.[1]

1 Corinthians 7:1 provides the crucial 'narrator's' comment here – 'now for the matters you wrote about' – leading to a string of specific questions, each introduced with the same tell-tale transitional marker, *Peri de* – '*now about* virgins' (1 Cor. 7:25), '*now about* food sacrificed to idols' (1 Cor. 8:1), '*now about* the gifts of the Spirit' (1 Cor. 12:1), '*now about* the collection for the Lord's people' (1 Cor. 16:1), '*now about* our brother Apollos' (1 Cor. 16:12). These are the issues the Corinthians wanted to raise with Paul. And under each of these 'headings' we get a fresh, contextualized example of Pauline pastoral wisdom in response.

In the section beginning at 1 Corinthians 8:1, the discussion takes us to the meeting point between pagan worship and food. As in every other major Graeco-Roman city of the period, cults and cult temples played a central part in the economic and social life of the Corinthian community, not least in the provision of food on account of the central significance of animal sacrifice in their regular rituals.[2] On festal occasions, meat offered to the gods could be consumed after the sacrifice at the temples themselves – indeed, many had dining rooms constructed especially for the purpose.[3] But the scale of the butchery also supported a 'takeaway' model, and Paul has both practices in mind as he wrestles with the question of whether followers of Jesus should participate.

The apostle's response to this issue still shocks many.[4] We're expecting brevity and clarity here – a simple 'yes' or 'no' seems as if it will suffice. But instead we get nuance. Lots of nuance. Nuance to the extent that, to some, it smacks of equivocation.

1 Corinthians 8:1–13 deals with 'eating in' and it opens with an enigmatic preview of the course Paul is about to steer. 'We all possess knowledge,' he says, quoting his correspondents (verse 1). But knowledge alone is an insufficient resource to respond to the question the Corinthians have asked. 'Knowledge puffs up while love builds up,' he continues. And building others up is the faith-authenticating emphasis he's longing to see worked out among his readers then and now (verses 2–3).

---

1 Hays 1997: 5–6.

2 See Parker 2011: 124–170; Burkert 1987: 55–66.

3 Thiselton cites a well-known invitation to just such a dining room from *Oxyrhynchus* 110: 'Herais asks you to dine in the room of the Serapheion at a banquet of the Lord Serapis tomorrow the 11th from the 9th hour' (see Thiselton 2000: 736; see also Murphy-O'Connor 2002: 164; Hays 1997: 137)

4 See Hays 1997: 134–135.

What was the 'knowledge' the Corinthians were appealing to? The answer comes in verse 4 with two more swift citations from their letter: 'An idol is nothing at all in the world' and 'there is no God but one'. These are truths Paul himself may have taught, and he certainly agrees with them in principle. He agrees so wholeheartedly, in fact, that he's inspired to compose one of the most remarkable declarations of God's unity in diversity found anywhere in early Christian literature (verses 5–6).[5] But all the way through the staggering restatement of the *Shema*, the classic Jewish daily confession, that follows – with Jesus incorporated alongside the Father into its fundamental definition of deity – we're expecting a 'but' and we're not disappointed.

For all their knowledge, for all its newly unveiled theological wonders, the Corinthians are still going to mishandle this matter of dining at local pagan temples if they fail to engage with it from a *pastoral* point of view (verses 7–8). Their knowledge may tell them that 'an idol is nothing' and they can do what they please with respect to idol food. But knowledge is not the only issue at stake here. There must be empathy for neighbour as well as theological precision if they're going to grasp the fact that exposing 'weak' believers to the self-same settings where they worshipped pagan gods in the past has the potential to defile and even to destroy them (verses 9–13).

How should we understand the contrast between 'the weak' and 'the strong' that Paul draws out here? Gerd Theissen sees the tip of a sociological iceberg poking through the surface of the text – the same iceberg that became visible in Chapter 1, where Paul reminded his readers about the state in which he first met them: 'Not many of you were wise by human standards; not many were influential; not many were of noble birth' (1 Cor. 1:26). The same iceberg returns into view in Chapter 11, where the ingrained social habits of wealthy members of the Corinthian congregations – dining at different tables and eating different food from their social inferiors – are seemingly being carried over into the celebration of the Lord's Supper.[6] But in Chapter 8, it's hard to divide the weak and the strong along the lines of social privilege. *Quality meats* were certainly reserved for the wealthy in Corinth, except on the rare occasions when benefactors laid on banquets for the entire population of the city.[7] But then, as now,

---

5 Note Richard Bauckham's penetrating analysis of this passage in Bauckham 2009: 210–218.

6 Theissen 2004: 121–143.

7 See, for example, Gill 1993: 336–337, citing the example of the wealthy first-century Corinthian magistrate Lucius Castricius Regulus, who once gave a banquet '[for all the] inhabitants of the colony' (The Inscriptions: no. 153). Note also the passage in Plutarch's *Table Talk* where we learn about a series of banquets at which Sospis, the president of the Isthmian Games, 'entertained a great many foreign visitors at once, and several times entertained all the citizens' (Quaest. Conv. 723A).

offcuts were cheaply available, and the text rebuffs our attempts to reduce the problem to a matter of rich believers flaunting their wealth in local temples while the poor looked on in envy.[8] The problem for the weak in 1 Corinthians 8:10 was that *they really could* emulate the behaviour of the strong. So what was the basis for the distinction?

A more promising path to interpreting Paul's language here involves a horizontal glance at the use of similar terms by his literary contemporaries. Clarence Glad has been the trailblazer here, with his fascinating thesis on 'strength' and 'weakness' as cyphers for maturity and immaturity in Hellenistic thought.[9] For Cicero, the weak were subject to 'bad habits and false beliefs' which '[turned] them in whatever direction they [were] inclined' (Leg. 1.29); for Seneca, weakness could be unlearned, but only through the 'toilsome' process of overcoming established vices and embracing unfamiliar virtues (Ep. 50.7–9).[10] Applying these insights to 1 Corinthians, Anders Eriksson thinks 'weakness' was a natural expression for Paul to use to describe 'the moral sickness [of] recent converts who were not yet able to make correct moral judgements'.[11]

Adopting this approach, we begin to see the basis for the curious division between the weak and the strong in the letter as Paul writes it. We don't have Jews and Gentiles in contrast here – weak Jews scrupulously avoiding pagan temples and strong Gentiles exercising their freedom to enter them. We have Gentiles *and Gentiles* in contrast – mature and immature Gentile believers with different degrees of detachment from their pagan past. The 'weaker brother' in Corinth doesn't falter because they're a Jew, striving to maintain 'redundant' Jewish laws. They're a Gentile and they falter, in Paul's own words, because '[they're] still so accustomed to idols that when they eat sacrificial food they think of it as having been sacrificed to a god, and since their conscience is weak, it is defiled' (1 Cor. 8:7). This is vitally important. Notwithstanding their grasp of the gospel and their wholehearted commitment to Christ, the person Paul describes here is still so affected by their years of pagan devotion and the contours of their inner life are still so shaped by its assumptions that

---

8 Against Theissen's assertion that regular meat consumption was a privilege of the rich, Meggitt argues that sausages, blood puddings and various unappetizing 'off-cuts' were commonly available at the *popinae* or 'cookshops' frequented by the *polloi* (see Meggitt 1994: 137–141).

9 Glad's work focuses on areas of overlap between Paul and the Epicurean philosopher Philodemus, whose handbook *On Frank Criticism* applies the labels 'weak' and 'strong' to individuals possessing greater and lesser degrees of moral and intellectual maturity (Crit. Fr. 7, 10, Col. XXIVa). In 1 Corinthians 8, Glad argues that, by participating in idol food, the strong hope to teach the weak by example (Glad 1995: 277–295).

10 See Malherbe 1994: 233–238.

11 Eriksson 1998: 143.

they cannot simply re-enter the world in which those associations were created without a reaction. However much they strive to eat idol food as a monotheistic follower of Christ, habit is pulling them in a completely different direction.

Anthony Thiselton highlights the *unconscious* nature of this threat to the weak: they sense the attraction of living like the strong, but they don't sense the danger of defilement.[12] David Garland describes it as a matter of reflexes: '[the weak] have a reflex reaction when it comes to idols… Eating sanctified food had always been an act of worship that honoured the god lurking behind the idol. Their minds are still infused with old conceptions that spring up involuntarily'.[13] For Richard Hays the immature believers in Corinth 'are so accustomed to thinking of the idols as real that they cannot eat the idol meat without conjuring up the whole symbolic word of idol worship; [and] they are dragged back into [it and] "defiled"'.[14] As they eat, the weak are drawn off into the familiar complex of fear and reverence that accompanied their eating in the past, only grasping the spiritual implications in the rear-view mirror, when their faithfulness to Christ – despite their pledge of unstinting devotion to him – has already been compromised.[15]

Neither must we miss the strength of Paul's language here. So, the weak in Corinth were struggling to detach from their past and felt occasional, unwanted twinges of familiarity as they sat and ate as Jesus-people in the pagan temples of Corinth. 'No big deal,' we think. 'It wouldn't have taken them long to get over it, and their participation was a potent picture of Christ's supremacy over every other claimed god and every other claimed Lord.' But if that's our conclusion here, we need to understand how violently Paul disagrees. Paul reserves some of the strongest language in the New Testament for

---

12 Thiselton 2000: 639–640. In dialogue with Eckstein, Thiselton associates weakness of conscience with 'merely routinized, unthinking, habituated action' (Thiselton 2000: 643; cf. Eckstein 1983: 232–256, 311–314). On the appeal of emulating the strong, see also Theissen 2004: 128–129). Garland analyses weakness and strength in terms of overactive and underactive states of conscience (Garland 2003: 381–382; see also Barrett 1971: 194–195). Jewett diagnoses among the weak Corinthians an inability to truly assimilate knowledge of the gospel on account of the 'dread of the idols' still affecting their consciences (Jewett 1971: 422–423).

13 Garland 2003: 380.

14 Hays 1997: 140.

15 See also Hays 1997: 142. 'Paul and the Corinthians share a common set of religious symbols and it is not in their choice of symbols that Paul finds fault with his converts. Instead, he is disturbed by the different manner in which the Corinthians construe the significance of these shared symbols' (Chester 2003: 214). In this case, the symbols of meat and drink are construed by the weak according to the Graeco-Roman religious culture in which they were immersed prior to their conversion (Chester 2003: 213–225). Theissen helpfully sketches Paul's concept of accountability for *both* conscious *and* unconscious intentions in his assessment of 1 Corinthians 4:1–5 (Theissen 1987: 59–66). Jeremias explores the intentions of the strong (Jeremias 1953: 151–152). Glad notes the inability of the weak to reach the same logical conclusions as the strong, *even if they accept the same premises* (Glad 1995: 285–286).

the pastoral risk this 'strong' approach is taking (1 Cor. 8:12–13). The weaker brother is 'wounded' and the stronger brother sins not only against him but against Christ. The weaker brother, 'for whom Christ died' – note how Paul drives home the value of the sentence's subject here to accentuate the impact of the verb – 'is *destroyed* by your knowledge'. This is a life and death issue. And to reinforce the point, he backs it up with an Old Testament allusion.

'Be careful, however, that the exercise of your rights does not become a stumbling-block for the weak,' he says (1 Cor. 8:9). It's a powerful image in and of itself. But the impact is even more pronounced when we reconnect it with its original context in Leviticus 19:14.[16] God's warning through Moses 'not to curse the deaf or put *a stumbling-block* (LXX: *skandalon*) in front of the blind' thunders against the mistreatment of those who are unable to perceive what's happening to them until after the damage is done – exactly the situation Paul envisages for the weak in Corinth. And neither is this his first use of 'stumbling-block' vocabulary in the letter.[17] In 1 Corinthians 1:23, the *skandalon* is Christ crucified – alluding now to Psalm 69:22–23, where the good gift of God becomes a stumbling-block to his enemies.[18] Read in the light of that earlier allusion, and the terrible possibility of stumbling over the fact of the cross, the point of Paul's logic in 1 Corinthians 8 is powerfully reinforced. The strong have to stop and consider what they're doing. Imposing their preferences on their unsuspecting weaker brothers can cause them to stumble over the stumbling stone, despite the fact that it's motivated by the purest theological principles.[19]

3 Weakness and Strength in Romans

Note, then, how all this prepares and equips us to rightly read the equivalent sections in Romans.

Romans presents us with new interpretative problems but also with an abundance of new material to work with. Unlike the Corinthian letters, the audience situation here is basically unknown to us. Paul had never previously visited the Roman church in person, and though he writes with *some* local knowledge, gleaned perhaps from his multiple contacts in the congregation

---

16 Rudolph 2011: 104–107. For instances of the specific association between stumbling blocks and *idolatry*, see LXX Josh. 23:13 and Hos. 4:17.

17 For a similar association between blindness and weakness compare Seneca Ep. 50.3 with Ep. 50.9.

18 On the different contexts in which Paul uses *skandalon* language, see Das 2007: 136. The Psalm itself is perhaps alluding to Leviticus, but with biting irony – if God's enemies stumble over even the good things he gives them, they are *truly* blind.

19 I am grateful to Dr David Rudolph for the germ of this connection between *skandalon* language and Paul's larger exploration of the accommodation theme.

(note the unprecedented extent of his personal greetings in Chapter 16), we have little more than speculation to guide us as we try to reconstruct the underlying needs. Paul is clear that he's writing to Gentiles, both in his introduction (Rom. 1:6, 13) and in his conclusion (15:15–16; 16:25–27). But only a brave (or reckless) reader would exclude Jews from the audience entirely when their state and fate is so central to his argument, and he applies it so carefully to both communities throughout.[20] In the passage that interests us in particular, in Romans 14–15, we do well to remember these lacunae in our knowledge and avoid jumping to peremptory conclusions about the situation on the ground.

The passage begins with two fascinating applications of Paul's larger theology of weakness and strength: food is the trigger issue once again in verses 1–4; in verses 5–9 it's special or 'sacred' days. Paul says nothing explicit about eating in pagan temples here, and the emphasis on vegetarianism is also distinctive to this passage (although he *does* make a point of his personal willingness to refrain from eating meat if by doing so he can guarantee the spiritual security of the weak in 1 Corinthians 8:13).[21] But the underlying principles are recognizably similar. Paul turns, once again, to stumbling-block language to explain his concerns, citing Leviticus 19:14 once again in his summons to brotherly accommodation (Rom. 14:13). And he does it, once again, in a context where the possibility of stumbling over the cross has already been established (Rom. 9:30–33; 11:7–12).[22] The seriousness of the situation is also reiterated in identically serious tones with stress laid, once again, on the danger that a person 'for whom Christ died' may be 'destroyed' (Rom. 14:15, cf. 14:20).

Speaking first to the strong (although they're not named as such until Rom. 15:1), Paul urges them to accept their weaker brothers 'without quarrelling over disputable matters':

One person's faith allows them to eat anything, but another, whose faith is weak, eats only vegetables. The one who eats everything must not treat with contempt the one who does not, and the one who does not eat everything must not judge the one who does, for God has accepted them. (Rom. 14:2–3)

How are we to make sense of the two groups he describes here? The conventional approach sees the weaker party as a Jew – not, of course, because there

---

20 The question of the composition of Paul's Roman readership is complex and thoroughly treated in specialist commentaries. Moo helpfully assesses the problems with assigning *either* an exclusively Jewish *or* an exclusively Gentile audience to the letter (see Moo 1996: 9–13).

21 See Moo 1996: 827–828; Hays 1997: 142.

22 Note that the scope of his Old Testament allusions has also now been widened to include Isa. 8:14 and 28:16.

was any Jewish law commanding abstention from meat (there wasn't) but be-cause, in diaspora settings, as we saw in Chapter 5, the kosherness of food couldn't always be determined or controlled by the eater and the only way to avoid all doubt was to avoid meat altogether.[23] The stronger party is a Gentile believer who sees all foods as clean as Paul does himself – much as the strong-er brothers in Corinth could claim him as a supporter in the matter of their 'knowledge'. Just as we saw in 1 Corinthians 8, Paul is strikingly clear about the strength of the 'strong' case here – 'I am convinced,' he says, *'being fully persuaded in the Lord Jesus,* that nothing is unclean in itself' (Rom. 14:14). But despite the strength of feeling he expresses, once again it's the strong who are asked to give way. The weak will be offended if their scruples are not accom-modated, even if they're no longer binding on Jewish Christians.

But this is not the only way to read the passage. Armed with our knowledge of the situation in Corinth, vegetarianism could also make sense if the weaker brother was a Gentile, not, I think, in the way Max Rauer once proposed – with the Gentiles in Rome pictured as former Neo-Pythagoreans like Apol-lonius of Tyana, for whom vegetarianism was an important expression of his religious convictions – but in the sense that a Gentile with a pagan past and with powerful habituated associations between eating meat and idol worship might renounce meat altogether (either 'eating in' or 'taking away') to avoid a damaging reactivation of those connections.[24] To be Gentiles, the weak here don't have to be clinging to practices learned in their pre-Christian past. The weak can be Gentiles who are struggling to *detach* from it. And this too makes sense of the logic of the passage. It might actually make *better* sense when we realize that, like 1 Corinthians 8 once again, the issue is not just *offending* the weak but leading them to the brink of spiritual destruction (Rom. 14:15, 20).

In verses Romans 14:5–9 we reach Paul's second case study in accommoda-tion which briefly flashes into focus before being absorbed into a more general discussion of the underlying principle:

One person considers one day more sacred than another; another considers every day alike. Each of them should be fully convinced in their own mind.

---

23 On the weaker party as a Jew, see Moo 1996: 826–833. See also Wright 2015: 634–635. David Rudolph provides an excellent introduction to the various models of accommodation practised by Jews in the time of Paul. Principled abstention from food prepared by Gentiles was a recognized manifestation of Pharisaic halakha (Rudolph 2011: 120–130). Several commentators note the vegetarianism of the Jewish priests sent to Rome under the procuracy of Felix as recorded by Josephus (Josephus Life 13–14). For other equivalent examples, see Barclay 2011: 41.

24 Rauer: 1923. Käsemann speculatively attributes the ascetic inclinations of the weak in Rome to 'syn-cretistic influences' affecting Jews in the city (Käsemann 1973: 352).

Whoever regards one day as special does so to the Lord. Whoever eats meat does so to the Lord, for they give thanks to God; and whoever abstains does so to the Lord and gives thanks to God. (Rom. 14:5–6)

Conventionally, once again, weakness is associated with Judaism here.[25] The Jew is the person who has scruples about sabbaths and Passovers and other important festivals, and the strong are those who '[consider] every day alike' – just as they consider every food alike. But all of this is just an assumption based on what we *think* Paul might have meant. It isn't actually *in* the text. And the text may actually speak against it.

Think for a minute about the order in which Paul introduces strength and weakness in this whole section of Romans. In Romans 14:2, the strong come first, and the weak were mentioned second:

One person's faith allows them to eat anything, but another, whose faith is weak, eats only vegetables. (Rom. 14:2)

The same pattern is observed in verse 3. And when the subject is resumed in Romans 15:1 we see it again:

We who are strong ought to bear with the failings of the weak and not to please ourselves. (Rom. 15:1)

The structure of Paul's argument in 1 Corinthians 8:1–13 follows the same basic pattern. In fact, the strong precede the weak in *every* Pauline instance of the contrast except here in Romans 14:5. So how would things look if it was not, in fact, an exception to the rule at all but actually conformed to it?

If the person who 'considers one day more important than another' is really *strong*, the natural reading of the data still points to the conclusion that they're a Jew. This person is a Jew who can keep on keeping the law without any negative effect on their faith in Christ (a Jew like Paul, perhaps, or Peter, James or John), the kind of Jew who knows that 'works of the law' like sabbath-keeping were never supposed to yield justification in God's sight (Gal. 2:15–16). But the weak person, now – the one who 'considers every day alike' – is a different kind of Gentile, not a *strong* Gentile who can do whatever they want, but a Gentile like we saw in 1 Corinthians 8:7 who spent their entire pre-Christian life

---

25 Moo 1996: 841–842; Wright 2015: 635.

keeping the sacred days of pagan gods and who now avoids anything even re-motely similar because they know the kinds of expectations such observances will reawaken. Perhaps, then, just like the weak in Corinth, we have Gentiles here striving to keep their distance from their pagan past. The difference is just that, in Romans 14, the source of the temptation is *Jews*.

4 Weakness and Strength in Galatians

How then does all this help us when we come back in to land in Galatians? The point is now clangingly obvious, I hope, in that all of it sounds *familiar*. Whether or not we accept the possibility that the 'weaker brothers' of Romans 14–15 included vulnerable *Gentile* converts of the same type we met in 1 Cor-inthians 8, the latter text presents a clear parallel to the situation in Galatia, with immature believers at risk of returning to the habitual norms of their pagan past:

> *Formerly, when you did not know God, you were slaves to those who by nature are not gods. But now that you know God – or rather are known by God – how is it that you are turning back to those weak and miserable stoicheia? Do you wish to be enslaved by them all over again?* (Gal. 4:8–9)

Like the 'weak' in Corinth, and in Rome, the Galatians were navigating this path into spiritual danger under the influence of mature believers with a dif-ferent approach to food and sacred days (and, of course, circumcision).[26] And, as in 1 Corinthians and Romans, so here – the consequences Paul envisages are potentially catastrophic:

> *Mark my words! I, Paul, tell you that if you let yourselves be circumcised, Christ will be of no value to you at all. Again, I declare to every man who lets himself be circumcised that he is obligated to obey the whole law. You who are trying to be justified by the law have been alienated from Christ; you have fallen away from grace.* (Gal. 5:2–4; cf. 1 Cor. 8:9–13; Rom. 14:20–21)

The strength of the warnings in each of these passages should weigh heavily with us as we assess this. I know of no other places in the Pauline epistles

---

26 If Clarence Glad's exegesis of 1 Corinthians 8:1–13 is on target, these 'other Christians' in Corinth, as also in Galatia, *intended* to educate not to destroy (Glad 1995: 280–283).

where words of equivalent force are used to sound a warning except perhaps the famous case in 1 Corinthians 5 where Paul talks about 'handing [a guilty person] over to Satan'.

It should also strike us that – sparing 1 Corinthians and Romans – the only other place Paul uses *skandalon* vocabulary is here, again, in the letter to the Galatians where the stumbling-block of the cross comes to his mind in Chapter 5. This stumbling-block would simply be effaced if he turned and preached a gospel where circumcision had some kind of residual instrumentality (Gal. 5:11). Each in their own way, both Romans and 1 Corinthians interact with this same idea.

Now, in those texts, as we saw, of course, the risk of stumbling over the cross is partnered with warnings about causing weaker brothers to stumble. And Galatians lacks such specific references, so perhaps it would be better to bracket it from our analysis? But what if the warnings are absent from Galatians because the time for warnings had already passed? What if Galatians lacks the expected component – the set piece citation from Leviticus 19:14 threatening destruction on the weak at the hands of the strong – because *the whole text* is in fact a response to the exact situation Moses sought to avoid, because it's a paramedic call out to the scene of an accident where the warnings of Leviticus 19:14 had not been heeded?

And if the reference in Romans to the person who 'considers one day more sacred than another' *really is* a description of strength, we have a parallel to Galatians in almost every respect. In Galatia, the Jewish Agitators held exactly the same opinion, and by imposing it on Paul's vulnerable readers they were ushering them to the same fate. If the Agitators are framed as the 'strong', the whole thing snaps into shape. And several other striking conclusions follow.

If the Agitators in Galatia are the 'strong', it should strike us especially that, in the other places where we meet 'strong' people, Paul *agrees* with them on their theological principles. Paul agrees with the strong in 1 Corinthians – idols are a vapour. And he agrees with the strong in Romans – nothing is unclean in and of itself. His problem with them isn't the inadequacy of their *knowledge* but the inadequacy of their *empathy*. They're like bulls running loose in spiritual china shops, proud of the precision with which they grasp their own freedoms but entirely unaware of the damage they're doing in the process.

If the Agitators in Galatia are the 'strong', we can position them, at least in principle, far closer to Paul than traditional readings allow. There may be good reasons not to do so, of course – they disagreed with him, certainly, on the necessity of circumcision, and almost as certainly they disparaged his claims to authority as an apostle.[27] But even when the anathemas are flying in Galatians 1:8–9, the overarching issue might still have more to do with their lack of pastoral good sense than with fundamental differences in theology. Paul accuses them of throwing the Galatians into confusion with the result that they're 'turning to a different gospel' (Gal. 1:6–7). But Peter himself is accused of something similar in Galatians 2:14, and that doesn't make him an apostate. Peter was failing to act 'in line with the truth of the gospel', he was '[forcing] Gentiles to follow Jewish customs' – though all he did in practice was omit to accommodate the weak. Might a similar omission in the practice of the Agitators stand at the root of the Galatian crisis?

Might Galatians in fact be *the crowning example* of the reality that weakness and strength have nothing to do with Jewishness and 'Gentileness' at all and everything to do with the extent to which the religious assumptions of our past, or of the cultures that surround us, remain viable beneath the surface of our real *but still fragile* convictions? Might the weak be not those who cling to outdated laws, but who wisely avoid situations where these assumptions can be reawakened, and who need the consideration of the strong to help them keep their distance?

And if the Agitators in Galatia are the 'strong', we can also see clearly that the issue in Galatia *really is* the 'salvation' of Paul's readers, even if it isn't directly about '"how to get saved" or "how to go to heaven"' as N.T. Wright has repeatedly pointed out.[28] In 1 Corinthians 8 and Romans 14–15, Paul is concerned about the *spiritual destruction* of the weak and how it can be avoided. If he's addressing weak believers on the brink of the same fate in Galatians then we're absolutely justified in reading the letter, as traditional readings always have, as a source of insight into the difference between the paths to spiritual life and spiritual death.

---

27 Barclay 1987: 73–93.
28 Wright 2021: 119 et passim.

9
Going Backwards in Galatia

Introduction

How, then, does all this look when we put the pieces together *in Galatians*? Let's start with a review of our progress so far.

In Chapter 4 we began to probe Paul's disconcerting diagnosis of regression in Galatia – disconcerting not just because it involves telling *Gentiles* who want to get circumcised they're going back to something they've done *before*, but also thanks to the problematic alignment it creates between his readers' past enslavement to the 'not-gods' and his own past enslavement under the Jewish law. Both of these states are described using *stoicheia* terminology in Paul's text (Gal. 4:3, 9). But what does he mean? Is he saying the Galatians are going back to the same state *he was in* before he accepted Christ as Lord? Surely this can't have been what the Agitators were offering given every other indication that they were Jewish *Jesus-followers*, not Jewish *Jesus-deniers* attempting to lure his readers away from Christ. And surely this also leaves us with an intolerably negative portrayal of the law, not just as a jailer (Gal. 3:22), nor even as a *paidagōgos* (Gal. 3:24), but as a cypher for the activity of evil powers. This is the problem we set out to solve in Part II of this book and, by so doing, to shine new light on the residual instabilities of the Old and New Perspectives summarized in Part I.

In Chapter 5, we explored the strengths and weaknesses of the most common response to this conundrum – the argument that the Galatian churches were populated with former Godfearers who were now reverting to that familiar lifestyle. Yes, it's quite probable that Paul's readers had significant past experience in local synagogues – especially if we locate them in the cities of southern Galatia mentioned in Acts 13–14. But no, it's highly improbable that they were returning to a 'Christianized' version of their former Godfearing behaviour with its easy integration of Yahweh-worship and other pagan cult affiliations. Circumcision was an expression of *exclusive* commitment, not an expression of commitment to just one element in a larger religious 'portfolio'.

And if the Galatians were simply moving 'in the general direction' of their Jewish past, why the big fuss? What wasn't there to like about Gentile converts embracing the same laws Paul and his Jewish apostolic colleagues were happy to embrace? Sure, it might have misread the time on God's eschatological clock. Sure, it might have underestimated the extent of Christ's achievements on their behalf. But it was surely better taken as a positive sign of commitment than as a step towards, or even over, the brink of apostasy (Gal. 5:2, 4).

In Chapter 6 we sought further insight by diving into the Galatians' pagan religious background. Clinton Arnold argued that legalism and fear marked their past pursuit of pagan gods, and it shouldn't surprise us to find them latching onto similar threads in the message of the Agitators. But his thesis concentrated on just one small subset of the data and neglected the fact that, for all its problems, Paul still considered his opponents' message a 'gospel' (Gal. 1:6, 8–9). Susan Elliott drew a parallel between circumcision and ritual castration in the Cybele cult, exposing the fascinating possibility that the Agitators' message *may have meant something quite different to the Galatians* than it did to the Agitators themselves. But the problem here was an overemphasis on ecstatic rites, and a failure to explain how an enthusiasm for circumcision with such esoteric origins could have gripped *a whole church*. En route, we assembled a realistic envelope of options for the Galatians' religious past and began to gesture towards its significance. The gods of first-century Asia Minor could be incentivized to bless in a variety of ways – through diligent observance of sacred days and dietary laws, through compliance with purity regulations, through the establishment of tangible, lasting expressions of devotion. In all but the most extreme cases, no bargains were struck; divine volition and chance remained determinative factors. But incentives were not for that reason thought ineffective, indeed many aspects of contemporary religious practice were specifically designed to *heighten* their effectiveness.

In Chapter 7, placing Paul in his apocalyptic context gave us a new interpretative framework for his remarks about going backwards. Whatever else regression means in Galatians, it must mean returning to the present evil age. But how should we understand this? Martyn focused on a return to the dualities that characterized life under pagan gods and under Jewish law but failed to explain the ongoing significance of dualities under the gospel. De Boer located a true point of contact between Jewish and pagan practice in their common concentration on calendrical rituals but failed to account for the extremity of Paul's warnings or for the pre-eminent importance of circumcision in the letter. Barclay led us to an (impractically?) broad reading of the equivalence between life under Jewish law and life under pagan gods – they were alike in their unlikeness to something *that was unlike everything*: life in the new creation, and to an (unrealistically?) narrow reading of the presenting issue – the Agitator's concept of *reciprocity* and the Galatians' customary pagan concept of reciprocity were essentially the same. Pitre et al. found a point of contact in subservience to angels but failed to account for the extent of Paul's concern without attributing the law to the interposition of evil powers and flirting with neo-Marcionism in the process.

In Chapter 8 we began to tack in a more promising direction, seeking clarification from Paul about the meaning of his regression language, and finding it in 1 Corinthians and Romans in the context of his teaching about the weak and the strong. In 1 Corinthians we found that the weak are not Jews but Gentiles, 'still so accustomed to idols that when they eat sacrificial food they think of it as having been sacrificed to a god, and since their conscience is weak, it is defiled' (1 Cor. 8:7). And the strong – despite Paul's evident agreement with them on the admissibility of eating food either in, or offered at, an idol temple – are warned in the strongest terms against causing their brothers to stumble. In Romans, the common assumption that the weak must be law-observant Jews was challenged with help from the data from Corinth. The weak could be Gentiles, the strong could be Jews, and vice versa – all of which became particularly interesting in Romans 14:5, where we found that Jewish strength, manifested as ongoing commitment to the traditional programme of sabbaths and festivals even after embracing Jesus as Lord, could lead to the destruction of weak Gentiles just as de Boer envisages in Galatia.[1] In Romans, as in 1 Corinthians, Paul reaches for stumbling-block vocabulary, and stresses the danger of spiritual destruction. Parallels in all these areas in Galatians suggest that Paul is not, in fact, as silent on the perplexing subject of regression as has previously been imagined. The whole letter can be fruitfully interpreted as a worked example of what happens in a church when Paul's later-to-become-standard warnings about accommodation are not observed.

Even from this summary of our findings thus far, it's apparent that much depends on our handling of Paul's elusive references to the *stoicheia* in Galatians 4:3 and 9 if we want to make sense of the Galatian situation. This interpretative crux demands our attention now as we begin to assemble our data into a coherent response to the regression problem.

---

1   See de Boer 2011: 252–261.

1 Returning to the *Stoicheia*

As we noted briefly in Chapter 7, for the past 50 years or so, the interpretation of *stoicheia* in Galatians 4 has been driven more or less determinatively by the work of Joseph Blinzler, whose pioneering reading rested on *quantitative* analysis.[2] Though working before the era of large-scale, digital, searchable archives of ancient texts, Blinzler established a pattern to which subsequent, database-driven research still very often conforms. Bringing together citations from '[all] the more well-known Jewish and Christian sources before and after Paul', he argued that the meaning of *stoicheia* in Galatians should be decided according to the sheer number of examples associated with each of the various interpretative options listed in standard Greek lexica.[3] And his research produced a clear result. Across the 175 texts he examined, Blinzler found that *stoicheia* meant 'basic materials' in 78% of cases, and in the 11 texts that contained the complete expression *stoicheia tou kosmou*, which Paul uses in Galatians 4:3, he found the meaning was 'basic materials' *in every case*. Subsequent, digitally assisted extensions of Blinzler's work by Eduard Schweizer and Dietrich Rusam served only to strengthen this seemingly bullet-proof result: *stoicheia tou kosmou* means physical elements in Galatians because that's what it means *everywhere else*.[4] On Blinzler's reading, in all likelihood, the elements Paul had in mind were the four basic elements of ancient cosmology – earth, air, fire and water.

But how can this conclusion be reconciled with the argument Paul is crafting? The belief that *stoicheia must* mean physical elements in Galatians has led, as we've already observed, to some strained interpretations of his thought (witness Martyn's 'dualities' reading) and to a slew of notable appeals to loosen the constraints. For Martinus de Boer, the phrase must be read 'in some other way, or perhaps better, in some additional way', to make sense of Paul's logic – leading to his distinctive conclusion that element worship, shading into veneration of the heavenly bodies, stands in the background of the Galatian crisis.[5] John Barclay is similarly unwilling to be bound to physical interpretations of *stoicheia*, taking it instead as a reference to cosmic norms. Pitre et al. interpret

---

2   See Blinzler 1963: 429–443.
3   Blinzler 1963: 439.
4   See Schweizer 1988: 455–468; Rusam 1992: 119–125.
5   de Boer, 2011, 253.

the *stoicheia* as angelic powers.[6] So how should we find our way amid all this confusion?

As a doctoral student, I completely reassessed the meaning of *stoicheia* in all the Greek texts that can be dated with confidence to the first centuries BC and AD.[7] Using the massive holdings of the Thesaurus Linguae Graecae database which far outstrip the resources available to previous generations of scholars, I identified 378 citations in total. I also carefully tracked the relationship between the meaning of each citation and the *genre* of the larger text from which it was drawn.

Looking first at the *prevalence* of citations meaning physical elements, my study validated Blinzler's results, albeit by a less dramatic margin. Citations meaning physical elements still accounted for the majority of the instances – 56% of the total. Taking the literary genres in which the citations appeared into consideration, however, I also found an extremely strong correlation between the meaning of *stoicheia* and the context in which it was used.[8]

In Blinzler's original dataset, it shouldn't surprise us that philosophical and scientific genres predominate. Philosophical and scientific works account for a significant proportion of *all* the texts that remain to us from the ancient world, and even more so when we restrict ourselves to examples that include the word *stoicheia*. Neither should it surprise us that *stoicheia* means physical elements in almost all of these citations. The equivalent English word 'elements' means *physical* elements in almost every citation drawn from similar genres today. But as soon as we move out of these genres, the picture, even in the texts Blinzler considered, changes dramatically. In contexts dealing with grammar and mathematics, with history and religion, *stoicheia* means physical elements in just 26% of his examples. In my extended dataset, that number drops to 15%. There is no intrinsic implication that *stoicheia* denotes physical elements in any of these contexts any more than there is an intrinsic implication that 'elements' today refers to oxygen or hydrogen outside the confines of a chemistry library. *Stoicheia* means letters, it means numbers, it means musical notes, it means elements of good behaviour – it means whatever the context demands it to mean in whatever situation it is used.[9] The

---

6   See also Arnold 1996: 55–76.

7   This sub-project was published independently in the *Journal for the Study of the New Testament*. See Martin 2018: 434–452.

8   This observation validates the basic thrust of Andrew Bandstra's undeservedly neglected, pre-quantitative study on the 'formal' character of *stoicheion*, (see Bandstra: 1964).

9   '[*Stoicheion*] receives its "specific content" from the context in which it is used' (Bandstra 1964: 33).

question we have to answer here, then, has to do with the context Paul establishes *in Galatians* – a context that seemingly has little to do with either science or philosophy.[10]

Now Blinzler, of course, claimed more than just a simple, statistical prominence for the meaning, 'physical elements' in his dataset. He also claimed that, with the addition of the genitive modifier *tou kosmou*, *stoicheia always* means physical elements. But this conclusion is similarly fragile. Ten of the eleven examples Blinzler appealed to here were drawn from philosophical and quasi-scientific texts where the meaning 'physical elements' should be expected. The conclusion tells us less about the addition of *tou kosmou* than it tells us about the function of *stoicheia* in these settings. Just because the English phrase 'elements of the table' means elements of the *periodic* table when we encounter it in a science textbook, it doesn't follow that it means the same thing in books about making furniture, or dinnertime etiquette.

But even if this observation is set aside, Blinzler's conclusion is still overdrawn. The references to the *stoicheia tou kosmou* he cites from *the Sibylline Oracles* refer to 'days and nights' and 'light' as well as air, land, sea and 'the vault of heaven' – hardly obvious candidates for the interpretation, *physical* elements (Sib Or. 2.207; 3.80; 8.337). In the Orphic Hymns, *stoicheia tou kosmou* refers to night and to various primeval deities (Orph. Hym. 5.4). Beyond Blinzler's original group of texts, the phrase *stoicheia tou kosmou* is used to refer to numbers (Pyrr. Hyp. 3.152.1) and to the names of the Titans (Zeno Test. Frag. 100.2). Antiochus of Athens uses it to refer to light as a transcendent power (Frag. Ap. 110.17). Clement of Alexandria uses it to refer to a range of subjects including ploughs, furrows, seed, rain, phases of the moon, seasons, night, planets and the sea (Strom. 5.8.49). In Tertullian's *Against Marcion*, it means basic elements of learning (Marc. 5:4).[11]

Quantitative lexical analysis, therefore, tells us next to nothing about the meaning of *stoicheia* in Galatians except that it means 'elements' of a type to be determined *by the context*.

---

10 'Paul's concern can hardly be to expatiate on the natural world as such. Something more is involved, and this is where the other proposed referential meanings of the phrase seem inevitably to come into play as attempts to make sense of Paul's text, even if there is no evidence for the meaning "heavenly bodies" or "elemental spirits" before the second or third century C.E.' (de Boer 2011: 253).

11 While it is impossible to date, or geographically locate, the origin of the Greek Magical Papyri with precision, it is striking that the only instance of the phrase *stoicheia tou kosmou* in this voluminous resource almost certainly refers to the twenty-four letters of the Greek alphabet (PGM: XXXIX.1–21; for Greek text, see Preisendanz 1931, vol. 2: 177).

2 Reading *Stoicheia* in Context

Furnished with some perhaps unexpected room for exegetical manoeuvre here, then, let's think about what the context in Galatians *actually requires*.

As we saw in Chapter 4, the most notable feature of Paul's use of *stoicheia* in Galatians is that it functions as *a bridge* capable of spanning Jewish *and* pagan religious experience. In Galatians 4:3 he describes his own *Jewish* past in terms of enslavement under the *stoicheia*, in Galatians 4:4–5 he even implies that *Christ* submitted to a similar enslavement, yet in Galatians 4:8–9 he uses *stoicheia* to describe his readers' past enslavement to *pagan* gods.[12] We also note that, in both instances where *stoicheia* appears, it's embedded in a discussion about *spiritual maturity*. In Galatians 4:3, Paul looks back to the situation experienced by Jews under the law, likening them to heirs who have yet to attain their majority. In Galatians 4:9, he looks back to the situation experienced by his readers worshipping pagan gods, not yet having attained (or, more accurately, not yet having *received*) knowledge of the true God. And in addition we note that the reference to *stoicheia tou kosmou* in Galatians 4:3 seems to refer to elements *of the old age* – a point that becomes only more striking when we read on to the end of the letter and meet the only other instance of the word *kosmos* in Paul's text (Gal. 6:14), a reference to the 'world' to which he now considers himself 'crucified'.

Setting aside familiar solutions for a moment and asking ourselves simply what *this usage* most naturally implies, the deeply surprising answer, I think, is that Paul is describing elements that are *morally neutral* in themselves. He's describing elements that can be *assembled* into an enslavement compatible with the outworking of God's larger covenant promises on the one hand (Gal. 3:17), *and* into an enslavement that's radically, *idolatrously* opposed to them on the other. The elements themselves have no *necessary* relationship to either of these outcomes. They're building blocks capable of constructing enslavements of different kinds.[13]

The *stoicheia*, then, are *basic components of religious practice*. They're the 'Lego bricks' of human–divine interaction: the purity rites, calendrical festivals, costly offerings and memorializations of devotion from which *every*

---

12 On the relationship between Christ and the *stoicheia*, note the striking repetition of the pronoun *hypo* (under) in Galatians 4:3–5 (see Martin 2020: 115–116).

13 Interpreters of the phrase *stoicheia tou kosmou* in Galatians must also consider the two parallel occurrences in Colossians (Col. 2:8, 20). As in Galatians, the lexical imperative to assign the meaning 'physical elements' proves unwieldy in practice (e.g. Schweizer 1988: 466–467). The alternative 'elementary principles', however, fits the context well and has rich support in the history of exegesis (see, for example, Lightfoot 1886: 178–179). Suggestions that the return to the *stoicheia* taking place in Colossae involved the invocation of personal spiritual mediators are adequately supported by the reference to the worship of angels in Col. 2:18 without forcing angelic overtones into the definition of *stoichiea* itself.

ordinary form of religious expression in the ancient world was assembled. After Christ's apocalypse – influenced no doubt by Jeremiah and Ezekiel – Paul seems to have believed that Jews and Gentiles alike were being ushered into a new era in which God's laws would be written on the human heart (cf. Jer. 31:33; Ezek. 36:24–27). Looking back to the old era, however, he sees enslavement to external religious rites. Jews were enslaved to them in the sense that, under Moses, their devotion was unavoidably constructed from these elements. But pagans too were enslaved to them as an index of religious duty – a duty which, in their case, led only to spiritual death.

2.1 Calendrical Observances

Looking back over our work so far, we've already noted several attempts to clarify Paul's use of *stoicheia* in the light of the surrounding context, each with their own strengths and weaknesses. For me, de Boer's reading stands out as the most satisfying, if only because the calendrical festivals he identifies as the basis of the 'enslavement' Paul is talking about in Galatians 4 were so uncontestably central to both Jewish and pagan life in the first century, bridging – as we've seen any coherent interpretation of *stoicheia* must – *both* worlds of experience. The reservation that this reading tells us nothing about circumcision and thus fails to explain the prominence of regression *throughout the letter* is significant and must be dealt with. But for now, let's defer consideration of this weakness and devote a few moments instead to cultivating the reading's strengths.

De Boer, we should note, doesn't equate calendrical festivals with the *stoicheia* directly – his definition of the word is still too tightly constrained for that. He claims, instead, that the *stoicheia* are heavenly bodies and that enslavement to the *stoicheia* in Galatians 4:9 is Paul's way of talking about his readers' former veneration of the sun, moon and stars which they *expressed through* their calendrical festivals. This, in itself, is not without problems. We've already seen that the evidence for pagan veneration of the elements in the first century is sketchy at best.[14] But for de Boer, this is still the place

---

14 See Chapter 7, pp. 96–100. Esau McCaulley's commendably creative reading of *stoicheia* in Galatians 4 founders here (McCaulley 2019: 178–182). McCaulley argues that the reference to *Jewish* enslavement to the *stoicheia* in Galatians 4:3 alludes to the covenant curse in Deuteronomy 28:64, condemning disobedient Israel to enslavement to 'gods of wood and stone', just like those worshipped by the Gentiles. Seeking a connection to Paul's *stoicheia* language, McCaulley appeals to Wis. 13.1–10, with its talk of Gentiles worshipping fire, air, water, stars and 'the works of human hands' as gods. But *stoicheia* language is not actually used in this text. The alleged connection depends on a further (unstated) bridge back to Wis. 7.1–2, and the assumption that first-century Jews would resonate with a description of themselves as 'enslaved to foreign gods' is also offered without proof. Clearly, Deuteronomy 27–30 informs Paul's use of curse vocabulary in Galatians, and we will explore this more fully in the next chapter. In Galatians 4:3 and 9, however, the suggested connection is far too tenuous to embrace with confidence, especially when we note Paul's willingness to quote Deuteronomy directly elsewhere (cf. Gal. 3:10).

we have to look if we are to understand the Galatians' former enslavement, and this makes his next move – from *pagan* to *Jewish* enslavement to the *stoicheia* – more than a little awkward. Whatever conclusions we come to about the Galatians' past practices, did Jews – did Paul himself, if Galatians 4:3 is to be believed – offer worship to the heavenly bodies in *their* life under the law? With the majority, de Boer answers 'no', and he's forced as a consequence to explain Paul's *stoicheia* language – as Barclay also did when he made the same argument – more as a rhetorical flourish than as a balanced reflection on the similarities between Jewish and pagan practice. Keeping the Jewish law was 'just as bad' as keeping the festivals of pagan gods for Paul – even if it wasn't strictly equivalent. But this blunts the force of his diagnosis of enslavement among the Jews to the point of near-redundancy.[15]

If we shed the constraint that *stoicheia must* mean physical elements, however, the difficulties de Boer is labouring under here start to melt away. If the calendrical festivals *themselves* are the *stoicheia* in Paul's argument – reading *stoicheia* now as *elements of religious practice* – we can readily see how *both* pagan and Jewish life might be construed as enslavement under them without resorting to speculation about element worship. On the pagan side of things we have ample evidence that participation in annual sacrifices, harvest thanksgivings and so on was a *necessity* for all who wished to maintain and enhance their chances of blessing from the gods.[16] And on the Jewish side, participation in sabbaths and annual festivals was similarly obligatory.[17] But here's the interesting part: if the *stoicheia* were calendrical festivals in Galatians – and we'll limit ourselves to that assumption for the sake of our argument for the moment – we can also see now why they might have been dangerous *for Gentiles but not for Jews*.

Remember back in Galatians 2:15–16 how Paul was quite relaxed about Jews keeping the law because they had learned at their mothers' knees that it was not, and never had been, a practical means to obtain justification in God's sight? Remember how Paul reiterated that thought in Galatians 3:6–14? Jews didn't see law as a means to obtain divine favour. Their hope

---

15 See de Boer 2011: 258. See also Barclay 1988: 63–64.

16 Note, for example, the first- or second-century confession of Gaius Antonius Apellas – found at Bahadınlar, 100 miles west of Pisidian Antioch – in which the delinquent is urged to change his ways not only by the gods but also, implicitly, by his peers. They summon him to attend 'the mysteries', fearing the consequences of his non-participation for the community (Beichtinschriften: no. 108).

17 Following Paul's logic back into Chapter 3, note that participation in annual rites like the day of atonement, not to mention a host of other regular sacrifices and thanksgivings, was an intrinsic part of living under the curse of the law, which constantly reminded Jews of the necessity of forgiveness. See Martin 2020: 131–139.

was covenantal – based on *God's* pledge in Genesis 15, and now realized in Christ (Gal. 3:13) – to bear the consequences of covenant non-compliance *both* for himself as covenant maker *and* for his people as covenant recipients. Jewish calendrical festivals, like every other part of their practice, were designed, at least in part, to articulate this hope – renewing and crystallizing dependence on God's mercy day after day, month after month, year after year.[18]

But for pagans, calendrical festivals meant nothing of the kind. Calendrical festivals – like other contemporary forms of religious devotion – expressed the expectation that the gods *could* be incentivized to bless. Sometimes these expectations were bold ('this rite will *oblige* the gods to bless me'), sometimes they were more modest ('this rite will *improve my chances* of being blessed, or at least of avoiding being cursed') – we saw examples of both types in Chapter 6 and a whole variety of options in between. But always the possibility of incentivization is present. And, for Paul, this was something authentic Jewish rites could never do. For Paul, divine actions *could* oblige human responses, but human actions *could never* oblige divine responses. Affirming the contrary in word or deed amounted to idolatry.[19]

So now we come at last to the point. Why were *Jewish* festivals dangerous *for recently converted pagans*? The answer is staring us in the face in the parallel passages in 1 Corinthians and Romans. *Recently converted* pagans were still so accustomed to *pagan* festivals celebrated in *pagan ways* that when the Agitators urged them to celebrate *Jewish* festivals in *Jewish* ways, the result wasn't what the Agitators were expecting. By putting the Galatians back in that familiar setting and exposing them once again to those familiar patterns of behaviour, all the hardwired reflexes associated with them in the past reasserted themselves – like my own experience with the electric toothbrush: standing in the same place, in the same posture, *and involuntarily doing the same thing I used to do,* despite the fact that it's no longer needed or appropriate. Even though Jewish festivals were *intended* to point in a very different direction, their similarity to pagan festivals at the level of pure practice reoriented them around totally different priorities. The Galatians *knew* what to expect from calendrical rites before the Agitators ever arrived. Whether they wanted to or not,

---

18 Jewish calendrical festivals carried a range of symbolic foci, see Morales 2015: 185–220.

19 See Martin 2020: 208–216. Commenting on Galatians 1:1–5, Barclay writes: 'A singular gift here embraces both Jews (Paul) and non-Jews (the Galatians), redeeming them from the grip of "the present evil age" (cf. 6.14)… *nothing in the rest of the letter* will indicate that the recipients of the Christ-gift were qualified to receive it' (Barclay 2015: 353; emphasis mine).

they couldn't stop themselves approaching them with pagan expectations –
celebrating the Sabbath, the Passover and all the other Jewish feasts as means
to incentivize their new God to bless them, just as they had sought blessings
from their old gods in the past.

Notice here the specific combination of ingredients that's bringing us at last
to a workable reading:

i. The *stoicheia* here are *elements of practice*. They're not objects of worship
(like the stars in de Boer's version of events), but mechanisms by which
that worship is enacted. They're neutral in and of themselves, acquiring
moral significance only as they're oriented towards particular goals and
augmented with particular expectations.

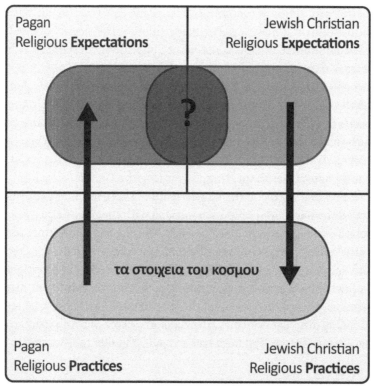

Pagan
Religious **Expectations**

Jewish Christian
Religious **Expectations**

?

τα στοιχεια του κοσμου

Pagan
Religious **Practices**

Jewish Christian
Religious **Practices**

Going Backwards in Galatia: Armed with Jewish Christian religious expectations, the Agitators encourage Paul's readers to embrace Jewish Christian
religious practices. Constructed from *the same stoicheia* as their former pagan
religious practices, these then reanimate their pagan religious expectations.

128

ii. We're working with an area of *genuine practical overlap* between Jewish and pagan religiosity – Jews and pagans were both familiar with the celebration of regular religious festivals, even if their expectations for what these celebrations might achieve were radically different.

iii. Like Paul himself in 1 Corinthians 8, we're recognizing the *tenacity* of these expectations – especially when they've been formed through years of repetitive reinforcement – and we're rejecting as unrealistic the common assumption that they ceased to be significant as soon as new religious convictions were embraced, however sincerely.

iv. We're fully exploiting now the observation that *the problem in Galatia might have had less to do with the message the Agitators preached than it did with the way the Galatians received it.* I don't imagine for one moment that the Agitators *taught* Jewish festivals as means to cultivate Yahweh's goodwill. What I imagine is that the Galatians *received* them that way and that, just like the former pagans in Corinth and Rome, they were exposing themselves to destruction in the process.

2.2 Thought Experiments in Regression

So far, we've simply taken de Boer's regression reading and reworked it according to the principles set out above. But other readings are capable of the same transposition, and working through that process – if only as a thought experiment – can help us as we begin to explore the potential of our new approach.

Angelic Powers

Like de Boer, Pitre et al. offered us another promising start point.[20] Though the evidence associating *stoicheia* with angelic beings in the first century is weak, Paul is clearly concerned about powers and authorities elsewhere (Rom. 8:38; 1 Cor. 15:24; Eph. 6:12, to name but a few examples), and, for many interpreters, the references to angels in Galatians 1:8; 3:19 and 4:14 tip the scales towards angelic interpretations of Galatians 4:3 and 9. The sticking point, as we saw in Chapter 7, is that the angels associated with pagan and Jewish worship are ineluctably *different*. In Paul's mind, the angels serving as mediators of Torah were holy and the 'angels' associated with pagan worship (divine messengers, local deities etc.) were wicked. Any attempt to equate them leads to an unsustainable denigration of the law. But none of this need concern us if we open ourselves up to the model I am now proposing.

---

20 Pitre et al. 2019: 64–94.

If the *stoicheia* are *elements of practice* in Galatians, the point of similarity between paganism and Judaism in Paul's argument shifts. Now we're no longer talking about pagan and Jewish angels with *common characteristics*. We're talking about veneration of – or at least subservience to – angels *as a common Jewish and pagan practice.* On this reading, once brought within the fold of Jewish law observance by the Agitators, the Galatians would have found themselves expressing dependence on the angelic mediators of God's law, and perhaps even appealing directly to them, as part of their new routines of worship (Gal. 3:19).[21] And all this would have been fine if they'd had no prior experience of similar forms of dependence, or of making similar appeals. But they did. And the objects of that dependence were so different that the practice now became dangerous to them in the same way eating idol food endangered the weak believers in Corinth. If this is really what was happening in Galatia, Paul's concern for his readers would have been driven by the realization that expectations formed in their minds through all the years they'd spent worshipping *pagan gods* were about to be rekindled in the practically similar context of venerating *holy angels* with disastrous results.

Now this, I stress, is a thought experiment – not to be confused for a realistic reconstruction of what was actually happening on the ground. Personally, I'm yet to be persuaded that veneration of angels really was prominent in any recognizable form of Judaism – let alone of Jewish *Christianity* – in the first century, and, like its counterpart focusing on calendrical observances, this reading does nothing to address the central issue of circumcision in the letter. It's *possible*, of course, that Paul consciously exploited the inherent flexibility of his *stoicheia* terminology to conjure overtones of submission to angelic powers in his argument. But my purpose here is simply to illustrate the explanatory power of the new reading of regression we're exploring and to clarify how it might be applied.

Physical Elements

Even robustly *physical* readings of *stoicheia* can be helpfully augmented by exploiting this new set of hermeneutical tools, although, as we saw in our work with Blinzler, we should no longer feel any *necessity* to prefer them.

Ernest Clark has recently argued that Paul's whole discussion of enslavement to the law and liberation at the coming of Christ in Galatians 3:23–4:7

---

21 As we noted in Chapter 7, Pitre's implicit move from reading Galatians 3:19 as a reference to the initial communication of the Mosaic Law to Israel through angels, mirroring well-established Second Temple Jewish traditions, to a reading in which subservience to angels and/or veneration of angels is a mainstream practice in first-century Judaism, is highly precarious.

might have been influenced by contemporary attitudes to fleshly existence.[22] Drawing on the prolific writings of the late second-/early third-century physician and philosopher Galen, and on Philo, Clark highlights their use of *stoicheia* vocabulary to describe the physical constituents of the body, which was thought to be constructed from earth, air, fire and water, like the humours in medieval medicine. Philo prescribes law (*nomos*) as his recommended treatment for derangement among the *stoicheia* and the physical and experiential consequences that flow from it – restoring life (Rewards 119–124), communicating righteousness (Moses 2.182–185, 215–216; Spec. Laws 2.62–63, 204; Rewards 22) and even facilitating qualification as an heir of Abraham (Heir 64–70, 98). Clearly this collision of terms and ideas familiar from the Pauline context demands our attention. But what might the significance be?

Clark argues that the Galatians were on the point of embracing an attitude to Jewish Law very much like Philo's – perhaps this was exactly what the Agitators were teaching? Reading the letter through the lens of regression, however, we can see how Paul's logic might be working without the need for quite such a precarious reconstruction of the background. Even if the Agitators had a recognizably *Pauline* perspective on law, Jewish *nomoi might* still have been dangerous for his Gentile readers if similar *nomoi* were familiar to them as *elements of practice* in the larger pagan quest for physical and spiritual wellness. If Paul's readers approached Jewish *nomoi* in the same way and with the same expectations that they approached the *nomoi* of their past – as means to achieve the outcomes they desired, returning to their former enslavement to self-sufficiency in the process – we can perhaps begin to appreciate the depth of Paul's concern.

Once again, as with Pitre's angelic powers reading, I'm yet to be persuaded that Clark's hypothesis can really bear the weight of Paul's larger argument. The suggestion that his readers in Galatia had acquired a recognizably Philonic attitude to Jewish law – either with or without the help of the Agitators – is intriguing but speculative. And this solution, once again, offers no explanation for their strange attraction to circumcision.[23] The flexibility of Paul's *stoicheia* vocabulary might perhaps be invoked again as a reason for incorporating 'physical' overtones within our interpretation of the letter. But for my own purposes here, I highlight them simply to illustrate the capacious scope of our conclusions about regression.

---

22 See Clark 2018. See also Wright 2021: 257–258.

23 Barclay considers the influence of a recognisably Philonic vision of circumcision as a possible explanation for its appeal among Paul's readers in his critique of Peder Borgen's interpretation of the letter, exposing the precariousness of the assumption that Philo's views were in any way representative of the wider landscape of Jewish thought (see Barclay 1988: 50–51).

3 Sketching the Galatian Crisis

Enough now, however, of adapted versions of regression hypotheses that already exist. How do the issues look viewed from the vantage point offered by our own long journey of exploration? Let's attempt a sketch of the entire situation.

I think the Galatian believers were probably very ordinary inhabitants of first-century Asia Minor at the point Paul met them. It's *possible* that they were particularly devoted to one specific cult, or particularly familiar with one specific form of worship, but I see no mandate for it in the text nor any need to assume it to explain the text. I'm content to position their religious experience somewhere in the centre of the envelope of possibilities we defined in Chapter 6, but equally content to entertain the possibility of variations from the centre to the edge in any given area.

Their geographical location will always, I suspect, remain a matter of debate, but, for the purposes of this sketch, I think the southern part of the Roman province of Galatia is the most likely option – consonant with the description of the first missionary journey in Acts 13–14. Southern Asia Minor was well-populated with Jewish communities in the first century, and Gentile readers living there might easily have been involved in Jewish communities prior to Paul's arrival – although this is by no means the only way to explain their evident underlying grasp of the basic Jewish story.[24] If I had to put a pin on the map to say where all this was happening, I would place it tentatively somewhere in or around Derbe, guided by the hint of a connection between Paul's flight to the city after his stoning in Lystra and his recollection of the physical infirmity that first brought him into contact with his readers in Galatians 4:13–14. If I had to name a date for this initial encounter, I would be aiming somewhere between AD 44 and AD 46, just a bit more than 10 years after his conversion/commissioning.

What all this means in practice is that I think we should picture Paul's audience as full and life-long participants in local pagan cults prior to his arrival, actively engaging in the calendrical festivals of both local and translocal gods (including the numerous festivals of the emperor cult), enjoying foods prepared in pagan temples, observing dietary laws and purity rites as each of these cults dictated, articulating their hopes and fears through prayer

---

24 Many scholars attribute this familiarity with Jewish themes to the ministry of the Influencers in Galatia (e.g. Dunn 1993: 9–11. See also Martin 2020: 38–40). Others attribute it to the earlier contribution of Paul and Barnabas (e.g. Nanos 2002: 76–77).

and votive offerings – always with the hope of cultivating divine favour – and all of this still loomed large in the rear-view mirror at the point the letter was written. I don't think it likely that the Galatians, as a group, practised magic or believed, as a group, that the gods could be positively coerced. Neither do I think they lived fearfully under the constant threat of divine judgment. But I do think it likely that they perceived themselves to be real players in 'the divine–human game', not equal by any means in terms of power and influence to the gods or to the overarching power of fate, but players nonetheless with the ability to incentivize the gods to bless by appropriate action, and to disincentivize them by its absence.

This is the context into which I think Paul preached his distinctive gospel message, with a particular emphasis, judging by the letter, on powerful, supernatural transformation by the Spirit (Gal. 3:2–5). Paul called the Galatians to turn from idols and to establish communities not unlike the synagogues and tradesmen's guilds with which they may have already been familiar, but with a new, and shockingly countercultural, disregard for race, gender and social status (Gal. 3:28).[25] He baptized them (Gal. 3:27), and I assume he also instituted the Lord's Supper among them – although 1 Corinthians is the only letter where he tells us anything about it. Besides this, I think he left them very little in terms of rituals to perform, very little even in terms of ethical commands – not out of carelessness or missionary inexperience but out of pastoral consideration for their weakness, as I hope to show in Chapter 11.[26]

Sometime after this initial visit, but before Paul wrote the letter itself – which I think we should slot into his larger biography at some point during the course of the second missionary journey, say, in late AD 48 or early AD 49 – the group we're calling 'the Agitators' came to prominence in the Galatian churches.[27] Here we must be particularly careful to avoid saying more than the text allows or overinterpreting Paul's highly polemical statements. What we can be sure about is simply that they were Jewish Christ-followers who urged the Galatians to accept the sign of circumcision, probably as part of a larger effort to recruit them as fully fledged Jewish proselytes. Paul hints that they were seeking to avoid persecution (Gal. 6:12), he goes a little bit beyond hinting that they doubted the legitimacy of his claim to be an apostle (Gal. 1:1, 11,

---

25 See Ascough 1998: 11–28, 71–94.

26 According to Barclay, Paul expected his converts to be 'led by the Spirit' (Gal. 5:18) and, '[i]f his experience at Corinth is anything to go by, it appears that he tended to underestimate the needs of his Gentile converts for basic moral instruction' (Barclay 1988: 71; see also 95, 115–119, 216–220).

27 It is *possible* that the letter was written based on information acquired on Paul's follow-up visit to the region, alluded to briefly in Acts 16:1.

20 etc.). But for the purposes of this sketch – and for exegesis more generally – despite the wealth of scholarly effort that's been devoted to this topic, I think there's nothing much to be gained by further speculation about their motives or their origins. I'm open to the possibility that they were visitors or locals (if pressed, I would say visitors), born Jews or converts (if pressed, I would say born Jews). I'm open to the possibility that they saw circumcision as making a necessary contribution to salvation or merely as a badge of membership in the covenant community. I'm open to the idea that they saw themselves as completing Paul's work or fundamentally redirecting it. None of this makes any difference at all to the problem in Galatia as I'm now expounding it, or to our exegesis of the letter in response to that problem. *The important thing is how their message was received.*

Put yourself in the Galatians' shoes for a moment. After years spent working on the practical assumption that the gods could be incentivized to give you what you wanted, Paul had come and overthrown the entire foundation on which those assumptions rested. That wasn't how the world really worked. 'God,' he said, 'wasn't made by humans, and blessings from God couldn't be secured by humans. God was the author and originator of it all. If humans were to be reconciled to him, he must accomplish the entire enterprise from his side. And *he has* now accomplished it, *in Christ.*' The Galatians received this with open arms as far as we can tell and set off attempting to integrate these massively angular convictions into their ordinary lives in the Graeco-Roman world.

Within a year or two, however – within three years at the most – the Agitators arrived with their own distinctive variation on this theme. God was the initiator, yes, Jesus was the saviour, yes, but visible conformity to the traditions of Judaism was also required if these aspiring Gentile sons and daughters of Abraham really wanted a share in the covenant promises.[28] Under pressure, Paul's immature converts began to give way. The whole thing sounded plausible – witness Paul's extensive efforts in the letter to clarify the relationship between the 'works of the law' and inclusion in the covenant. But the reason it was dangerous was this: when his converts in Galatia started celebrating Jewish Sabbaths, when they embraced Jewish food laws, when they accepted circumcision, *all of it* was activating their old religious habits. The problem wasn't that the Agitators were presenting these things as 'meritorious

---

28 As Barclay has so helpfully shown, Sanders mistook uniform agreement among Second Temple Jewish authors on the principle that God's initiative to bless human beings is always prior for a more general principle that Second Temple Jewish texts are uniformly gracious. The conclusion depends entirely on what we think *grace* actually means (Barclay 2015: 151–158).

works' – although they may have been. The problem wasn't that they were presenting them as boundary markers – although they may have been doing that too. The problem was that all of these rites had practical analogues in the Galatians' pagan past, and as they embraced the former the expectations associated with the latter were coming back to life.

We've already seen how calendrical festivals were part of this past, and associated – at least as far as Paul was concerned – with assumptions that were incompatible with his gospel. Like the converts in Corinth with habituated reflexes linking eating in idol temples with thinking of idols as gods, the Galatians couldn't participate in sabbaths or Passovers without triggering their own set of habituated reflexes telling them how God ought to act in response. I don't think the Agitators were aware of this – *the Galatians themselves* may not have been aware of it until it was too late (cf. 1 Cor. 8:7–13). But whatever the extent of the Agitators' pastoral foresight, or lack of it, marching the Galatians back to those familiar patterns of regular rites was making them think like pagans again. And the same thing was true of the rest of the Agitators' demands.

If the allusion to dining in Galatians 2:11–13 and the prominence of food issues in the parallel discussions of strength and weakness in 1 Corinthians and Romans is anything to go by, dietary restrictions were also on the Agitators' agenda in Galatia. And if the Galatians were habituated – as we have every reason to believe they were – to the dos and don'ts of pagan worship and to restrictions about what could be eaten, or not eaten, touched, or not touched, in that context, it's easy to imagine how expectations associated with the one could revive and reattach themselves to the other.

If the Galatians had any experience of votive offerings – which also seems certain given the sheer frequency with which they appear in the archaeology of the region – we have a model that can perhaps help us make sense, even of Paul's remarks about circumcision. Prior to his arrival we should imagine the Galatians as participants in a culture where costly, tangible, lasting offerings were used to express personal commitment to the gods. The chances of divine favour could be enhanced in various ways: placing votives in the sight line of the god's statue, placing them 'under his hand' – as we read in Aelius Aristides (Hier. Log. IV.45–7) – or in shafts bored into the walls of his sanctuary. There is evidence that votives could be 'recharged' using candles.[29] All of this was

---

29 See Van Straten 1981: 74. Petsalis-Diomidis interprets Aelius Aristides' entire physical substance as a votive offering within the narrative of the *heroi logoi* (Petsalis-Diomidis 2010: 133). In one particularly striking example, the request that Aristides 'cut off some part of [his] body for the sake of the well-being of the whole' is remitted by the dedication of a ring to Telesphorus (Hier. Log. II.27).

designed to maintain and/or enhance the devotee's prospects of blessing from the gods. Not infrequently, these offerings would have conformed to a pattern that scholars today describe using the vocabulary of *reification* – the symbolic surrender of valuable possessions, even body parts, to the gods in the belief that, owning them themselves, they would take all the more care about their preservation thereafter. If these were the habits of Paul's readers in the past, it isn't hard to see how circumcision fitted in. Show me a Jewish calendrical festival and it's easy to see its potential for incubating previously dormant pagan religious expectations. But how much more so circumcision, with its permanence, with the high degree of personal cost and with the tangible handing over of a physical piece of oneself to God. Perhaps this even begins to account for the Galatians' willingness to participate?

But even if the Galatians were unconscious of this connection and their motive for submitting to circumcision was attributable simply to the forceful arguments and personalities of the Agitators – a combination which is now, I think, beyond the reach of authoritative reconstruction – we can still see why *Paul* would have feared for their spiritual futures on this basis. Then as now, when we act in ways that are strongly associated with specific intellectual or spiritual prompts in the past, our minds and bodies start working backwards, and the effect rekindles the cause that originally produced it. In the past in Galatia, minds told bodies that making offerings to the gods made them look on humans with favour. And after years of reinforcement, years of solidifying that connection, mere participation in the same kinds of action spoke the same principle back, unbidden from body to mind.[30] Circumcision celebrated God as the covenant maker, the initiative taker, the unilateral benefactor, but, in the hands of the Galatians, it must have *felt* like a sure-fire way to get his attention and secure his good will.

So why did Paul write as he wrote? Now at last I think we can see it. He wrote in response to the imminent danger that his readers were returning to the expectations of pagan religion even as they embraced Jewish law. He didn't write because Jewish laws were dangerous in and of themselves – if the Agitators are the strong in this 'weaker brother' scenario, remember, Paul probably agreed with them on the underlying principle: legal observances were permissible for a Christian, even if they were no longer obligatory. No, Paul wrote because Jewish laws were dangerous for recently converted pagans. And the danger is quite simple to explain: even among an audience who had voluntarily

---

30 The insight was inspired, in part, by Bessel Van Der Kolk's extraordinary book, *The Body Keeps the Score* (van der Kolk: 2014).

renounced their pagan past, Jewish observances presented the perfect petri dish for regrowing their former religious expectations in the present.

Paul stressed regression throughout the letter because regression *really was* the heart of the problem. Insistence on keeping *Jewish* laws was ushering his readers *back* to the enslaving norms of their *pagan* religious background. He used *stoicheia* vocabulary because it allowed him to describe the *religious practices* common to both of these worlds. I don't think he had a particularly rarefied connection in view here, no special rite or secret handshake that Jews and Galatian Gentiles shared and thought about in exactly the same way. Quite the opposite. Paul was casting the net wide and setting the bar low – aiming at sacred days, costly sacrifices, dietary restrictions and purity laws. Religion worked like this all over the world, not just in Palestine or Asia Minor – that's another reason why I think he talks about the *stoicheia tou kosmou*.

Did enslavement to the *stoicheia* include calendrical festivals? Paul tells us himself that it did (Gal. 4:10). Did it include veneration of angels? I don't think it's likely, but we can't rule it out. The problem in Galatia, though, wasn't limited to, and it isn't completely explainable by appealing to, any one of these specific connections. The point, I think, for Paul was that religion in the old age, whether Jewish or pagan, was characterized by a whole set of generic practices, that were difficult to embrace in one form without bringing back the assumptions associated with another.

Why did Paul talk about enslavement? He was enslaved to the *stoicheia* in his own past in the sense that Jewish legal rites were unavoidable for anyone who wanted to lay hold of the gracious promises of the covenant. The *paidagōgos* of the law led its pupils back to the classroom again and again to be educated in advance of their ultimate graduation. But the enslavement Paul envisaged for the Galatians was far worse. Under the guise of Jewish observances Paul feared their return to a divine–human interaction devoid of grace, where humans were players at the table in a game they could never win. Paul warned them of a slavery that would cut them off from the benefits of Christ (Gal. 5:2) even as he acknowledged that circumcision had no value in and of itself (Gal. 5:6). How was that possible? Because circumcision was merely a practice – a *stoicheion* – the blessing or the curse of which lay in what the circumcised person believed it would achieve.

Part III
GOING FORWARDS
WITH PAUL

10

Faith and Works, Law and Gospel

Introduction

Now we come to the fun part. Armed with the revised sketch of the underlying Galatian situation emerging from our work in Chapters 4 to 9, we now return to the interpretative problems broached in Chapters 1 to 3, asking ourselves whether things look any clearer with regression re-established in its rightful place as a structuring theme. Deferring until the next chapter consideration of the integrity of Paul's argument – the classic question of how his stern warnings in the first part of the letter fit or don't fit with his prescriptions for living by the Spirit in the second – we'll begin with the problem of Paul's attitude to the law.

Galatians is celebrated by some and slated by others as the place above all places in Paul's letters where the strength of his antipathy to law is most clearly visible.[1] And, as we've seen, there are plenty of texts to call on to support that conclusion. The letter as a whole clearly associates law with 'the present evil age' from which Christ has delivered us (Gal. 1:4). Paul recounts how he himself turned his back on a past marked by legal observances (Gal. 1:13–17). Unlike those who are 'from faith' (*ek pisteōs*) in Galatians 3:6–9, the people Paul describes as 'from the works of the law' (*ex ergōn nomou*) in Galatians 3:10 are 'under a curse'. Law is a jailer (Gal. 3:23), a 'guardian' (Gal. 3:24–25), a slave-master (Gal. 4:3–5) – keeping its charges under close supervision until the coming of better things. On the strength of this evidence alone, it isn't hard to see how the letter has come to play a key role in the classic law–gospel dichotomy that characterizes so many branches of Protestant theology.

But we've also noticed contrary threads running through Paul's argument. Far from pointing to a law–gospel *dichotomy*, Paul himself seems to think his argument in Galatians 3 points to a law–gospel *harmony*, the former

---

1 Martyn, in particular, seems to relish what he perceives to be Paul's thoroughgoing negativity about the law and the old age with which it is associated in the letter (see, for example, Martyn 1997: 370–373).

complementing the latter and playing 'a constructive role' in the outworking of God's larger plan.[2] The account of Paul's interactions with the apostles in Jerusalem in Galatians 2:6–10 is hard to fathom on the basis of Pauline hostility to law in all its forms. Why would he positively underline his willingness to divide the work of gospel proclamation with law-observant Jewish Christians like Peter, James and John if he really wanted to condemn any and all interactions with the Jewish law as retrograde and toxic to mature faith in Christ? Most Bible-reading Christians are aware of Paul's classic rhetorical question and answer: 'Is the law, therefore, opposed to the promises of God? Absolutely not!' But in a blind trial, not many, I suspect, would locate it correctly as an integral part of his argument in Galatians 3:21 ahead of, say, Romans – where he expresses similar sentiments (Rom. 3:31; 7:7; 10:4).

In Chapters 2 and 3 we noticed how awareness of this problem yields a variety of interpretative responses. Under the New Perspective, the issue with law is no longer its purported function as a basis of acceptance in God's sight but its function as a boundary marker. Law observance is problematic only to the extent that it is *required* for inclusion in the believing community. Law, in and of itself, is not the problem – indeed it can have, and it does have, a positive function when viewed in its proper place within the larger redemptive historical narrative. Reformed readings in the Calvinist tradition also preserve a positive role for law even in the present.[3] But it's hard to see how either approach quite does justice to Paul's positive engagement with the Jerusalem apostles or the wider witness to his ongoing commitment to legal observances in the Corinthian letters and in Acts (see 1 Cor. 3:21–23; 15:3–11; 2 Cor. 11:24; Acts 14:1–3; 21:17–26).

Armed with our new understanding of regression as a threat to the faith of recently converted Gentiles, however, the pieces begin to fit together more naturally.

With all other credible interpretations of the letter, and especially with interpreters stressing the importance of Paul's *apocalyptic* perspective, we can affirm that the problem with law in Galatians originates in the great change of eras the apostle sees accomplished in the life, death and resurrection of Jesus. It's a feature of the new age of gospel outreach to the nations. *But what is its precise shape?*

Our work so far suggests that Paul's problem with law was not founded on some kind of *inherent* legalistic bent in Judaism from which he was desperately

---

2   Hays 2015: 1098.

3   See Chester 2017: 114–121.

trying to keep his readers separate. Notice especially the word *'inherent'* here. I'm not arguing that Jews were *immune* from legalism – any more than any other subset of fallen humanity – or that there isn't *any* evidence of Jewish legalism in the period in which Paul was writing. I'm arguing that there is nothing *inherently* legalistic about Judaism, and that in Paul's mind, wherever it existed, Jewish legalism represented a fundamental misunderstanding of, and departure from, the principles on which God's covenant with his people was founded (Gal. 2:15–16; 3:6–9). With due deference to the many helpful studies that now exist on the role of works in final justification as Jews conceived it, I think we should still be fundamentally *encouraged* by E.P. Sanders' basic insight that Jews of the period in general seem not to have thought like this – attributing their acceptance with God to the extent of their obedience.[4] It would be a tragedy of gigantic proportions if they had.

But this doesn't entail a matching affirmation of the idea that Paul's problem with the law was founded on its boundary-marking function. It's possible, of course, that the Agitators in Galatia really *did* see Jewish law as a boundary marker and insisted on circumcision among Paul's converts for this reason – believing that a law-observant lifestyle was the only credible place from which to lay hold of the promises to Abraham. But the letter to the Galatians wasn't written to the Agitators, and projecting this assumption onto them is conjecture not exegesis. The letter to the Galatians was written *to the Galatians* (remember you paid good money for this book!) and *their response* to Jewish law is the problem Paul writes to address.

With the Radical New Perspective, then – and carefully following Paul's logic in Galatians 2:15 – we should affirm that the people who had the problem with law in Galatians were not Jews at all but 'sinful Gentiles', and the problem itself *wasn't* a Jewish problem. This doesn't, of course, entail a matching affirmation of extant Radical New Perspectives on the problem itself – none of which does justice to the severity of Paul's warnings. We don't have to assume that Jewish observances were illegal for Gentiles (Thiessen) or that we can come to adequate interpretative conclusions simply by camping on Paul's distinctive eschatology – arguing that conversion to Judaism was no longer appropriate for Gentiles in the new age because it undervalued the accomplishments of Christ (Wyschogrod).[5] I think we should assume that Paul is simply showing the same pastoral sensitivity to the enduring legacy of his readers'

---

4 On the role of works in final justification, see especially Gathercole: 2002.

5 See Thiessen: 2016; Wyschogrod 2004: 188–201; 'The revelation of Jesus as Christ and the apocalyptic point of view that Paul adopted as a result led him to believe that it was no longer necessary or appropriate for Gentiles to become Jews' (Eisenbaum 2009: 171; see also Eisenbaum 2009: 232).

former religious affiliations that he shows in 1 Corinthians and Romans. He's concerned that *Jewish* law is being received and practised among the Galatian Christians with assumptions about its purpose and efficacy derived from their *pagan* past.

1 Justification

What then does this do for a passage like Galatians 2:15–16 with its classic dichotomization of works and faith:

> *We who are Jews by birth and not sinful Gentiles know that a person is not justified by the works of the law, but by faith in Jesus Christ. So we, too, have put our faith in Christ Jesus that we may be justified by faith in Christ and not by the works of the law, because by the works of the law no one will be justified.*

The towering significance of these words in the history of Christian theology can hardly be overestimated. Paul's striking threefold juxtaposition of faith and works has played a central role in shaping doctrinal formulations of justification – viewed by many as *the* key Protestant theological distinctive – for centuries.[6] Little wonder that the challenge posed to traditional interpretations by the New Perspective has proved so explosive.

Old and New Perspectives concur, of course, on the foundational lexical observation that justification is *primarily* a legal image – communicating the status of a defendant in a court when the judge pronounces their acquittal.[7] It says nothing at all about *actual* guilt or innocence. It simply indicates a *status* of rectitude before the judge on the basis of which no sanctions will be carried out against the justified individual. Differences emerge immediately, however, as soon as we consider how Paul puts the word to work.

Under the Old Perspective, crudely speaking, the contrast between faith and works in Galatians 2:15–16 maps to the contrast between Christian and Jewish takes on *the basis* of justification in God's sight. 'Faith' is the basis of the Christian hope. It is trusting in Christ's accomplishments and not in our own, trusting that 'in him' – no longer living ourselves but Christ living in us, as Paul describes it in Galatians 2:20 – God acquits us though, in reality, we are guilty. 'The works of the law,' by contrast, are the basis of the Jewish hope – or

---

6   Riches offers a helpful overview of major interpretative takes on the passage in Riches 2008: 114–137.

7   See Schreiner 2010: 155–157; Wright 2009: 49–51, 65–72.

at least the hope of the particular Jews Paul is confronting in the letter – as he seems to affirm with his quote from Leviticus 18:5 in Galatians 3:12: 'The person who does these things will live by them.'

All this changes, however, under the New Perspective, where Paul's bold statements about the faith of Abraham as an 'advance announcement' of the gospel (Gal. 3:7–8) are combined with Sanders' bold insistence that Second Temple Jews were not, in fact, legalistic. If Jews – Jews like those influencing Paul's readers, as the argument normally runs – believed they were already accepted in God's sight on the strength of their connection to Abraham prior to, and irrespective of, any 'works of the law' they might perform, and if the Galatians were being encouraged to think the same, then what could Paul have meant by this contrast between faith and works? In what sense *did* Jews perceive themselves to be justified by works if it wasn't in this fundamental matter of acceptance with God?

These questions lead us to distinctive New Perspective interpretations of justification like that of N.T. Wright, who acknowledges the word's implicit legal overtones but complements them with emphases on family and covenant.[8] In Galatians 2, this move is grounded on Wright's sense that membership of the single new family that Christ is forging from Jewish and Gentile strands – irrespective of their established cultural norms – is the key issue emerging from Paul's discussion of Peter's poor behaviour in Antioch (Gal. 2:10–14).[9] What does justification mean when read against this background? For Wright it means having a justified sense of confidence that one is indeed included in this new eschatological community – a sense of confidence based on faith in Christ's accomplishments, not on embracing Jewish works.

Much has been said in praise and in critique of this reading, and this is not the place for a thorough review of the debate. What I want to do here, in the light of our work on regression, is simply to ask if this remodelled version of justification really reflects the problem as Paul conceives it. For all the clear blue water Wright establishes between himself and traditional interpretations here, he still sees the problem in Galatia as *a Jewish problem*.[10] Our work on regression, however, encourages us to see it as *a Gentile problem*. And we can see that difference playing out in the exegetical details.

In Chapter 2 above, we noticed that the question of membership of God's covenant family – though it undoubtedly *arises* in Paul's retelling of the

---

8   See Wright 2009: 72–79; Wright 2021: 191–193.

9   Wright 2009: 93–97 et passim. See also Wright 2021: 120.

10 Eisenbaum sees the same underlying feature in the work of James Dunn (Eisenbaum 2009: 215).

Antioch Incident – is *not*, in fact, the point on which his logic culminates as he steers from Galatians 2:10–14 into Galatians 2:15–16 with its famous faith and works dichotomy. The point to which his recollection of events is driving is that Jewish Christians like Peter can unwittingly *force* their Gentile brothers and sisters to follow their customs and lead them astray from the gospel in the process. With inclusion in the family at the front of his mind, Wright argues that 'the urgent question is not "whether someone has a righteous standing before God"' – whether or not they are 'saved'.[11] But, as we saw in Chapter 8, if our reading of the underlying problem in Galatia is on target, that is *precisely the question* Paul has in his sights. Paul is trying to help the Galatians respond to a new set of influences that directly threaten their salvation by resurrecting their former religious assumptions, even in the act of submission to the Jewish law (Gal. 5:2, 4).

Read from the perspective of regression as the letter's central pastoral concern, then, the works of the law that Paul warns about in Galatians 2:15–16 are not Jewish works embraced *in a Jewish way* with *Jewish* assumptions and priorities, but Jewish works embraced *in a Gentile way* with *Gentile* assumptions and priorities. In Paul's mind, Gentiles lacked the protections afforded to Jews schooled in the gracious origins of God's election from the cradle. Jews knew – or at least they ought to have known – that their legal observances were contextualized *within* this larger vision of divine–human interaction. This is why Paul could position the Jewish law as a *paidagōgos* (Gal. 3:23–29) – supervising God's people until, and with a view to, the ultimate *christological* resolution of the inherent Old Testament tension: 'How can a holy God dwell among sinful people?'[12] But Gentiles were not so fortunate and, while their pagan presuppositions retained their vigour and plausibility, law, for them, was a threat.

Gentiles already had a category for the kinds of things Jews did when they celebrated their festivals and memorialized their acts of devotion. And if they did those kinds of things again, whatever new convictions they'd come to in the interim, Paul was wise enough to know that that category would reassert itself. The Galatians would find themselves playing the divine–human game again, even though the pieces on the board were Jewish pieces. Even as they embraced Jewish feasts and the quintessentially Jewish rite of circumcision, suppressed but nonetheless still-potent religious instincts would be

---

11 Wright 2021: 119–120.

12 Hays rightly resists simplistic articulations of the idea that the law as *paidagōgos* was intended 'to lead us to Christ' but mutes, in the process, the important educational overtones of the metaphor Paul chooses. The role of the *paidagōgos* was not only to supervise and guard children in Graeco-Roman households but also to escort them to and from school (see Hays 2015: 1097–1098).

reanimated – telling them that, by doing so, their new God could be incentivized to bless them in much the same way that their old gods had been incentivized. And this for Paul was a spiritually life-threatening situation.[13]

This is why the anathemas are flying in Galatians 1. This is why Paul thinks that, if his readers submit to circumcision, 'Christ will be of no value to [them] at all' – even as he affirms that circumcision itself is morally neutral (Gal. 5:2, 6; 6:15). Paul stresses the antithesis between justification by faith and justification by the works of the law *in Galatia* because, *in Galatia*, works of the law have the capacity to undermine faith even though they're readily compatible with faith *in Jerusalem*. The problem *in Galatia* is the problem of how recently converted Gentiles *respond* to law, using it – whether they mean to or not – as a means to maximize their chances of obtaining the blessings they desire.

By acknowledging New and Radical New Perspectives along the way, then, we've come, perhaps unexpectedly, to a vision of justification not so different from the Old Perspective but with a much wider applicational scope. Read through the lens of regression, the faith–works dichotomy in Galatians *really does* contrast two different ways of thinking about status before God. It contrasts an approach that, in Paul's mind, characterizes the entire Judeo-Christian story from Abraham forward with an approach characteristic of *pagan* thought: that divine favour can be courted and expedited by careful cultivation.

This, of course, was exactly the approach the Reformers critiqued in medieval Catholicism and that *they thought* they saw mirrored in first-century Judaism. What they saw in the mirror in fact, however, was paganism. And the distinction is vital to our understanding of the implications both then and now. Justification by faith embraces dependence on Christ and repudiates the possibility of incentivizing God to bless. It leans on Christ's credentials in the divine–human relationship, not on our own; it focuses its expectations on Christ's practice, not on human practices whether Jewish or pagan. Justification by faith embraces what *God* says we need, it renounces angling for what *we* think we need. When it looks across the room at its polar opposite *it doesn't see Judaism, it sees idolatry* – where the self creates and controls the gods we worship. Justification by faith renounces ingenuity as a means to attain God, or to persuade God, it lays it down as a means to *serve* God. It's not a new life we summon up or 'identify with' by our own strength and power; it's the radical renunciation of the very idea that summoning up or identifying with a

---

13 Recall the comparably drastic language to which Paul feels forced to resort in 1 Corinthians 8:11 and Romans 14:15, 20.

new life is either possible or beneficial. It *isn't* narrowly focused on the scarcely penetrable attractions of Judaism in first-century Galatia. The issue is vast and existential – and absolutely significant for the present day.

With 'works of the law' safely domesticated as a reference to *Jewish* festivals and circumcision, many modern Christians find the thunderous affirmations of Galatians 2:15–16 strangely remote and irrelevant: 'Justification is by faith in Christ and not… by something I will probably never encounter, let alone have any active interest in.' But as soon as we see that Paul's problem is the importation of *pagan* religious assumptions into our regular expressions of Christian devotion, the issue becomes *intensely* relevant. The world we live in today has greater similarities to the pagan world of Paul's day than it has had at any other point in the intervening centuries. We may not worship Cybele or Mēn in local temples as Paul's readers did before he met them, but the conviction that there are things we can do in the present to maximize our chances of blessing in the future is the very lifeblood of Western culture. This is how we think about money, career, appearance and physical fitness. Astute investments in the now improve our chances of experiencing what we perceive ourselves to deserve in the not yet. Most of us have probably never even considered the possibility that immersion in these modern preconceptions subconsciously influences the expectations with which we approach our God. But if Galatians is allowed to speak clearly across the centuries, it tells us – and we'll explore this much more fully in Chapter 14 – that, to the extent these cultural norms shape and drive our Christian devotions, *we're not in fact Christians at all*.

2 Obeying the Law

Next, we come to the question of the extremity of Paul's warnings. We have, I think, already answered the key question here: why does Paul think embracing Jewish law is a salvation issue for his Galatian readers (Gal. 5:2, 4)? Not because it undervalues the work of Christ – though it surely *does*. If undervaluing the work of Christ was really a fast track to apostasy in Paul's mind, this wouldn't be the only letter to begin with the kind of rhetorical firework display we see in Galatians 1:8–9. Neither are the warnings attributable to some kind of legal obstacle to Gentile proselyte conversion, as suggested by Matt Thiessen.[14] The extremity of the warnings should be attributed to the fact that, if the Galatians (or anybody else for that matter) approach Paul's God – the God of Abraham, the Father of 'the Lord Jesus Christ' who is characterized above all other things

---

14 Thiessen 2016: 73–101.

by incongruous *grace* (Gal. 1:1, 3) – on assumptions appropriate to an alternative pagan god, they're placing themselves beyond the help of the gospel.

The situation is analogous to Luke's description of Simon Magus in Acts 8:9–25, who hears the good news of the kingdom announced through the ministry of Philip and shows every sign of true conversion, including baptism, before being re-exposed to the distinctive patterns of his former life as a wonder-worker when Peter and John arrive in Samaria in the power of the Spirit, and reverts to the assumptions with which those patterns were still associated in his mind – offering money in exchange for a share of the apostles' abilities. Peter's rebuke on that occasion sets Simon outside the boundaries of the Christian community pending radical repentance. Fearful that he may be about to witness something similar in Galatia (Gal. 4:11), Paul's warnings are similarly dire.

One specific warning that still demands our consideration here, however, is the remark that separates Paul's striking forebodings of apostasy in Galatians 5:2–4:

Again I declare to every man who lets himself be circumcised that he is required to obey the whole law. (Gal. 5:3)

How should we respond to the apparent imposition of an obligation here on anyone who submits to circumcision, be they Christian or not, to embrace Torah in its entirety? Does this tell us that continued observance of the Jewish law is more than just *an acceptable option* for Jewish believers after the coming of Christ, and that it is, in fact, a necessity? And, if so, does the same thing hold today?

This question, once again, is hotly debated, with the continuance of the obligation to obey standing close to the centre of many Radical New Perspective and Messianic Jewish readings.[15] Careful exegesis of the autobiographical material in Galatians 1 and the Antioch Incident in Galatians 2 – often seen as proof texts for the idea that Paul had abandoned his former life of law observance – certainly keeps these alternative interpretations on the table here. The emphasis in Paul's description of his 'previous way of life in Judaism' (Gal. 1:13–14) lies not so much on his renunciation of Jewish law as on his

---

15 'Paul lived and died as a Jew' (Eisenbaum 2009: 5; see also Eisenbaum 2009: 134–135, 150–153, 208–239 and Fredriksen 2017: 86). Eisenbaum helpfully challenges the prevalent assumption that obligatory Torah observance was viewed as a liability and not as a good gift from God (see Eisenbaum 2009: 76–77). David Rudolph mounts a detailed exegetical defence for ongoing Pauline law observance in 1 Corinthians 9:19–23 (see Rudolph: 2011).

renunciation of his prior vocation as a persecutor of the church. And, in the Antiochian context (Gal. 2:11–14), we've already noted that eating with Gentiles involved no necessary violation of Torah – especially if the Jews involved provided their own food.[16] But even *with* these acknowledgments, it's hard to imagine a Paul who believed in mandatory, ongoing law observance for Jewish Christians saying the words, 'I died to the law so that I might live for God' (Gal. 2:19, cf. Rom. 7:4–6), or 'the law was our guardian until Christ came that we might be justified by faith. Now that this faith has come, we are no longer under a guardian' (Gal. 3:24–25), or 'I am convinced, being fully persuaded in the Lord Jesus, that nothing is unclean in itself' (Rom. 14:14). So how should we interpret Galatians 5:3?

Regression, once again, points to a solution here. First, in Galatians 5:3, we should note that the expansive scope of the warning – 'I declare *to every man who lets himself be circumcised…*' – is restricted in practice, not least by the verses either side of it, to the audience of the letter: 'every one *of you* who let's himself be circumcised' better captures Paul's intention. Paul's remarks about obedience here are made *within the Galatian context*.

Second, we should note – as we've already argued extensively above – that the underlying problem in Galatia was *the power of pagan religious habits*. Circumcision – though neutral in and of itself (Gal. 5:6) – was spiritually dangerous for Paul's readers because, like calendrical observances and dietary laws, it could trigger the reanimation of their former religious assumptions, cutting them off from the grace available in Christ (Gal. 5:2, 4). The Galatians wouldn't be able to claim reliance on God's incongruous goodwill if they were actually placing confidence in this kind of costly personal sacrifice. That may not have been their *intention* in submitting to circumcision. But, in Paul's mind, that's where the power of their habits was going to lead them.

Third, we have to ask ourselves whether Paul would have believed there was any hope for Gentile believers who entangled themselves again in this kind of effort to cultivate God's favour. This is the question Paul's statement about '[obeying] the whole law' in Galatians 5:3 is, I think, designed to answer. And the answer he provides makes sense if we understand the underlying problem. There *would* be hope, says Paul – in theory – *but only for someone who was totally law observant*. God's favour, he says, *can in principle be cultivated* – but

---

16 See Rudolph 2011: 130. See also Eisenbaum 2009: 100. The NIV over-translates Peter's opening statement on arriving at Cornelius's house in Acts 10:28: 'You are well aware that it is against our law for a Jew to associate with or visit a Gentile.' The Torah forbade neither associating nor visiting. It forbade *ritual uncleanness*, which was easier to avoid by keeping company only with Jews but this was by no means a universal mandate (see Bruce 1988: 210; Eisenbaum 2009: 105).

only by total obedience. And this, as we've already observed several times, is not a practical path to justification in his mind.[17]

Now we should note that Paul doesn't make any comment here on the question of what 'total obedience' would actually look like. Debates between Old and New Perspectives on this point typically founder on the question of whether or not Paul thinks obeying 'the whole law' means living a life of sinless perfection.[18] Certainly no robust case can be made for that reading here. Paul simply argues that any Galatian Christian who submits to circumcision will be liable to comply with everything the law demands, which could in principle include compliance with its protocols for atonement in the event of transgression.[19] But the point Paul is making here is that – in practice – nobody *does* offer this kind of compliance.[20] This is why the passage runs on directly from the hope of verse 3 to the hopeless prospect of verse 4. Any attempt to be justified by law – to attain favoured status in the sight of God by keeping his commands – ends in alienation from Christ.

With regression restored to its original position at the centre of Paul's diagnosis of the problem in Galatia, therefore, we find ourselves confronted with an apostle who is positive about law observance for *Jewish* Christians – witness his endorsement of the law-observant mission to Jews in Galatians 2:6–10. As we'll see more clearly in the next chapter, we can even imagine him being positive about law observance for *Gentile* Christians – subject to their attainment of sufficient maturity that, like the strong in Corinth, they can participate, even in activities strongly associated with their pagan religious background, without unwittingly reactivating the expectations that went along with it

---

17 Note here N.T. Wright's summary of Ezekiel's reception of Leviticus 18:5 in Ezekiel 20:11, 13 and 21, 'Yes, God did give Torah with the aim of bringing life, but it hasn't worked out that way' (Wright 2021: 205).

18 See Gombis 2007: 83.

19 '[Paul's] point cannot be that the Law requires sinless perfection, for the Law contains extensive provisions to provide atonement and forgiveness of sins,' (Hays 2015: 1138, see also Hays 2015: 1086; Eisenbaum 2009: 81, 88).

20 'Paul has already unconditionally asserted that no one can be rectified by the law (2:16; 3:11)' (Hays 2015: 1138). The counter-text to which appeals are frequently made here is Phil. 3:6 where, reflecting on his own past experience as a Pharisee, Paul tells us that his obedience was 'faultless'. Here, though, I think we're compelled to note that Paul is talking about something slightly different. BDAG highlights the fact that, in wider Graeco-Roman usage, the underlying Greek adjective *amemptos* (blameless) is used to refer to 'persons of exceptional merit' not to describe a state of sinless perfection (see Arndt et al. 2000: 52; on the use of *amemptos* and the related adverb *amemptōs* in 1 Thess. 2:10 and 3:13, see also Weima 2014: 152–153, 241). Paul's emphasis in Philippians 3 is on an outward assessment of legal compliance in comparison to his Jewish peers, not on justification in the sight of God who sees and transforms the heart (compare Psalms 143:2, to which Paul himself alludes in Galatians 2:16). On similarities and differences between the situation Paul describes in Philippians 3 and his expectations for Christian obedience, see also Bockmuehl 2006: 202–203.

(1 Cor. 8:1–13). But he doesn't endorse law observance for Gentile Christians who are weak. And he doesn't think law observance is obligatory for Jewish Christians in the new age in which its role as a *paidagōgos* now stands complete (Gal. 4:25). He can see good reasons for keeping it – not least, presumably, the law's ongoing capacity to helpfully contextualize Christ's ministry.[21] And, all things being equal, perhaps ongoing legal observance would have been his own preferred mode of practice.[22] But whenever he had to choose between law observance and 'forcing' vulnerable Gentile believers 'to follow Jewish customs' and so lose their grip on the gospel (Gal. 2:14), his instinct was always to refrain in accordance with the broader principle of accommodation formalized later in 1 Corinthians and Romans, failure to appreciate and apply which shapes the entire context of the Galatian crisis.

3 The Curse of the Law

In Chapter 4, we introduced the disconcerting diagnosis of regression in Galatia as the crowning example in a long list of interpretative problems in the letter. Since then, we've explored the counterintuitive possibility that applying our attention to that specific difficulty might shed new light on all the others. And the results are exciting. Justification emerges in fresh perspective when viewed from this unfamiliar vantage point. And the same goes for the mysterious extremity of Paul's warnings. But what about the most hotly debated issue of all – Paul's notoriously dense interaction with the curse of the law in Galatians 3:10–14?

The first thing to note as we approach this challenging text is the context. Whatever else it does or doesn't teach us, Galatians 3:10–14 serves the purpose of summoning Gentiles back from their newfound enthusiasm for Jewish law

---

21 Isn't it striking that, on the Emmaus road, the very first thing the risen Jesus does to explain all he has just accomplished in his death and resurrection is point to 'Moses, and all the Prophets'? (Luke 24:27, cf. 24:44).

22 Astute readers will ask whether this reconstruction is adequate to explain Paul's response to the accusation he faces on returning to Jerusalem after the third missionary journey in Acts 21. Reports are circulating in the city that he '[teaches] all the Jews who live among the Gentiles to turn away from Moses, telling them not to circumcise their children or live according to our customs' (Acts 21:21). James and his fellow elders urge him disprove these allegations with a show of legal observance at the temple '[so that] everyone might know that what they have heard about you is nothing, and that even you yourself conform, obeying the law' (Acts 21:24 – translation mine) and Paul enthusiastically complies. The text is ambiguous about the specific point Paul's legal observances were intended to make. Was the goal to prove that Paul was law observant after the fashion of the law-observant believers in Jerusalem – details of which we lack? Or was it to prove something about his practice among Jewish converts in the diaspora by showing that *even he* kept the law? Either way, there is nothing here to suggest that Paul thought law observance was obligatory. All we have in this text is a strong denial of the allegation that he spoke against circumcision among Jewish Christians – a denial that Old and New Perspectives struggle to accommodate, but which the reading presented here wholeheartedly embraces.

to the emphasis on faith and transformation by the Spirit that seems to have so marked their conversion (Gal. 3:1–5). It also stands as a counterpoint to Paul's description of the faith of Abraham in which he articulates his conviction that God's mode of dealing with human beings in the new age inaugurated by Christ's life, death, resurrection and ascension stands in direct continuity with the covenant that anticipated it in the old age (Gal. 3:6–9). The relevance of all this to the discussion about the curse of the law that follows becomes immediately obvious when we notice the very deliberate way in which Paul resumes these threads in his conclusion in Galatians 3:14:

> *He redeemed us in order that the blessing given to Abraham might come to the Gentiles through Christ Jesus, so that by faith we might receive the promise of the Spirit.*

But how do we get from the one to the other?

Paul begins with a provocative comment based on a citation from Deuteronomy. In direct contrast to his remarks about those who are 'from faith' immediately beforehand (Gal. 3:7–9), Paul tells us that '[all those who are from the works of the law] are under a curse as it is written, "Cursed is everyone who does not continue to do everything written in the Book of the Law"' (Gal. 3:10 citing Deut. 27:26). Having paid careful attention to Galatians 2:15–16 in the foregoing chapters, we should immediately be alert now to the possibility that the expression 'all who are from the works of the law' need not necessarily refer to people practicing the Jewish law with *Jewish* priorities. But whoever they are, Paul certainly expounds their fate with reference to a quintessentially *Jewish* story. The quote from Deuteronomy transports us to the climactic moment in the Exodus narrative where Moses prepares the people of Israel to receive the law of God, together with its attendant blessings for obedience and curses for disobedience, in an elaborate ceremony to be performed on the slopes of Mount Gerazim and Mount Ebal in the Promised Land after they cross the Jordan. The cited text is the concluding summary statement of the law-proclamation part, immediately prior to the recitation of the blessings and curses, and its summarizing function is brought out especially clearly in the septuagintal text that Paul reproduces, with its stress on the necessity of *total* obedience: 'Cursed is everyone who does not continue to do *everything* written in the Book of the Law.'[23]

---

23 The citation is actually compounded from Deuteronomy 27:26 LXX and either Deuteronomy 28:58 or 30:10 LXX, which contribute the phrase 'everything *written in the book of the law*', indicating an inclusive reference to the entire law of Moses (see Hays 2015: 1087).

Much has been made of Martin Luther's belief that Paul's use of Moses' words here contradicts their meaning in the original Deuteronomic context. So Timothy Gombis: '[Paul] claims in v.10a that all those who advocate faithfulness to the Mosaic law are accursed, and he substantiates this with a quotation from Deuteronomy in v.10b stating that those who fail to remain faithful to the Mosaic law are under a curse.'[24] This objection fails to grasp the reality that Galatians 3:10a does not describe '"those who do the Law," but rather "those whose identity is derived from works of the Law"'.[25] It also takes far too narrow a view of the narrative trajectory of the passage from which the citation is drawn. There are dark forebodings of Israel's future unfaithfulness here even if we broaden our interpretive horizons no further than Deuteronomy 27–30.

But, of course, there's no reason to stop there and tie everything Paul has to say about the curse of the law to the threat of exile that Moses develops in Deuteronomy 28, as if exile was an end in itself. If the post-patriarchal storyline from Exodus forwards is read rightly as a series of recapitulations of the foundational story of creation and fall, Israel's failure to keep the law is an entirely predictable component of the plot and the exile itself, however terribly it looms over the rest of the story, still serves only to illustrate the more fundamental estrangement of human beings from their maker that originates in the garden. Ironically, the expectation that Israel will not keep the law – presented as the missing 'third term' in an incomplete Pauline syllogism in many *Old Perspective* readings of Galatians 3:10 – is in fact a straightforward consequence of the redemptive historical exegetical strategy that characterizes leading *New Perspective* interpretations of the text.[26]

So, what does Paul mean when he talks about the curse of the law in Galatians 3? Regression begins to help us here when we start to see the connections between Galatians 3:10–14 and the two passages to which we've already given detailed consideration in this chapter.

The quoted text from Deuteronomy: 'Cursed is everyone who does not continue to do *everything written in the Book of the Law*,' finds an echo in the now-familiar words of Galatians 5:3–4:

Again I declare to every man who lets himself be circumcised that he is required to obey the whole law. You who are trying to be justified by the law have been alienated from Christ; you have fallen away from grace.

---

24 Gombis 2007: 82–83.

25 Hays 2015: 1087. See also Martyn 1997: 236–240, 299, 307–308.

26 See Wright 2021: 201. Paul may be making the same point about the Agitators in Galatians 6:13: 'Not even those who are circumcised keep the law.' His peculiar use of the present passive participle *hoi peritemnomenoi* and the polemical context of his remarks, however, make this a precarious foundation for theological generalizations (see Martin 2020: 42–43).

Here we have the obligation to obey and the curse applied directly to the Galatian situation. Moreover, we also have a sense of what is *actually* going on: if the Galatians embrace the Jewish law they will do it with an old age mentality – thinking, as they used to think, that religious works will give them status in the sight of God, however maximally or minimally Paul's reference to complete obedience is construed.

And this realization should shape our understanding of the curse in Galatians 3. Israel too lived under the old age paradigm before the coming of Christ, with laws to keep which held out the promise of justification to any that could keep them. But, as we also saw in our work on Galatians 5:3, in practice nobody could. Nobody could stand justified before God on the basis of their obedience – irrespective, once again, of how maximally or minimally the reference to complete obedience is construed. Now, of course, in reality, Israel's experience of the old age paradigm was very different from that of their Gentile neighbours because Jewish religious laws did more than just demand compliance: they pointed backwards to God's solemn pledge to bear the consequences of Abraham's – and his descendants' – covenant faithlessness, while simultaneously cultivating a longing for its fulfilment. That's why Paul could embrace legal observances for Jews even as he ruled them out in the most strenuous terms for Gentiles. The old age had always been 'old age *plus*' for the people of God in Paul's mind – the cold and rigid principle that 'the person who does these things will live by them' (Gal. 3:12 citing Lev. 18:5) *plus* the shining if ambiguous hope that 'the righteous will live by faith' (Gal. 3:11 citing Hab. 2:4).[27] But none of that in any way mitigated the reality of the curse in the face of which faith spoke its words of comfort. In the biblical worldview, the curse is Edenic – threatening everyone everywhere since the third chapter of Genesis.

Tracking back to Galatians 2:15–16 yields further regressive insight on the remaining components of the argument. In Chapter 2 above, we saw how Galatians 3:11, complete with its quote from Habakkuk 2:4, follows the logic of Paul's earlier faith and works dichotomy precisely. Now we can see how it invites the same interpretation. Justification here, as there, is a matter of right standing before

---

27 Just like Deuteronomy 27:26, Paul's quote from Leviticus 18:5 carries with it strong reasons to anticipate that the command it contains cannot be kept. In its context in Leviticus, the command 'the person who obeys them will live by them' is positive, urging the Israelites to embrace God's law and enjoy his blessing. As Josh Willits has helpfully demonstrated, however, in its subsequent use in later Old Testament and extra-biblical Jewish texts, Leviticus 18:5 is used in different ways. Note especially the three citations of Leviticus 18:5 in Ezekiel 20:11, 13 and 21, charting the relationship between Israel's repeated disobedience and God's mercy, and the citation in Nehemiah 9:29 which integrates the text of Leviticus into an articulation of national confession (see Willitts 2003: 105–122).

God. The means by which that right standing is appropriated is not the abundance or creativity of religious works, as the Galatians were formerly wont to think, but faith. And the object of that faith is now revealed – not just in the hints of Habakkuk, but in the concrete accomplishments of Jesus Christ – coming and taking the consequences of his people's covenant unfaithfulness on himself as foreshadowed by the procession of the smoking brazier and the blazing torch between the split pieces of Abraham's original covenant-making sacrifice.[28]

The point of the whole, then, is that Israel, like every other race, lay under the curse associated with the old age, however clearly or inchoately the affected individuals understood it. Israel's privileged position as the bearer of the promises of future deliverance expressed in the Abrahamic covenant meant they were not helpless before that curse. They were summoned to faith – a faith whose true and ultimate object Paul believed had now been revealed (Gal. 3:13). But the purpose of the passage in context is a warning to the Gentile Galatians that embracing Jewish law would not simply propel them into the privileged position of Jewish Christians who could keep the law even in the new age and benefit in the process. The Galatians' instinctive response to law had been shaped under the old age proper, not under *old age plus*. And, for Paul, law embraced *that way* was a high road to accursedness.

4 Jewish Legalism

It should be clear by now that reading with the grain of the regression narrative in Galatians removes the obligation to pit Paul against Jewish legalism in the letter. But it all still begs the question, 'what about the many other places in Paul, and in the New Testament more broadly for that matter, where we *do* read negative things about Jews and the law?' Galatians may no longer seem quite such a natural home for this interpretation as it once did, but what about, say, Romans 10:2–3, where Paul solemnly testifies about his Jewish contemporaries that:

> they are zealous for God, but their zeal is not based on knowledge. Since they did not know the righteousness of God and sought to establish their own, they did not submit to God's righteousness.

---

28 Galatians 3 is a particularly clear example of the more general truth that when Paul cites an Old Testament text, he has an eye on the whole passage from which it comes, not on the quoted words only. Galatians 3:8 famously invokes the words of Genesis 15:6, but the subsequent formal establishment of a covenant relationship between God and Abraham (albeit a highly unusual one in which God binds himself to bear the consequences of faithlessness on the part of *both* the covenant maker *and* the covenant recipient) is clearly in view as the logic unfolds in Galatians 3:15–18 (note Hays' helpful comments on *Metalepsis* in Paul in Hays 1989: 14–21 et passim).

Or what about Luke 18:9–14, where we find Jesus in dialogue with a group of Jews who are 'confident of their own righteousness' and who '[look] down on everyone else'? Don't these passages rather suggest that Jewish legalism *was* the foil against which early Christians defined their gospel, however much we might protest that, in Galatians, it wasn't?

Now, of course, the first thing to say here is that Jewish legalism *absolutely* should be acknowledged as *a possibility* in other places. The argument presented in this book deals with Galatians specifically, and I'm very far from trying to replace the unpleasant notion that first-century Jews *in general* were legalists with the equally bizarre idea that first-century Jews *in general* were in some way *impervious* to legalism. Paul *does* make the case in Galatians, I think, that – unlike Gentiles – Jews had every reason *not to be* legalists. Their law was founded on, and always anticipated, the gracious forgiveness of God. But he doesn't deny that Jews *could* forget, misunderstand or distort this great truth, and something very much like that might well explain the contents of Luke 18.

In Romans 10, I suspect we need to pay more careful attention to how the state of unbelieving Jews looked to Paul *at the time of writing*, and not from a vantage point located 2,000 years later from which it's all too easy to collapse the events of Christ's life and ministry into the subsequent story of the emerging church. For Paul, the key issue in Romans 9–11 was the fate of Jews who had still quite recently rejected their Messiah, with gigantic consequences for the value of their legal observances. Prior to Christ's coming, the legal infrastructure of Judaism supervised and guarded God's people until the revelation of God's ultimate plan to save (Gal. 3:23–25). All hopes focused on the law ultimately terminated on his shoulders. But after he had come, after he had come *and been rejected*, this connection between law and hope was severed in Paul's mind, even while Jewish legal practice continued unabated. Law no longer carried Jews who saw and spurned God's Christ to Christ as it did for those who accepted him and continued to live law-observant lives. Law functioned now only as a measure of their personal righteousness, a measure which Paul – as we've already seen in Galatians 5:3–4 – considered unfailingly unfavourable.[29]

This, I think, is the problem Paul also discerns in 'the present city of Jerusalem' in Galatians 4:25, illuminating his logic with a subtly contextualized allegorical reading of the Hagar and Sarah story.[30] Paul looks at his Jewish contemporaries and sees people who have settled for Ishmael – people

---

29 I think Paul also makes the same case in Romans 2:1–3:20, but that is another project.

30 See Elliott 1999. Pitre et al. provide a helpful overview of eschatological expectations for the heavenly Jerusalem in Pitre et al. 2019: 82–88.

who have waited in vain for the heaven-sent child of promise for so long that they've eventually replaced him with something more down-to-earth – a messiah modelled more on contemporary national renaissance stories than on the pattern established in their own scriptures. When at last God's Isaac came, the substitute was more palatable than the reality and they refused him. And it is this rejection that explains their present state of enslavement (Gal. 4:25). For if the hope born out of the experience of enslavement under the law is rejected in the end, all law has left to offer Jews is the same thing law offers Gentiles. And its consequences are tragically the same.

11
Growing to Maturity

Introduction

Like so many of his letters, Paul's letter to the Galatians ultimately traces a path from the indicative (statements about what is) to the imperative (instructions about what ought to be).[1] Unlike the other examples, however, the transition from the former to the latter in Galatians is so puzzling that many respectable commentators have suggested they were aimed at two quite different factions in his audience. Some have argued that the whole thing is a mash-up of two quite different original sources.

In the indicative material (roughly, Gal. 1:6–5:12) Paul warns his readers against law – and Old and New Perspectives alike, including the interpretation offered in this book, all have their own take on what the underlying problem with law might have been. In the imperative material, however (also known as the 'ethical section' of Galatians – roughly, Gal. 5:13–6:10), Paul turns around and gives his readers laws to keep, including a comprehensive list of virtues to practise and vices to avoid (Gal. 5:19–23), culminating in a command to 'fulfil the law of Christ' (Gal. 6:2) that few can read in context without a double take. Integrating these two seemingly incompatible threads in Paul's logic into a single whole without relegating the imperatives to the category of a banal afterthought – a fate which, as we saw in Chapter 8, also commonly afflicts the imperatives in Romans – is a vital test of a complete and faithful interpretation of the letter.

A quarter of a century after its original publication, John Barclay's book, *Obeying the Truth*, is still by far the most insightful response to this exegetical conundrum, and his classification of the various interpretative strategies that have been attempted over the years provides us with a helpful way into the problem.[2] Barclay divides the participants in the debate into two broad categories: those who think Galatians 5:13–6:10 is 'wholly or largely unrelated' to

---

1 Betz 1979: 255–256; Dunn 1993: 285; Madsen II 1998.
2 Barclay 1988: 9–23.

the rest of the letter and those who 'attempt to integrate [it] into the interpretation of the... whole'. In the former camp, he notes examples where the ethical material is dismissed as a later interpolation, or as a generic grab-bag of admonitions with no connection to the specific circumstances addressed in the earlier chapters.[3] In the latter camp, he notes attempts to relegate Galatians 5:13–6:10 to the status of a clarifying appendix, and 'two fronts' hypotheses in which Paul tackles two contrasting forms of disaffection with his gospel at the same time, one leading towards Judaism (favoured by a putative legalistic faction) and the other towards paganism (favoured by a putative libertine faction).[4] Barclay himself belongs squarely in the integrationist camp but elegantly evades the extremities of the extant solutions with an original solution of his own.

Barclay argues that the jarring switch to ethics in the second part of the letter should be attributed to Paul's naive missionary tactics – his reliance on the simple proclamation of Christ crucified (Gal. 3:1) and subsequent transformation by the Spirit to lead his Galatian converts to maturity.[5] Capitalizing on the 'moral confusion' that this approach left in its wake, the Agitators won a hearing among Paul's readers by offering them *lots* of guidance, *lots* of structure, in the form of obedience to the Jewish law.[6] Paul had to hastily erect some basic moral scaffolding to counter this threat. But Barclay doubts his skeletal response would have really measured up to the gravity and plausibility of the Mosaic alternative.[7]

1 Regression Meets Ethics

At first glance, the conclusions we've come to about regression in the foregoing chapters make the problems here worse not better.

I argued above that Jewish law was dangerous for Paul's Galatian converts because they already had a category for the kinds of practices law observance

---

3   On Galatians 5:13–6:10 as a later interpolation, see, for example, O'Neill 1972: 65–71 (Thomas Witulski employs a similar strategy to account for the oddity of Paul's claim that his readers are returning to paganism in Galatians 4:8–20 – see Witulski 2000: 71–72). On Galatians 5:13–6:10 as a generic set of admonitions, see, for example, Dibelius 1936: 157–160.

4   On Galatians 5:13–6:10 as a clarifying appendix, see, for example, Burton 1921: 290–291. On 'two fronts' hypotheses, see, for example, Ropes 1929: 25–27. Justin Hardin's contribution to the debate represents a more recent embodiment of this interpretative approach (see Hardin 2008: 140–142). See also Kahl: 2009.

5   See Barclay 1988: 70–71; see also 95, 115–159, 216–220.

6   See Barclay 1988: 218.

7   See Barclay 1988: 170.

entailed. Jewish sabbaths and special days were superficially similar to the high days and holidays of the pagan religious calendar. Jewish concerns about dietary restrictions and ritual purity were mirrored at multiple points in the customs of local cults. Circumcision bore a superficial resemblance to the pagan practice of dedicating votive offerings, even though – as was also the case with special days and diets – the underlying expectations on the Jewish side of things were *very* different. But the point is that recently converted Gentiles who'd spent their entire former lives pursuing pagan practices *with pagan expectations* couldn't be expected to have acquired some kind of *immunity* against the reanimation of those expectations simply because they were Christians. Give them similar religious practices to participate in – even practices that were only *tangentially* similar – and the same old network of assumptions was there ready to be resumed. That's the whole point of Paul's *stoicheia* language in Galatians 4:1–11. He ties Jewish and Gentile experience *together* at the level of basic practices to expose the danger that, despite a wealth of higher-level differences, embracing the one could reactivate the assumptions associated with the other, leading to spiritual destruction.

All this yields an elegant explanation of the situation in Galatia, making sense of many of the incongruities in Paul's text along the way. But now it seems to run aground on Paul's imperatives. If regression is really the key problem Paul addresses, why don't his prescriptions in the ethical section at the end of the letter fall under the same sentence? What was so bad about *Jewish* practices that made *them* likely to trigger the reanimation of the Galatians' pagan religious presuppositions in a way that the practices *Paul himself* was now advocating wouldn't? Scholars are divided on the exact extent to which Paul's vice and virtue lists here and elsewhere were influenced by pagan prototypes, but even the existence of a recognizably common category to which they all belong begs this question.[8] How could he hope to give his readers lists of things to do and things to avoid without reawakening their former assumptions about what this kind of moral compliance could achieve? The late second- to mid-third-century church father, Origen, memorably comes

---

8   For a comprehensive treatment of the relationship between vice and virtue lists in the New Testament and the Hellenistic prototypes popular in the time of Paul with a particular focus on Galatians 5:19–26, see Longenecker 1990: 249–252. The list of cardinal virtues and vices in Aristotle's *Rhetoric* (Rhet. 1.9.4–14) affords an early parallel, but New Testament lists were more probably influenced by Stoic prototypes (e.g. Seneca Brev. Vit. 10.2–4; Epictetus Disc. 2.8.23; Cicero Tusc. 4.7–8). See also Dunn 1993: 302; Oakes 2015: 175. The charter of the private cult in Philadelphia discussed in Chapter 6 affords an interesting insight into the use of vice and virtue lists in contemporary pagan religious contexts (see Barton et al. 1981: 7–41). While noting the generic form of the vice and virtue lists, Breytenbach convincingly demonstrates the unique character of the examples in Galatians (Breytenbach 1996: 138–140).

up against exactly this problem in his response to the philosopher Celsus who argued that Christians should take part in pagan sacrifices. Origen cites Paul's warnings about the observation of 'special days and months and seasons and years' in Galatians 4:10 but is then obliged to face the obvious rejoinder that *Christians themselves* observe special days in the form of 'the Lord's Day… the Preparation [day] … the Passover [and] Pentecost' (Cels. 8.22). So, do we need a rethink?

Before we get into the substance of this question, we should at least pause first to think this through from *Paul's* point of view. We're dealing with a letter that records Paul's perception of the problem in Galatia yielding insights into his understanding of the Christian gospel in the process. But we shouldn't necessarily be looking to it for a similarly sharp analysis of his proposed solution. Perhaps it's enough simply to note that he *raised awareness* of the dangers associated with embracing familiar-looking religious practices in a way that the Agitators did not? Paul may not have entirely removed the risks associated with navigating from one set of habituated convictions to another but, with his help, his readers were at least no longer flying blind.

We might also highlight the fact that the imperatives of Galatians 5:13–6:10 seemingly occupy quite a different 'register' to the specifics of Jewish law observance that were causing all the trouble in the Galatian churches. Paul has his mind on relational ethics here – love for neighbour (Gal. 5:14), love for others, peace with others, forbearance of others, kindness to others, goodness to others, faithfulness to others and gentleness with others (Gal. 5:22–23); he wants his readers to restore sinners in their fellowship gently (Gal. 6:1), to carry one another's burdens cheerfully (Gal. 6:2) and to resist pride and unhelpful comparisons with other people (Gal. 6:4–5); he wants them to share all good things with their instructors (Gal. 6:6). None of this is particularly reminiscent of the Agitators' insistence on traditional observances connected with diet, calendar and physical distinctiveness from people of other views or ethnicities.

A critic might respond that Paul *did* actually institute formulaic rites in Galatia as well. Galatians 3:27 makes it clear that his readers submitted to baptism, probably during Paul's initial visit to the region, and we have no reason to believe that he *didn't* introduce the celebration of the Lord's Supper, even if there's no positive evidence to say that he did. And yet Paul seems to be at pains to stress the *differences* between circumcision and baptism as initiatory rites, even as he reinforces the symbolic continuity from the one to the other. Baptism, unlike circumcision, is for Jew *and Gentile*; baptism, unlike circumcision, is for slave *and free* (remember, slaves *were* circumcised as members of

Jewish households, but freemen were not – cf. Genesis 17:27); baptism, unlike circumcision, is for male *and female* (Gal. 3:28).[9] And of course baptism involves no obvious cost to the recipient – all of which distinctives considerably diminish its potential to reactivate the expectations associated with votive offerings and other similar pagan practices.[10]

It's true that the Lord's Supper really did share many features in common with contemporary pagan religious practices which often gravitated around food.[11] And it's striking that, in the only Pauline letter that discusses it, the Supper has become a living illustration of exactly the same kind of problem we're discerning in Galatia, with rich Christians claiming the best seats and the best portions of food and excluding poor Christians *in just the same way they did as devotees of their pagan gods in the past* (see 1 Cor. 11:17–34).[12] But the key thing to recognize here is that, while Paul's prescriptions for Christian living clearly failed to *eliminate* the risk of triggering habituated pagan religious assumptions, they still did a better job of protecting his converts against them than the Agitators were doing with their pastorally reckless insistence on submission to Jewish law – and the danger was further reduced by Paul's exposure of the whole issue in his warnings.

The fundamental problem with the question we're wrestling with here is the implicit assumption that *some* religious systems are apt to reawaken entrenched religious expectations from the past and *others* are not. But there is no basis for this kind of simplistic binary logic. Paul wasn't presenting the Galatians with a choice between Judaism and anti-Judaism – he himself was encouraging Gentiles to 'Judaize' to the extent that he insisted on exclusive devotion to the one God of Israel; the difference was just that he didn't insist

---

9   Esau McCaulley provides a helpful summary of the interpretative options for Paul's famous statement of Christian inclusivity in Galatians 3:28 en route to the fascinating proposal that it deliberately contrasts the state of things *as they were* under the Torah with the state of things *as they are now* under the gospel with respect to the question of *inheritance*. Under Torah, Gentiles could not inherit, and neither could slaves or women, but now in Christ they can (McCaulley 2019: 162–170). If this were really Paul's intention, however, it seems strange that he fails to place the newly enfranchised group *second* in all three couplets. I agree that Paul is contrasting life under the old and new ages here, and on the strong connection McCaulley makes between Galatians 3:28 and the letter's key themes. By focusing on circumcision not inheritance in my own reading, however, the second group in each clause *really is* the focus of blessings in the new era: the sign of covenant inclusion is now opened up to Gentiles, to uncircumcised freemen and to women (noting, of course, that all three categories overlap).

10 Along with recognizing – and cultivating – divine favour, votive offerings in the ancient world were also used in the interests of social signalling – indicating piety, wealth and status to one's peers (see Linders 1987: 118).

11 See Borgen 1994: 30–59.

12 See Theissen 2004: 145–174; Winter 2001: 142–158; Ascough 1998: 91–93.

on Torah observance as well.[13] So we're dealing with *a question of degree* here. As we saw in Chapter 9, Paul talks about the *stoicheia tou kosmou* in Galatians, in part, because *every* real-world manifestation of organized religion exhibits some level of dependence on a common set of fundamental religious practices.[14] The question we have to ask in validation of our thesis is not whether Pauline Christianity *eradicated* these *stoicheia* completely but whether it consciously minimized exposure to their associated risks. And here we can answer resoundingly in the affirmative, not just because of the differences between his own and the Agitators' commands but because of differences in how he thought these commands would be realized in practice.

2 Spiritual Transformation

Paul's understanding of the practical, ethical implications of faith in Christ is grounded in the ministry of the Spirit.[15] In Galatians 6:7–9, he provides his own interpretation of the ethical material he's just laid out:

> *Do not be deceived: God cannot be mocked. A man reaps what he sows. Whoever sows to please their flesh, from the flesh will reap destruction; whoever sows to please the Spirit, from the Spirit will reap eternal life. Let us not become weary in doing good, for at the proper time we will reap a harvest if we do not give up.*

The reaping and sowing imagery here neatly connects to Paul's earlier presentation of the fruits of the Spirit (Gal. 5:22–23), but now the focus shifts from the fruits to the root from which the fruits will spring. Fleshly intentions yield fleshly actions, and spiritual intentions yield spiritual actions. As Jesus himself says in Luke 6:45, 'it is out of the abundance of the heart that the mouth speaks' (NRSV).

Relating this principle to the *stoicheia* imagery of Galatians 4:1–11, it's apparent that all 'elements' of religious action – be they sacred days, dietary laws, offerings, prayers or whatever – have the capacity to do good or harm, to be

---

13 '[Paul's] gentiles were to act "as if" they were Jews without, for males, receiving circumcision. By radically, exclusively affiliating to Israel's God, Paul's *ethnē* were to assume that public behaviour universally identified, by pagans and Jews alike, as uniquely Jewish. That is to say, Paul's gentiles – by the normal and contemporary definition of the term – Judaized' (Fredriksen 2017: 112. See also 125, 157).

14 e.g. Weiss 1995: 139: 'It would seem to be the case that all human societies organized with some kind of established priesthood, and some kind of astrological world view, have determined that sacred days are to be distinguished from profane ones.'

15 See Fee 1994: 420–469.

used to celebrate freedom or to inflict slavery, according to the intentions of the heart that drives them. When intentions are worldly, religious actions – like every other kind of action – have worldly points of focus and serve worldly purposes. And if worldly intentions drive religious actions for long enough, the connection between them becomes so strong that even when the intentions are renounced, renewed experience with the actions they once animated immediately reawakens them. Renunciation of intentions, then, is not enough. Intentions have to be utterly and radically *transformed* to protect the heart from the long reach of its past influences. *This transformation* is the focus of the ethical material in Galatians, and for Paul it's entirely bound up with the Spirit's work.

The point emerges clearly when we trace the developing idea of spiritual transformation through the letter. 'Spirit' vocabulary appears for the first time in the blunt challenge Paul issues to his readers in Galatians 3:2–3:

> *I would like to learn just one thing from you: Did you receive the Spirit by the works of the law, or by believing what you heard? Are you so foolish? After beginning by means of the Spirit, are you now trying to finish by means of the flesh?*

Spirit and flesh – and their respective partners, 'faith' and 'the works of the law' – are placed in direct opposition here. 'The flesh' is the direction in which Paul's readers are turning; the Spirit points in the opposite direction. But Paul gives us no information about the Spirit's role in inner transformation just yet.[16] The presence of the Spirit is a diagnostic for real relationship with God, but the argument has to develop a little before we discover how he expects the diagnosis to be taken.

Galatians 4:6 offers the first clear insight into the Spirit's distinctive work at the climax of Paul's paired explanations of the apocalyptic transition Christ has accomplished from slavery to freedom and from minority to majority, not just for Jews but for Gentiles as well. In striking contrast to the spiritual self-sufficiency that so marks the religious inscriptions of the region, the Spirit

---

16 Barclay is surely right to associate *sarx* and *kosmos* in his assessment of the Spirit–flesh dualism of Galatians 5–6 and to note the similar role that *sarx* and the *stoicheia tou kosmou* play in Paul's argument (Barclay 1988: 206, 209–210). Indeed, his assessment of *sarx* as 'an umbrella term' in Galatians, capable of encompassing pagan and Jewish behaviour and denoting that which is 'merely human' is very similar to the interpretation of the *stoicheia tou kosmou* offered in this thesis. Perceiving the essential moral neutrality of the *stoicheia*, however, guards against his overdrawn conclusion that 'by putting Judaism under the category of *sarx* and *stoicheia tou kosmou* [Paul] appears to be dismissing its value altogether' (Barclay 1988: 210).

of the Son liberates childlike dependence among God's people, marked by the distinctive cry, 'Abba Father!'

In Galatians 5:5–6, this contrast is developed further. Paul tells the Galatians that the Spirit will enable them to wait for the righteousness they hope for by faith – tying faith and Spirit together in the lives of believers once again and gesturing towards the striking new stance he expects from them in the realm of religious actions. This is what it looks like to be free from enslavement to the *stoicheia*, whether you're a Jew or a Gentile: to know that whatever actions you perform, your hope of righteousness doesn't depend on them. It can't be, and it doesn't need to be, drawn down towards you by careful cultivation of the gods like the healings and good harvests the Galatians hoped for in the past. It's a hope for which you wait, not resignedly nor sceptically, but 'eagerly', as Paul puts it, because God can be trusted to give it when *he* sees fit.

The celebrated vice and virtue lists of Galatians 5:19–26 are contextualized by Paul's explanation of freedom in Galatians 5:13–14. True freedom is not freedom *from* restrictions on fleshly behaviour but rather freedom *for* humble service epitomized by the love command which Jesus also cites from Leviticus 19:18 in Mark 12:29–31. And the key to this life of freedom, once again, is the Spirit (Gal. 5:16). It is the Spirit who transforms the heart, and the Spirit who grants freedom from the otherwise irresistible attractions of 'the flesh'.[17] Spiritual transformation involves such a fundamental reconstitution and empowering of the intentions that believers are enabled to resist patterns of behaviour that previously held their intentions captive (Gal. 5:17).[18]

The vices listed in Galatians 5:19–21 are hard indeed to reconcile with conventional pictures of Paul's Galatian correspondents moving towards Judaism out of a sense of genuine concern to complete their identification with the Abrahamic family, or even for more pragmatic reasons like avoiding persecution. Paul has some lurid warnings for his readers here which seem to have been chosen with care for this specific setting, despite the formulaic nature of the genre in which he operates.[19] Debauchery, idolatry, witchcraft and

---

17 See Martyn 1997: 289–294.

18 This is not, however, the process by which Paul expects his readers to complete their deliverance from the curse of Galatians 3:10 (contra Wilson 2007: 117–138). Paul ties redemption from the curse decisively to the accomplishments of the cross (Gal. 3:13).

19 H.D. Betz interacts at length with Hellenic and Jewish parallels to the paraenetic material in Galatians 5–6 concluding that its Christian meaning is 'secondary' and the content largely generic (see Betz 1979: 305). Barclay, however, finds substantial problems with the parallels Betz adduces, drawing attention in particular to the difference between lexical parallels and true parallels in context, concluding that the comparison is 'considerably more complex than Betz's treatment suggests' and arguing for substantial situational sensitivity on Paul's part as the author/compositor of this material (Barclay 1988: 176, 217–218). For an analysis of the unique character of the Galatian vice and virtue lists with respect to similar material in other Pauline letters, see also Breytenbach 1996: 138–140.

drunkenness are perhaps particularly improbable accusations for an audience animated by the desire to complete or at least to regularize their new affiliation to the God of Israel.[20] But if we perceive the cause, at least in part, in the reactivation of their former pagan expectations, it's quite natural to assume that behaviours associated with these expectations through long exposure to the religious culture of the region – and considered not only acceptable but thoroughly conventional within that culture – might also be reasserting themselves. There's nothing in the vice list that seems altogether implausible as an allegation Paul might have made against the practices of contemporary Anatolian cults.

But the striking point to which Paul is driving here is *the contrast* between the vices and the virtues. The vices are 'acts', but the virtues are intentions. The vices come from 'the flesh', but the virtues come from the Spirit. Paul's vision of spiritual maturity doesn't involve replacing one set of religious actions with a completely different set of actions that are somehow incapable of triggering the expectations associated with the first. Paul is arguing for a transformation of the heart that, in time, allows actions – even familiar, habituated actions – to be practised in a new way (Gal. 6:9). The virtues Paul describes here are the new principles according to which a believer's spiritual actions should be undertaken. These are the new expectations Paul expects to see gradually overwriting the old as the Spirit works.

3 Symptomatic and Systemic Responses to the Galatian Problem

If our analysis is on target here, what should strike us immediately, then, is that the supposed incompatibility of Paul's warnings and his ethics may actually be illusory. With regression established as the principal problem in Galatia, Paul's indicatives and imperatives emerge clearly as an attack on the same problem *from two different directions*. He begins with *symptomatic* treatment (dealing with the presenting manifestation of the problem) and then progresses to *systemic* treatment (dealing with its underlying cause). Or, to pick up the analogy we sketched briefly in Chapter 8, if Galatians is a paramedic callout to the

---

20 While Barclay does an admirable job of demonstrating the compatibility of these warnings with the Galatian situation considered more broadly, the prevalence of scholars drawing other conclusions here still highlights the fundamental difficulty of combining the vice list with a portrait of the Galatians as pious to the point of embracing Jewish law and suffering merely from 'moral confusion' (Barclay 1988: 19–22, 218). On the increasing interest in sociological explanations for the Galatians' change of allegiances, see, for example, Barclay 1988: 56–60.

scene of an accident where 'strong', mature, Jewish Christianity has smashed into 'weak', immature, Gentile Christianity without so much as touching the brakes, and his warnings – 'Have nothing to do with these people!' 'Flee from the Law!' 'Don't even think about getting circumcised!' – equate to the initial response of putting out the fire, pulling the victims clear of the wreckage and so on, his ethics equate to a treatment plan designed to steer his injured readers through recovery and rehab and set them back on their own two feet. Paul doesn't want vulnerable Gentile Christians to live their whole lives avoiding all contact with anything and everything that might trigger a resumption of their former pagan religious expectations. Sure, he wants them to avoid such triggers *while their vulnerability lasts.* But he also wants them to grow up and experience such a transformation by the power of the Spirit that they can live and participate resiliently in the pagan culture that surrounds them without fear of capitulating once again to its norms.

With his warnings about Jewish legal observances in the first part of the letter, Paul deals with the specific practices that are reawakening the Galatians' habitual religious expectations. With his ethics in the latter part of the letter, he urges them to embrace a spiritual renovation that will blunt and deaden those expectations, gradually consigning them to the past. As we saw in Chapter 9, Paul *really does* believe that the new covenant promises of Ezekiel and Jeremiah are coming true before his eyes, and that a new age of inner transformation by the Spirit, removing hearts of stone and replacing them with hearts of flesh, has dawned. In Corinth, he holds himself up as an example of maturity along these lines – as one who has 'become all things to all people' and who no longer has any fear that embracing other people's practices will produce harmful side effects. The same hope is even more evident at the tipping point between indicatives to imperatives in Romans 12:2: 'Do not be conformed to this age but be transformed by the renewing of [your] mind' (translation mine).[21] And it also gives us a compelling account of the imperatives in Galatians.

---

21 The point comes tantalizingly close to full realization in Craig Keener's exploration of this pivotal Pauline antithesis. 'Being conformed' and 'being transformed' are both *passive* ideas in Paul's text – the world from which his readers would been delivered would conform them to its norms once more; the Spirit who is now at work in them would transform them into the likeness of Christ. Keener also helpfully highlights the connection back to the corrupt state of the pre-Christian mind in Romans 1. But he fails to engage with the striking implication of Paul's argument that the conforming power of the present age requires *ongoing resistance* on the journey towards Christian maturity, or to note the outworking of that implication in the subsequent chapters of the letter, not least in Romans 14–15. See Keener 2016: 152–158.

Is Barclay right, then, to attribute the problems in Galatia to *pastoral naivety* on Paul's part during his initial encounter with his readers? Certainly, he left them with a gospel light on rules and formal ritual requirements, light perhaps to the point where he insisted on baptism and communion alone. But I think we can attribute this now more to *astute pastoral policy* on Paul's part than anything less flattering.[22] Paul was well acquainted with this region – he spoke the local languages and understood their cults.[23] If 1 Corinthians and Romans are anything to go by, he was well aware of the risk that pagan spiritual assumptions could rear their heads again even in the context of belief in Christ if he gave them hooks to hang on. Paul knew that if he led with Jesus *plus* vice and virtue lists, or Jesus *plus* a host of Jewish laws, his message would land in terrain shaped by entrenched pre-existent pagan assumptions, producing a faith of Jesus-themed externals draped over the mannequin of the Galatians' pagan past.

So, his strategy was to start with the basics, trusting to the Spirit to initiate the process of overwriting past habits and closing down unhelpful mental pathways. In time he hoped to see his converts grow to such a point of maturity that they could eat in pagan temples (1 Cor. 8:4–6) and perhaps even participate in Jewish rites. He certainly seems open to the *possibility* that his Gentile co-worker, Titus, might be asked to accept circumcision in Jerusalem when he takes him there, although in the event, of course, it doesn't happen (Gal. 2:1–5). The purpose of the ethics in Galatians, then, is to point the way towards spiritual maturity along a distinctive new age trajectory.[24] The transformation Paul longs to see among his readers is not that which characterized the era before Christ's appearing. It was a transformation led by the Spirit, empowered by the Spirit – a transformation of the mind and heart enabling a completely new approach to familiar actions.

---

22 Notice that re-establishing regression at the heart of our understanding of Galatians *also* undermines incoherence and developmental models of Paul's thought based on the idea that his later, seemingly more moderate, statements about Jewish law point to significant shifts in his theological opinions over time (for developmental readings, see Drane: 1975; Hübner: 1984. For incoherence readings, see Räisänen: 1983). Our work in Galatians suggests that Paul is simply practising what he preaches – accommodating his statements about the law (and indeed the extent of his own legal observances) to the needs of his audience.

23 On Paul's familiarity with local languages see Acts 14:11. On the evidence within Galatians that Paul was familiar with local cults see Chapter 6, pp. 72–73.

24 Fee hints in this direction by positioning the ethical material in Galatians 5 and 6 as the answer to the question about spiritual maturity posed in 3:3: 'Are you so foolish? After beginning by means of the Spirit, are you now trying to finish [or 'trying to attain *completion*'] by means of the flesh?' (Fee 1994: 421).

12

Pastoral Priorities

Introduction

Now let's begin to think about the implications of all this for the life of the church. In this chapter, I want to further develop the realization that the underlying problem in Galatia was a failure of accommodation – a failure on the part of 'strong' Jewish Christians to anticipate the impact of their actions on the 'weak' Gentile Christians Paul was writing to. If accommodation stood as close to the heart of Paul's pastoral priorities as our work so far suggests, the consequences – both for our understanding of the early church and for our own pastoral priorities today – are significant. After that, in the two remaining chapters, we'll follow the story of Paul's priorities from the New Testament era through to the now, opening our eyes to the effects of their marginalization over the centuries and our ears to their urgent call to action in the present.

1 Accommodation and the Agitators

Let's get started by reacquainting ourselves with the group that stands at the centre of so many attempts to decipher Galatians – the Agitators. Old and New Perspectives alike typically read the letter as a more or less clear window on their distinctive views, locked in a titanic clash with Paul's own.[1] In this book, however, we've been exploring the possibility that Galatians was written primarily to pastor *its readers' reaction* to the Agitators' ministry, a reaction that may have stood at some distance from the Agitators' actual intentions. Clearly Paul had some real problems with these individuals – their contribution to the Galatian situation leaves him needing to reassert the legitimacy of his apostleship (esp. Gal. 1:11–2:10), and he has significant doubts about their motives and integrity (Gal. 4:17–18; 5:7–12; 6:12–13). Paul condemns their ministry as the proclamation of 'a different gospel' in Galatians 1:6–9 – a distortion

---

1 For presentations of the Agitators on a variety of quite different collision courses with Paul, see Dunn 1993: 9–11; Martyn 1997: 302–306; Nanos 2002: 106–108, 193–199; Schreiner 2010: 49–52.

of the good news about Christ. But even this has to be read in the light of his comments about Peter's failure to '[act] in line with the truth of the gospel' in Galatians 2:14. Very few interpreters see that as an indication of *apostasy* on Peter's part.

As the substance of the letter unfolds, Paul's critique focuses much more clearly on the effect of the Agitators' demands *on Gentiles* than it does on any specific affirmations or denials they may have made. It still speaks to all the same arterial theological issues for which it's become known over the centuries: justification, union with Christ, covenant and spiritual transformation shine out among a host of other major themes – all the more brightly, I think, when read against the readers' pagan background. But we shouldn't jump too quickly to the conclusion that there were fundamental disagreements *between Paul and the Agitators* in any of these areas.[2] Their message may have been 'another gospel', but it was still recognizably *a gospel*.[3] Working with the information the letter actually provides, Paul's problem with the Agitators seems to have been *less theological than it was pastoral and missiological*. It had to do with their cavalier attitude to their hearers' past religious experience, their heedlessness to the possibility that what seemed good *to them* might actually be a source of incalculable harm *to their audience*. And this should be given due weight as we seek to make sense of the strength of Paul's reaction.

Let me illustrate. Suppose you get together with some well-meaning friends from your church and attend an open meeting of a local Alcoholics Anonymous group, aiming to learn and encourage and help. You sit and listen as the participants tell their stories of drink-related chaos – lost jobs, broken marriages, estranged friendships – and at the end you feel thoroughly heartbroken and convinced of the value of talking about it. 'This is great,' you blurt out, 'and it's such a shame it has to stop now. Let's, er... let's all go round the corner to the pub and carry on the conversation!' And, with that well-meaning gesture, you send your newfound friends back to the abyss. Even when our intentions are good, it's possible to do great damage and justly incur great displeasure through insensitivity to issues in the background. The leaders of the AA group here would obviously be apoplectic.

Now, of course, I'm not suggesting the Agitators in Galatia were really *this benevolent* to Paul or to his project. The thesis of this book can

---

2 Barclay's cautionary remarks about *Mirror Reading* remain a helpful guide to exegesis here (see Barclay 1987).

3 See Barclay 2015: 392.

accommodate more positive interpretations of their actions than conventional exegeses allow, for sure. But it can also accommodate negative interpretations too. The point I'm arguing for here is simply that we don't know enough to adjudicate where to place them on this spectrum. And I *don't think we need to know* in order to explain the material we *do* have or to meaningfully interpret it.

It doesn't matter that we can't say precisely who the Agitators were, or where they came from, or why they thought circumcision was an essential step for Gentile converts to take. The key lesson for us to learn here has to do with the impact of their demands *in this specific setting.* They marched in among the Galatian Christians without a thought, it seems, for the past from which Paul was so delicately trying to disentangle them. They had no sense of the Galatians' sensitivity to religious law-keeping as a familiar category and no sense of the collateral damage that would be inflicted by leading them back to those familiar practices with all their familiar associated expectations. The Agitators drew a blank in the realm of *accommodation.* And, for Paul, this was an absolutely vital component of Christian maturity.

2 The Parting of the Ways

This realization, I think, has some major implications for the way we think about the early history of the church. Let's start with one of the hottest topics in this field. When did the division between Christianity and Judaism first take place? Or, more specifically, when did the church of Jesus cease to be a single movement in which Torah observance for Jews and Torah non-observance for Gentiles were *both* considered legitimate responses to the gospel, notwithstanding the difficulties of brokering the relationship between them?[4]

That things started out this way seems difficult to deny. Galatians itself testifies to the existence of a substantial community of Torah-observant Jesus-followers in Jerusalem several years after the commencement of concerted Gentile outreach. And in Acts we see the same phenomenon on several occasions, complete with an account of the efforts that were made to

---

4   Dunn rightly draws attention to the fact that there were several noteworthy 'partings of the ways' between Christianity and Judaism during the early Christian period. Among Jews who were unable to countenance a separation of religious and ethnic identity, the point of fracture must have been very early, and the same goes for Jews unwilling to accommodate Christian worship as a legitimate species of monotheism (see Dunn 2006a: 301–302). The specific question I have in mind here, however, is an inner-Christian question: when did the attempt to reconcile law-observant Jewish Christianity and non-law-observant Gentile Christianity within a recognisably single movement cease to be a viable project?

normalize this unprecedented religious and social innovation (Acts 11:1–18; 15:1–35; 21:17–26). However, 350 years later – as we saw in Chapter 2 – John Chrysostom saw the world very differently. Torah-observant Christianity in Chrysostom's Syrian Antioch had become a repellent contradiction in terms, and law-observant Jewish Christian congregations had retreated into the shadows. But when and why did this great shift take place?

Thanks, in particular, to the legacy of the German theologian and flag carrier for the massively influential Tübingen School, F.C. Baur (1792–1860), for the past 200 years the standard answer to the 'when?' part of this question has been that it happened *very early* in the church's development.[5] Baur thought he saw Jewish (nationalistic) and proto-Christian (universalistic) inclinations in tension *even in Jesus' concept of his own vocation.*[6] But the key text undergirding the idea of an early, irrevocable parting of the ways among his followers, was, and has remained, Paul's description of the Antioch Incident in Galatians 2:11–14.[7] Though Luke may have drawn a discreet veil over the details, Paul's raw recollections of the event have been widely assumed to testify to the existence of (at least) two distinct factions in the early church with two very different visions of the gospel – a Pauline 'law-free' faction worshipping a Jesus posthumously elevated to super-human status (the so-called 'Christ of Faith') and a Petrine law-observant faction devoted to the much more ordinary, much more *Jewish,* 'Jesus of History'.[8] It should hardly surprise us that interpretations of Galatians have been dominated by the idea of conflict between *Jewish* groups on this basis. The Agitators are pre-assigned roles in Baur's anti-Pauline faction, or something like it, before the remainder of the letter has even been consulted.

Our work on regression in the foregoing chapters, however, offers a completely different way of understanding these events. We're no longer left asking whether (and, if so, when) Paul and Peter made things up after their shocking theological falling out, because – if the Antioch Incident bears any

---

5 Dunn provides a very helpful summary of the process that leads from Baur's iconic rejection of Christianity's Jewish origins to contemporary perspectives placing a much greater emphasis on continuity (see Dunn 2006a: 1–23).

6 See Baur 1878: 49; highlighted in Bockmuehl 2006: 127.

7 See Baur 1878: 54–55. See also Dunn 2006a: 172–179.

8 Dunn 2006a: 6–12. The Baurian model has, of course, been substantially undermined in recent years by more realistic assessments not only of the dating and integrity of the New Testament documents, but also of the *Pseudo-Clementine Recognitions* on which he placed great emphasis (see Baur 1878: 55; see also Bockmuehl 2006: 125; Jones 2014: 25–26). The testimony to Paul's continuing respect for, and deference towards, Peter and the other apostles in 1 Corinthians. 15:3–11, however, has always strained the credibility of reconstructions in which the Antioch Incident leads to an immediate and irrevocable breach (see Bockmuehl 2006: 112, 135).

resemblance to the situation in Galatia to which Paul applies it – it wasn't a shocking *theological* falling out at all. The Antioch Incident was certainly shocking, and embarrassing. But it was a difference nonetheless between two leaders with a common understanding of what God had done in Christ (Gal. 2:15–16). The Antioch Incident was a clash between Paul's and Peter's evolving concepts of the *consequences* of these convictions – of how they should impact the behaviour of Jewish believers and Gentile believers in situations where the two communities mixed. Like Paul's later confrontation with the Agitators in Galatia, it was a clash *in the realm of accommodation* more than it was a clash between fundamentally different concepts of faith. And far from deserving its later reputation as a unique 'sliding doors' moment in the history of the church, it emerges instead as an exchange that typifies the challenges of the period. The Antioch Incident gives us a glimpse into the necessary, and indeed Spirit-inspired, process of discovery that ultimately produced the mature treatments of weakness and strength preserved for us in Paul's later letters.

Many commentators think Galatians was written *before* the Jerusalem Council of Acts 15, concluding that – at the time of the Antioch Incident – no significant collective attempt to resolve the question of Jew–Gentile accommodation had yet been undertaken. In Chapter 1, I briefly sketched the case for placing its composition *after* the Jerusalem Council. But even if the apostles had already come to the united view on circumcision for which that gathering is principally remembered, a myriad of other practical issues still remained to be worked out, not least the matter of communal eating that flares up here. And these weren't simple questions – they were pastorally complex. Remember Paul's problem in Antioch wasn't restricted to Peter withdrawing from fellowship with Gentiles. He was also concerned about the possibility that Gentiles would feel obliged 'to follow Jewish customs' (Gal. 2:14) – leading presumably to the same kinds of dangers that dominate the remainder of the letter, viz. the reanimation of their pagan religious expectations. Peter is portrayed as unaware of this possibility. But that shouldn't surprise us. By this stage, Paul was a veteran of several years standing, proclaiming the Jewish Messiah and planting churches among Gentiles like his friends in Antioch. It should strike us that his disappointment in Galatians 2:10–14 is focused *particularly* on the capitulation of his travelling companion Barnabas who should have known better. But none of this points to a dispute about what Christ had done or how it was to be appropriated. It points instead to a debate about pastoral tactics in a context where the protagonists were learning all the time.

3 Accommodation in Paul

Notice also what this does to the profile of accommodation in the larger landscape of Pauline theology. I've already made the case that we should be paying closer attention to this in 1 Corinthians and Romans based on the merits of the relevant passages alone (1 Cor. 8:1–13; 10:23–11:1; Rom. 14:1–15:13). But if Galatians joins the chorus as a letter-length case study in the importance of accommodation and the seriousness of the consequences that follow when it's neglected, the case for giving it detailed consideration becomes overwhelming. Accommodation of difference emerges as arguably the single most important topic in Pauline ecclesiology.

Churches, by their very nature, are constructed in the midst of difference, epitomized in Paul's time by the foundational difference between Jew and Gentile. True, they're built around the great levelling reality of the cross – the realization in history of the fundamentally Jewish principle that *all* the children of Abraham are accepted by God because he bears the obligations of *the recipients* of his covenant and not just his own obligations as its author. But the survival and effectiveness of each fellowship, as Paul conceives it, still depends *entirely* on the Spirit-empowered willingness of its members to invest time in understanding the strengths and vulnerabilities of their brothers and sisters and to respond by laying down their own preferences in the interests of others.

David Rudolph draws out the Jewish roots of this key idea in his thought-provoking monograph, *A Jew to the Jews*. Judaism in the first century, he reminds us, was *pluriform* – raising questions about allowable interactions with Gentiles and with Jews of differing opinions and answering them in a whole variety of different ways long before they emerged as live issues in the church.[9] Pharisees resolved these tensions by adopting practices *stricter* than their own when circumstances required it, mirroring Paul's advice to 'the strong' in Romans and 1 Corinthians. And to facilitate fellowship with *less strict* Jews, and even Gentiles, they invited them into their own homes, or visited on the condition that they could bring their own food or omit to eat dishes proscribed by their own dietary laws.[10] None of this tallies well with the common suggestion that Paul's application of recognizably similar principles to the life of the

---

9   Rudolph 2011: 116.
10   Rudolph 2011: 121–130.

church amounted to little more than offhand pragmatism, mere scribbles on the back of the ecclesiological envelope.[11]

The circumcision of Timothy reported in Acts 16:3 and noted at several earlier points in this book, of course, represents an important test case for this claim. Doesn't the fact that the event took place *in Lystra* – in the very same region to which Galatians was probably written – undermine the suggestion that Paul was driven by a principled desire to accommodate the weaknesses of local Gentiles? If Jewish rites were poised to reactivate pagan religious sensibilities in the Galatian churches, why not here as well? But in reality, the very opposite is true. Paul's teaching about the weak and the strong in Romans and 1 Corinthians requires an assessment of weaknesses and strengths and the risks associated with each *on a case-by-case basis*. Just because Paul was in close physical proximity to the destination of Galatians when he visited Lystra tells us almost nothing about the outcome of this specific calculation. Arguing that Paul should have refused to circumcise Timothy in Lystra is like arguing that because I know one person in Oxford who needs cancer treatment, *everyone* in Oxford needs cancer treatment. It doesn't make any sense.

Just because the events took place *in Lystra* tells us *nothing at all* about the pastoral wisdom of circumcising the son of a Jewish woman and a Greek (Acts 16:1) considered Jewish by virtue of his maternal ancestry, and set to minister in a world where Jews were expected to be circumcised – and where the opinion that neither circumcision nor uncircumcision meant anything was held by only a tiny minority (Gal. 5:6; 6:15).[12] Paul clearly judged that the imposition of 'strength' implicit in travelling with an uncircumcised Jew posed a greater risk to the spiritual health of scrupulous Jews going forward than circumcising him did to the vulnerable Gentiles in Timothy's home town. Remember, the danger that pagan religious expectations would be reactivated was live only among Gentiles who felt compelled to follow Jewish customs *themselves* (Gal. 2:14; 6:12), but that can hardly have been the tenor of Paul's ministry in Lystra. Circumcising Timothy may even have given him an opportunity to explain

---

11 Rudolph 2011: 12–13. On Pauline accommodation as evidence of unprincipled pragmatism, see Räisänen 1983: 71–72. Rudolph concludes that Paul remained Torah-observant throughout his Christian life, modelling a liberal halakhah that did not require proactive inquiries about where the food he was offered as a guest came from and accommodating the norms of others on the Pharisaic basis (Rudolph 2011: 204–208). Whether or not we accept this analysis, it *does* at least support a vision of Pauline practice in which *the initiative lay with him* to accommodate the norms and scruples of Jews and Gentiles with practices different from his own in the manner best adapted to their edification. If the argument of this book is on target in Galatians, failure to accept this responsibility and to take this initiative on the part of the Agitators is the dominant factor in Paul's disaffection with them.

12 See Cohen 1999: 308–340.

why he believed the rite was both unnecessary and inadvisable for Gentiles, facilitating the edification of both groups.

Paul clearly believed that thoughtful reflection on our weaknesses and strengths, and on the weaknesses and strengths of others, was a vital duty for every member of a functional church. There must be a willingness to take the specific needs of each person we meet into account, not fearing to come to different conclusions in different situations. The very thing that constitutes strength in one scenario can *be* weakness in another, and vice versa. And there must be an understanding that spiritual growth is threatened as much by the lingering plausibility of expectations formed in the past as it is by any more obvious factors in the present. Jesus himself tells us in Luke 11:24–26 that, when an impure spirit is expelled from a person and returns to find the house of their life swept clean, it resumes its former occupation – taking other spirits more wicked than itself along for the ride – and 'the final condition of [the] person is worse than the first'. Paul planted churches and built congregations on the assumption that every believer had responsibility for every other in the battle to stop that happening.

4 Accommodation Today

So why have we lost this in the modern church?

Contemporary models of discipleship expand at length on the right way to build young Christians *up* in faith, but I hear almost nothing about what we're building *on*. We assume that every convert enters the church as a *tabula rasa*. Visible interest in Christianity is sufficient to assume all past and concurrent interests void of significance, despite the fact that they're often contesting the same space and building with outwardly similar materials. It doesn't cross our minds to think that inconsiderate incorporation of practices that are already associated with secular expectations in our lives outside church – or with any other set of counter-Christian expectations for that matter – are likely to stay associated with those expectations when we come in.

And this isn't happening because the world has taken it into its head to emulate the church. It isn't that universities and shopping malls and sports teams have set out to create social contexts that look like Christian teaching settings, or corporate prayer, or worship – leaving Christians with a distorted sense of what they're doing in church in the process. No, the logic is moving in the other direction. It's happening because – thinking to repurpose them for spiritually fruitful ends – the church is embracing the *stoicheia* of the secular world and weaving them into the very fabric of discipleship.

What do we think Paul would say to this? Knowing all we know about Galatians now, what do we think he would say about the wisdom or otherwise of positively embracing the practical cues of the culture around us? At minimum, I think, he'd be urging extreme caution, and among the vulnerable 180-degree change of direction.

To embody Paul's pastoral priorities even to some small extent in the modern context, we first need comprehension of what's going on around us. It's a striking feature of Paul's ministry in Galatia that he understands his readers' pagan context and *he knows what it signifies*. He doesn't just look at their pagan rites and set himself the challenge of extracting his readers from them. He looks at their pagan rites and sees *what they think those rites accomplish*. It's subverting and supplanting *that* which counts for him as authentic discipleship. 'You can take a young convert out of paganism, sure,' he says, 'but have you given any thought to the challenge of taking paganism out of the convert?' For Paul that question is both vital and unanswerable, with merely human resources. Bravely exorcizing the assumptions of the non-Christian world from our souls by willpower alone is an exercise in deckchair rearrangement on a sinking ship. Paul's prescription, as we see in the latter part of Galatians, is spiritual transformation.

But neither is this a summons to otherworldly cultural detachment in the church. That isn't Paul's vision of maturity at all. Paul doesn't want his readers to *stay* in the intensely vulnerable place in which he finds them, where they simply can't participate in anything remotely like the world they're trying to leave without triggering the resumption of its expectations. Paul wants his readers to grow up, to become resilient. He wants them to become as he is, able to return to their pre-Christian context without bringing its assumptions back from the dead, and to embrace other people's pre-Christian contexts too where needed. But the way they're going to get there is a process of development. It takes time and deliberation and careful pastoral investment to grasp the reality that 'justification *is by faith*', whatever generation we live in and whatever contemporary norms we've imbibed with the alternative routes to 'justification' they've bequeathed to us.

In modern churches, more often than not, we get this absolutely the wrong way round. We think the people who need cultural relevance are the newcomers and we allow the experienced saints who might actually be able to handle it to retreat into Christian enclaves that wouldn't resonate with a contemporary cultural cue if it jumped out and bit them on the nose. Paul saw maturity as a qualification for constructive engagement with counter-Christian assumptions, not as a free pass to avoid or to belittle them! The church needs ambassadors who can engage sympathetically with the norms of the world around them like Paul did, without degenerating into a superficially Christian pastiche of those norms that has nothing decisive or redemptive to say to them.

And while this paradigm stands, we're raising generations of Christians with profound problems under the surface. If the world has taught us that every major activity we participate in is part of the same divine–human game Paul encountered (masterfully rebranded now, of course, to accommodate the scruples of an atheistic age), and if, far from resisting the game, or even plugging along contentedly alongside it, the church has actually embraced its outward manifestations in the name of disciple-making, the Christianity we're cultivating may actually have more of paganism about it than it does anything recognizably connected to the Bible. Even in churches with healthy attendance numbers, Paul might still have us in his sights with the chilling warning of Galatians 4:11: 'I fear for you, that somehow I have wasted my efforts on you!' If the Christianity we've acquired is really just another way to maximize our chances of blessing and get the future we think we deserve, it doesn't matter if we have a great conversion experience to look back on in the past – the Galatians had that too (Gal. 3:2–5). In Paul's view, *it isn't Christianity at all.*

13
Voices From the Past

Introduction

Might the church have lost something vital, then, on the long journey from Paul's vision of church planting and disciple-making to our own? Certainly, it hasn't always been the case that the possibility of regression to counter-Christian modes of thought has been neglected, or that their propensity to inhabit and ultimately to co-opt and direct superficially Christian practice has been so badly underestimated. In this chapter we'll briefly review this story of waning awareness, noting that the 'regression reading' of Galatians developed in this book is anything but new, and that its steady eclipse over the centuries has robbed us of a vital set of tools for guarding against pagan religious motives and guiding young believers towards maturity.

1 Recognizing Regression – Ignatius, Justin, Origen

Our story begins – like so many other attempts to chart the emerging norms of the ancient Christian church – with the extraordinarily early letters of Ignatius of Antioch which transport us back to the early second century.[1] Composed, as tradition has it, in the course of the elderly bishop's journey from Syria to Rome to face execution, the letters provide us with fascinating glimpses into the lives of the churches in the major cities of Asia Minor along his route. Writing to Christian communities in Ephesus, Tralles and Smyrna, Ignatius focuses on the emergence of proto-docetic scepticism about Jesus' physical existence. Writing to Magnesia and Philadelphia, he concentrates on the question of unity, pointing in each case to the temptation to embrace Jewish customs as the key divisive issue.

---

1 Eusebius locates Ignatius's death under the reign of Trajan (AD 98–117, see Eusebius, *Hist.* 3.36). Scepticism about the authenticity of the letters and the suggestion that they were composed under gnostic influences have not met with broad acceptance (see Weijenborg: 1969; Joly: 1979; Hübner 1997: 44–72; in response see Ehrman 2003: 209–213; Foster 2012: 3392–3395).

In the letter to the Philadelphians, we run into a situation with marked parallels to the one Paul faced in Galatia. Jewish Christians were visible and influential among Ignatius's readers, as were Gentile converts to Judaism – who probably *weren't* Christians given the way he pushes the two groups apart (Phld. 6.1). But wherever the encouragement to embrace Jewish customs was coming from, Ignatius's warning to the Philadelphian church is strikingly reminiscent of the logic we've been exploring in this book. To a congregation tempted to embrace Torah, he says, 'Flee then the arts and plots of the ruler of this age' (Phld. 6.2). How can that make sense? If he's alluding to Galatians with these remarks about the present evil age (cf. Gal. 1:4), we should assume, I think, that it makes sense in the same way it makes sense *there* – as a warning about Jewish practice reawakening the norms and assumptions of his readers' pagan past.[2] In the letter to the Magnesians, the underlying situation is less clear. But Ignatius's reiteration of the connection between embracing Judaism and reversing the salvation historical clock is once again reminiscent of Galatians (Mag. 10.3), and his remarks about believers living in Judaism 'not [having] received grace' (Mag. 8.1) remind us very plainly that there was *something* about being a Gentile convert that made Jewish practice dangerous for them, threatening the very core of their Christian profession.[3]

Ignatius, like Paul, is open to the idea of a distinctively Jewish form of Christianity – although he gives us very few details about what that might actually involve. But he's also aware of the danger of regression – and of the possibility that conversion may never actually happen in the first place – if Jewish modes of behaviour are made obligatory for Gentiles. More than half a century on, the pastoral lessons of Galatians were still very obviously paramount in Ignatius's mind. And the same thing remains true moving forward another half a century to the works of Justin Martyr.[4]

Justin is known to us principally through two extensive treatises – *The Apology* and *The Dialogue with Trypho* – the latter of which portrays him in debate with a learned Jew, marshalling arguments to prove that Jesus was indeed the

---

2 Barclay uses Ignatius's letters as evidence for the strength and influence of *local* Jewish communities in Asia Minor (Barclay 1996: 280). For another allusion to Paul's argument in Galatians, compare Phld. 7.2 with Galatians 1:11–12. Schoedel argues that the 'injection' of circumcision into Ignatius's argument at Phld. 6.1 is itself an allusion to Galatians with no concrete point of reference in the Philadelphian context (Schoedel 1985: 202–203). Ignatius's remarks associating the old age with 'magic' and 'evil' at Eph. 19.3 represent a particularly interesting point of contact with the Galatian situation.

3 'For Ignatius the teachings and myths of Judaism are "old" (cf. Mag. 9.1; 10.2) – a term that he uses to describe what is opposed to God (cf. Eph. 19.3)' (Schoedel 1985: 119; cf. Wyschogrod 2004: 193).

4 On the date of Justin's *Dialogue*, see Marcovich 1997: 278; Marcovich 1994: 11. On the relationship between the final form of the *Dialogue* and putative earlier versions, see Horner 2001: 19–23, 61–63.

Jewish Messiah.[5] In Chapter 46 of the *Dialogue*, Justin's interlocutor broaches a question that is also vital for our understanding of Galatians: is it possible for those who 'even now desire to live in observance of the precepts of the Mosaic law, and yet believe the crucified Jesus is the Christ of God… [to] be saved?' (Dial. 46.1). By the time we reach Chrysostom, of course, Galatians was being used as a basis to deny this possibility in the most strident terms. But Justin is still open to something much more like the reading of the letter we're exploring here. 'Such a man *will* be saved,' he says, 'unless he exerts every effort to influence other men (I have in mind the Gentiles whom Christ circumcised from all error) to practice the same rites himself, informing them that they cannot be saved unless they do so' (Dial. 47.1, emphasis mine).[6] Like Paul, Justin is entirely opposed to the idea that submission to the Jewish law is *obligatory* for Gentile converts – but not just because he thinks they have everything they need without it. Justin thinks Jewish legal observances can actively undermine a Gentile's faith. Even if they continue to profess confidence in Christ, he judges it only 'probable' that such a person will be saved (Dial. 47.3). For a clear sight of why an early Christian author might think this way, however, we have to jump forward another century to the works of the towering scholar and prolific sermon writer, Origen.

Origen's interaction with regression in Galatians should interest us if only for the fact that he returns to the theme so many times and in so many different contexts. In his *Homilies on Leviticus*, he reflects on the destruction of the temple in Jerusalem and its legal rituals as an example of God's providential care for weak believers in the new era of mass outreach to the nations (Hom. Lev. 10.1.4). If its observances had continued, he says, the health and growth of the church would have been hindered. With the temple and its rites eliminated, however – bridging now to Galatians 4:9 – he fails to see how anyone could reasonably 'turn again to the weak and worthless elements' (Hom. Lev. 10.2.3).[7] Regression returns to the surface in his *Homilies on Jeremiah*, providing ammunition for a withering critique of scrupulous sabbath observances (Hom. Jer. 12.13.1). And, in his commentary on John's prologue, Origen reaches for it again, this time to explain what he considers the typically Gentile tendency to drift over time from worship aimed directly at the incarnate

---

5 On the *Dialogue* as a witness to Jewish–Christian interactions, see Horner 2001: 181–185; Murray 2003: 91–99.

6 Justin immediately concedes that not all Christians are so generous (Dial. 47.2).

7 The implication that returning to the *stoicheia* is a sign of 'weakness' for Origen is interesting in and of itself given the proximity we've detected between Paul's pastoral strategy in Galatians and his subsequent teaching about the weak and the strong in 1 Corinthians and Romans.

Son to worship mediated through the Jewish law that points to him (Comm. Jo. 2.21–33).[8]

By far the most substantial and interesting interaction with regression in Origen's writings, however, is found in his *Homilies on Exodus* where Galatians is used as a commentary on the ongoing influence of Egypt in the lives of the Israelites even after their redemption from slavery. Origen's preference for 'spiritual interpretations' might be a little bit disorienting for us here. In the passage where Moses heals the waters at Marah (Exod. 15:26), he takes the waters as an image of the law, the wood Moses throws into them as an image of the gospel and 'the diseases of the Egyptians' from which God promises to deliver them – on condition of obedience – as love of the world and the observation of 'days and months and times... [seeking] for signs [and clinging] to the courses of the stars' (Hom. Ex. 7:1–2, citing and expanding on Gal. 4:10).[9] The underlying point, however, is fascinating. The Israelites in the story *don't* satisfy the condition of obedience, and they return to the norms of their pagan past. They claim to worship the God who delivered them from Egypt (Exod. 32:4), but in reality they worship a golden calf, rearticulating the familiar idolatry of their former lives. And this for Origen is the lesson for today. Embracing Jewish Law is turning from pure water back to bitter water. It may be aimed at the God of the Bible in name, but the underlying motive, the underlying attraction, the underlying vacuum it fills, is pagan.[10]

2 Resisting Regression – Tertullian, Cyprian, Origen

In his book, *The Patient Ferment of the Early Church*, Alan Kreider confronts us with portraits – gathered mainly from the second, third and fourth centuries – of churches that still understood the significance of habituated pagan expectations in the process of Christian discipleship. His conclusion – that their catechetical practices were deliberately designed to overwrite converts' former habits, replacing them with Christian reflexes capable of withstanding

---

8 A similar logic undergirds Origen's citation from Galatians 4:10–11 in Contra Celsum (Cels. 8.21).

9 In his homilies on Joshua, the wilderness wanderings of the Israelites are likened to the period of catechetical instruction prior to baptism designed to purge the candidates of 'the darkness of idolatry' which they have only 'recently forsaken' (Hom. Jos. 4.1).

10 Commenting on Exodus 5:23 in Hom. Ex. 3.3, Origen highlights the fact that it is only when a person has stood up in resistance to their religious past that it begins to trouble them and to exert a contrary force on their affections. Sensing the same dynamic at work in his congregation, he urges them, like the Israelites, but using the words of Galatians 5:1: 'Stand, therefore, and do not again submit to the yoke of slavery.'

immersion in a pagan society – is strikingly relevant for our work in Galatians. Here we have not just letters and sermons but tangible examples of what it meant for Christian communities to put Paul's vision of accommodation and spiritual growth into practice, and glimpses, perhaps, of what it might mean to embody it today.

In *The Martyrdom of Perpetua and Felicitas*, set in Carthage in AD 200 and edited in the view of many by the noted Christian convert and author Tertullian, we meet two women of different ages and social classes who, in the extremity of their suffering in the arena, revert not to familiar pagan patterns of superiority and inferiority but to Christian patterns of sisterhood deliberately instilled by regular repetition through the practice of the church.[11] Tertullian places a similar emphasis on intentionally displacing pagan norms when he contrasts Christian gatherings with the private associations or *collegia* that served as social hubs for pagans with similar professional and religious interests in the period. Their leaders are chosen not 'by rota or "for a price" but because of their maturity and character' (Apol. 39.4). They welcome members irrespective of their sex, status or financial means.[12] Their focus is on discipline, and on 'internalising the teachings of Christ'.[13] This picture sheds light on Tertullian's description of his own conversion, emerging from the pagan society he embraced as a younger man and shedding its assumptions. 'Christians are made, not born,' he famously tells us (Apol. 18.4). Discipleship involves 'reformation of character' through a deliberate process of replacing former actions and former expectations with new ones (Apol. 3.3–4).

Remaining in Carthage and moving forward a single generation, the biography of Bishop Cyprian tells a similar story. In his Letter to Donatus, Cyprian looks back on his former bondage to the 'innumerable errors of [his] previous life' – practices and modes of thought that, either innate or acquired, had 'become inveterate by long accustomed use' and 'radically ingrained' (Don. 3–4). The tipping point, he tells us, came at his baptism – conjuring up a vision of immediate deliverance from the baggage of his former life, perhaps, if we think, as modern Christians tend to think, of baptism as a *start point* for Christian discipleship and not as a milestone along the journey. But for Cyprian and his contemporaries, the proper place of baptism was considerably later in the process, after a period of catechetical formation typically lasting *several years*, and focused on laying down new habits and new practices

---

11 Shaw 1993: 30–31.
12 Kreider 2016: 56–62.
13 Kreider 2016: 57.

in place of their destructive predecessors.[14] Even when baptism lay in the distant past, Cyprian urged vigilance, lest 'the old enemy creep upon us again' (Don. 4). Emerging from, and surrounded by, a pagan culture, Cyprian was hyper-aware of the lingering influence of former religious habits and the vital importance of confronting and replacing them in the new life of Christian discipleship.

Origen embodies a similar vision, likening catechesis to the Israelites' journey through the wilderness, and baptism to the crossing of the Jordan in yet another interpretative variation on the Exodus story (Hom. Jos. 4.1). Catechumens, he tells us, should begin with a diet of 'milk' – light on profound spiritual truths and heavy on 'the correction of morals and amendment of discipline' (Hom. Judic. 5.6). Former patterns of behaviour and their associated expectations should have been identified and deliberately weakened before the serious building could begin. Participants in the process were kept at a distance from full participation in the Christian community until their period of probation was completed.[15] The approach seems scarcely believable from the vantage point of modern evangelistic rallies pushing for conversions and hoping discipleship will somehow take care of itself. But this is the infrastructure that propelled the church through what history now reveals to have been a period of staggering growth.[16]

3 Disregarding Regression – Gregory Thaumaturgus, Gregory the Great

Even within this period, however, scrupulous pastoral awareness of the kinds of danger that Tertullian, Cyprian and Origen detected in their congregants' habituated pagan norms – and that Paul detected in the habituated norms of his readers in Galatia – was not quite as uniform as we might hope. Kreider himself identifies a worrying break with the established pattern in the ministry of Gregory Thaumaturgus, whose fast-paced contribution to the Christianization of Pontus in northern Asia Minor depended more on his gifts as a charismatic speaker and wonder-worker than on the kind of cumbersome catechetical infrastructure favoured by his slower-moving contemporaries. Gregory believed his hearers would accept Christ more readily if they were

---

14 Kreider 2016: 152–178.
15 Kreider 2016: 178–182.
16 For adventurous and conservative estimates of early church growth see Stark 1996: 4–13 and MacMullen 2009: 98–104, respectively.

allowed to preserve their familiar pagan practices, albeit in suitably altered forms. Noticing the popularity of *Refrigeria* – banquets held in veneration of the dead at local burial grounds and generally accompanied by a good deal of drinking and merrymaking – Gregory repurposed these occasions as commemorations of local Christian martyrs.[17] His expectation, according to his biographer, Gregory of Nyssa, was that 'when with the passage of time their life had been naturally transformed to what is more noble [and] more and more strict, their faith would be directed to that end' (Life of Gregory 95–96). Paul, one suspects, would have questioned whether this would indeed have been a 'natural' development.

The same transmutation in missionary tactics can be seen in progress in the career of Pope Gregory the Great (AD 540–604). In the course of two letters written within a month of each other to King Æthelbert of Kent (c. 589–616) and to the Abbott Mellitus, both preserved in Bede's *Ecclesiastical History of the English People*, Gregory articulates a shift in strategy from the destruction of pagan shrines on the northern frontiers of Christendom (Ecc. Hist. 1.32) to a new approach involving the preservation of existing holy sites and festal days in the hope that they could be repurposed for Christian worship (Ecc. Hist. 1.30). James Russell believes this led directly to the 'Germanization' of Christianity in Europe in the seventh and eighth centuries.[18] There is, of course, no question that Gregory *intended* to create a doctrinal hybrid. His plan was simply to embrace the externals of pagan religion in order 'to facilitate a smooth transition' to orthodox Christian worship.[19] But, as Carol Cusack notes perceptively, 'form and content are not so easily separable... form sometimes determines content'.[20] And this, of course, is exactly the danger that seems to have so troubled Paul in Galatia.

Ignoring it bequeathed to future generations a Christianity with direct lines of descent back to the burial customs and sacrifices of paganism.[21] In theology, pagan warfare vocabulary was adopted to express key Christian concepts of sin and salvation.[22] In literature, Beowulf emerged in a Christianized world, engaging in Davidic conflict with the offspring of Cain (*Beowulf*

---

17 Though martyr-day celebrations are considerably better documented, the practices associated with pagan *Refrigeria* are still accessible to us through archaeological sources and poetic fragments (see MacMullen 2009: 76–80).

18 Russell 1994: 183–184.

19 Cusack 1998: 179.

20 Cusack 1998: 179. See also Russell 1994: 180.

21 Cusack 1998: 76–77, 109.

22 Russell 1994: 40, 163, 206.

102–114, 1260–1268) but with the ethics of a traditional Germanic hero.[23] In the Saxon retelling of the canonical gospel narratives, *Hêliand*, Jesus mutates into a great chieftain with a retinue of warrior – companions, travelling between the 'hill forts' of Judea, and entrusting the Lord's prayer to his followers as a repository of 'secret runes'.[24]

In some situations, pre-existent pagan religious norms survived as an act of conscious, principled resistance to the unwelcome imposition of Christianity.[25] But in others more like the situation described in Galatians, the process was unconscious. Careless evangelists left a 'void' where old convictions and old practices used to be, and the 'sense of loss… created the conditions for a restoration of the old faith, only slightly altered'.[26]

4 Regression and Retrojection – Luther

Much has been written about the exegetical strengths and missteps of Martin Luther in the debate between Old and New Perspectives over recent decades, based more often than it ought to be on caricatures of the great Reformer's thought instead of nuanced readings of his own material. Stephen Chester's book *Reading Paul With the Reformers* has done a great deal to challenge and change this situation and I, for one, stand in his debt for the unusual clarity he brings to the themes of law, grace and righteousness in Christ – both in Luther's thought and in the writings of other leading Reformation scholars, each of whom had their own particular emphases and parts to play in the development of the larger movement. Chester forcefully challenges several orthodoxies of contemporary Pauline scholarship – not least the idea that Luther espoused an entirely extrinsic, even 'fictional', vision of justification, or Krister Stendahl's influential suggestion that mainstream Christian teaching about 'salvation' owes more to Luther's introspective conscience that it does to Paul's actual experience of conversion/commissioning.[27] One element of the modern

---

23 Cusack 1998: 110–111; Russell 1994: 178–179.

24 Cusack 1998: 129–130.

25 Russell 1994: 142, 159. From a very different cultural context, Nicolas Saunders' account of the retention of pre-Columbian religious norms in Mesoamerica after the Spanish conquest through the surreptitious use of the sacred stone, obsidian, in crosses and church buildings, is a paradigmatic example of syncretism as principled resistance (Saunders 2001: 220–236).

26 Taylor 2007: 441. See also Cusack 1998: 178.

27 For stereotypical portrayals of Luther on both these fronts, see Eisenbaum 2009: 48–54. For Chester's nuanced response, see Chester 2017: 121–135, 175–217, 341–346. On extrinsic righteousness, note Chester's helpful emphasis on union with Christ in Luther's thought and the contrast with Melanchthon (Chester 2017: 183–193, 241–261).

critique that emerges unscathed from his analysis, however, is the frequently repeated assertion that Luther read the excesses of medieval Catholicism back into the Judaism of the first century.[28]

Allusions to this feature of Luther's work in contemporary Pauline scholarship are often unsubstantiated, and even when citations are provided, on closer inspection, the parallels have more to do with the relationship between Catholic practice and Judaism *as Luther knew it* than Catholic practice and Judaism *as it existed in the time of Paul*.[29] That he believed this deeper level of relationship existed, however, is undeniable. In his lectures on Galatians 3:2, a striking aside on Acts makes the point explicit:

> *Thus in Acts you will find the comments, the experiences, and the sermons of the apostles, as well as examples in support of this argument against the stubborn notion of the righteousness of the Law. For this reason we ought to love this book more and read it more diligently; for it contains very firm testimonies that can comfort and sustain us against the papists,* who are our Jews *and whose abominations and pretenses we attack and condemn by our doctrine in order that we may make clear the blessings and the glory of Christ.*[30]

Or again in his lectures on Isaiah 28:15:

> *Thus the monk says: 'If I have kept my vow, I cannot possibly be lost,' and he draws the conclusion: 'Everyone who has kept this rule, has eternal life.' There, faith, fear, and the Word of God are neglected, and they rely on their traditions, convinced that if they keep these, neither death nor hell can harm them. We see this covenant very plainly in the rules and monastic orders of the papists,* and such were the Jews. *Trusting in their own righteousness, they rejected Christ.*[31]

---

28 See Chester 2017: 3, 361.

29 Dunn states boldly that, 'as Luther had rejected a medieval church which offered salvation by merit and good works, the same, it was assumed, was true of Paul in relation to the Judaism of his day' (Dunn 2006b: 336–337). The citation from Luther's *Table Talk* used to justify this claim, however, is drawn from a discussion of Anton Margaritha's *Der gantze Jüdisch Glaub*, focused on the relationship between Catholicism and contemporary Jewish practice (see Luther 1967, vol. 54: 436–437). The same thing applies to Saperstein's excerpts from *On the Jews and Their Lies* and *Against the Sabbatarians* (see Saperstein 1989: 30; Luther 1971, vol. 47: 65–66, 177).

30 Luther 1963, vol. 26: 207–208; emphasis mine.

31 Luther 1969, vol. 16: 228; emphasis mine.

Recognizing and wrestling with this feature of Luther's theology forces Chester into a delicate balancing act. On the one hand he acknowledges its implicit misrepresentation of first-century Judaism – Judaism was not, and never should have been, positioned as a monochrome legalistic foil to Paul's theology of grace. But on the other hand, he affirms the juridical roots of Paul's justification language and resists the suggestion that it can be entirely explained by appealing to the boundary-marking function of legal observances.[32] Jews *must* have believed their works played some kind of role in establishing status with God for Paul's logic to work. Following Gathercole, Chester appeals to their significance in final justification.[33]

Whatever the strengths and weaknesses of this assessment of works in Jewish thought, however, the question posed in *this* book is whether this both/and reading is really what the text of Galatians *demands*. If Paul was not, in fact, critiquing Judaism in his remarks about law at all, but a pagan misappropriation of Judaism – a misappropriation driven by habitual exposure to pagan religious norms and pagan attitudes to religious works – *and if Luther had known it* – the parallel he strove to establish between the abuses of his own time and the situation into which Paul wrote might have come out very differently.

Luther was reading Galatians in a world that had lost touch with the importance of regression. Judaism was the problem the letter appeared to deal with, and Judaism was consequently the natural target for comparison with similar problems in the present. But if Luther had read the text like Ignatius or Origen, it's hard to imagine he could have made the same mistake.[34] Luther was living in an era when the thing Paul opposed *really had* become mainstream Christianity; his error was simply his assumption that the thing was *Judaism*.[35] Luther was living in an era when the church had embraced *pagan* norms in the hope that their adherents would advance more readily, and thus more rapidly,

---

32 'If it is unconvincing to understand obedience to the whole law almost exclusively in terms of self-achieved works-righteousness, is it any more convincing to understand it almost exclusively in terms of the boundary-marking function of the works performed?' (Chester 2017: 349).

33 Chester 2017: 352–354.

34 Fascinatingly, Chester sees something very close to this insight in the works of John Calvin. Calvin, he tells us, 'refuses to find anything inherently wrong with the Jewish practices of Paul's opponents' (Chester 2017: 141). And then he quotes from Calvin's commentary on Galatians 2:14–15: 'The use of ceremonies for edification was free so long as believers were not deprived of their liberty... Paul was worried not so much about ceremonies being observed as that the confidence and glory of salvation should be transferred to works' (see Calvin 1854:65).

35 Might the realization that defending the gospel against Medieval Catholicism *did not*, in fact, entail a balancing denigration of Judaism have moderated the gross excesses of Luther's later anti-Semitism, expressed most infamously in his 1543 tract, *On the Jews and their lies* (Luther 1971, vol. 47: 121–306)? One can only hope so.

to spiritual maturity. But the result had been the very opposite. Read with this understanding of the context, Luther's parallel wasn't so much wrong as it was *misaimed*. He *thought* he was reacting against a Christianity with Jewish underpinnings. What he was reacting against, in fact, however, was a Christianity still carrying within itself the religious norms of paganism – norms acquired along a journey stretching from first-century Asia Minor all the way to medieval Europe.

14

Challenges and Opportunities for the Present

Introduction

Reading within the larger story of the church's emergence from the Patristic era and its journey via the Reformation to the present day, we're better equipped, perhaps, to approach the storm and stress of contemporary debates about Old and New Perspectives on Paul with a proper sense of proportion. But none of this dulls the significance of the issues at stake.

In Galatians, Paul begins on a note of grace: 'Grace and peace to you from God our Father and the Lord Jesus Christ' (Gal. 1:3). But what *was* this grace? The question no longer admits a simple answer. Was it God's Riches At Christ's Expense, as the old mnemonic goes – with 'characteristically Jewish' scrambling to foot the bill ourselves as the foil? Or was it acceptance in the community of believers for everyone and an end to circumcision and other traditional Jewish 'boundary markers' in the process – nothing to do, in fact, with striving to impress God or its futility, but a watchword for the new age of Gentile inclusion? Was 'grace' Paul's way of stressing God's role as the initiative taker reaching out to humanity, or was it something more radical? Was it his way of positioning God as the incongruous giver, blessing the unlovely in spite of their unloveliness? And where did it *come from*? Was it a product of Paul's conversion *from* Judaism, signalling the scale of his renunciation of the legal observances that marked his past? Or was it in itself a Jewish concept – or at least a *recovery* of a Jewish concept – a product of Paul's commission as a prophet *within* Judaism to preach Jesus as the Jewish Messiah with a host of recognizably Jewish consequences?

Reconsidering Galatians has led us to an unfamiliar coalition of responses to these familiar questions. By and large we've *affirmed* traditional readings of faith and works in Paul – here indeed is the great negation of the idea that God's favour can be *earned*. But none of this has implied or required the traditional 'balancing' assertion that *Jews* thought otherwise. The problem Paul was pastoring in Galatia flowed directly from his readers' *pagan* preconceptions.

We've affirmed the *unity* of Jews and Gentiles in Christ, but we've discovered, in the process, that each group required *different* pastoral responses when it came to questions about the law. The whole letter, in fact, tells us as much about pastoral and missiological good sense as it does about first principles in theology, especially when we read it in the context of Paul's larger commitment to accommodating the particular vulnerabilities of the weak.

And all of this has lead us to some striking conclusions. If embracing Jewish law in Galatia really meant going backwards to a *pagan* past, *Judaism itself was not the problem*. The problem, at least as far as Paul perceived it, was pagan religious *habits* – the deep-rooted connections that existed between the offerings and festivals that characterized the Galatians' past and the sense that, by doing these things, it was possible for them to gain some small measure of control over their future. *That set of assumptions* was coming back to life among Paul's readers, summoned by their immersion in the superficially similar practices of Jewish Christianity. The problem wasn't the practices themselves, of course – food laws, festivals, circumcision – which obviously embodied completely different expectations for the Agitators who promoted them *whatever conclusions we come to about who they were and where they came from*. The problem was the pagan assumptions these practices reawakened – the whole system of interacting, and negotiating, with the gods that accompanied them as an intruder into the Galatians' new relationship with the God of Israel. Paul never intended to position *Jewish law itself* as a threat in Galatians, he never dreamed of institutionalizing Christian aversion to Jews or the Jewish scriptures. Sure, he saw the acute danger of imagining God could be *incentivized* to bless his people. But he didn't see it in Moses. He saw it in the assumptions that had been pressed into his hearers through their life-long exposure to pagan religious norms.

Justification as Paul used the word, then, absolutely had to do with the status of divine–human relations. It stood for acquittal *in God's court* – for inclusion, acceptance, righteousness *in God's sight*, neither obtained, nor augmented, by religious actions. But for Paul, this didn't stand in contrast to Judaism – this was a fundamentally *Jewish* idea. The problem in Galatia was the Galatians' perception that they had a part to play in cultivating divine goodwill, and justification by faith was Paul's devastating counterpunch. God couldn't be obliged to give his people what they wanted or perceived themselves to deserve, and it was madness to imagine otherwise if they grasped, even in the faintest outline, the superiority of his foresight and beneficence, and the depth of their indebtedness.

Neither was Paul's emphasis on transformation by the Spirit a mere afterthought, disconnected from the remainder of the letter. It was a vital, forward-looking prescription for the Galatians' growth and resilience. Paul understood enough of his readers' past to sense – and fear – the triggers that could bring it back from the dead. But he wasn't content just to wrap his readers up in cotton wool and hope they never encountered anything like it again. Sure, he began by barking out commands designed to extract them from immediate danger. But at the same time, he urged them to embrace a programme of inner renewal capable of overwriting their former spiritual instincts, gradually withering well-worn mental pathways and substituting weakness with strength.

And all of this receives an extra twist when we begin to see how this dominant concern for Paul – this issue that stands in the background of Galatians and which resurfaces in the form of detailed, positive teaching in 1 Corinthians and Romans eclipsing, if sheer column inches are a reliable guide, every other ecclesiological topic he covers in the process – has faded from view almost completely over subsequent centuries. All who share the conviction that all scripture has relevance for all God's people at all times will doubtless be disturbed to think that this could ever have happened.

But still the question remains – what is the relevance of all this for the present day? Our churches are no longer populated with former devotees of Cybele and Zeus. And much though it might interest us – and help us – to read Paul against this background, it doesn't change the fact that the pagan religious rituals of first-century Galatia are long forgotten. Doesn't locating the problem Paul sought to address in his readers' pagan background rob Galatians of its capacity for contemporary application even more effectively than attaching it to the rites and mores or first-century Judaism?

1 Pagan Post-Modernity

The purpose of this final chapter is to begin, at least in some small way, to expose how very wrong this assumption is, and how very important and urgent it is for the church to wake up and realize it. Though the rites and rituals of Zeus and Cybele may well be dead and buried, *the assumptions they embodied are alive and well,* and all the more potent for the fact that we fail to recognize them for what they are.

Think back with me to our work on the context of Galatians, turning your mind from the 'what?' to the 'why?' *Why* did Graeco-Roman pagans in the first century make offerings to the gods, and celebrate their festivals, and comply with their prescriptions? The question is broad, and any answers we give here must reflect this breadth – and the difficulties of interpreting the data that remains to us. 'It was tradition.'[1] 'It was fear.'[2] 'It was the desire to define and police communal "forms of life".'[3] None of these one-size-fits-all explanations will do. All of them played a part, no doubt, in the whole we're trying to describe, but none of them can describe it adequately on its own. Throughout this book we've resisted essentialist portraits of the situation Paul wrote to address, seeking instead to present an *envelope* of motivational possibilities in the Galatians' religious background. But however we draw the boundaries of that envelope there's no avoiding the conclusion that, to a greater or lesser degree, every probable reconstruction of first-century Galatian society includes the idea that human actions could effectively incentivize the gods to bless.

For some, that belief was very tentative: 'I participate in this rite *in the hope* that my chances of blessing will be improved, or that my chances of being cursed will be reduced.' For others, it was confident, perhaps even manipulative: 'I make this offering and I place it in the sight line of my god in the *expectation* of her response. I've honoured her more than my neighbours, and I expect to be blessed more than my neighbours. I've entrusted articles of value to her and she will act now to defend what is hers.'

But either way, whether faltering or forceful, the underlying ethos here includes the sense that *something* can be done, that there is something *I can do*, to promote favourable relations with the gods, or with fate, or with whatever it is that I perceive to stand as a gatekeeper to the blessings I desire. There is *something* I can do in the present to maximize the possibility of blessing in the future. *And this is the assumption that still drives the societies we live in.* We may not express it through devotion to obscure first-century deities, but as citizens of the post-modern world, the conviction that we can maximize our personal chances of blessing *by what we do* is as fundamental to our sense that life is worth living, as its erosion is fundamental to our experience of despair.

The world around us shouts that investments in our careers will bring us the futures we crave. If we act smart in the present, if we follow our dreams, if we give ourselves to the process of gaining qualifications and building networks, our chances of blessing will be improved. And if it doesn't happen, we can feel rightly aggrieved. We do what's needed, and we expect to be rewarded. We make sacrifices for our career and we observe its rites and festivals. And in return we get a seat at the table, and cards in our hands, in our negotiation with whatever it is we think controls our future.

---

1 See Parker 2011: 3.

2 See Arnold 2005: 435; Wilson 2007: 72–79.

3 The use of the phrase, 'form of life', hints here at a Wittgensteinian interpretation of pagan religious actions. See Wittgenstein 2009: §241.

Fitness and physical appearance are the same. If we act smart, if we follow our dreams, if we give ourselves to the process of getting that look, of hitting that weight, of achieving that time, our chances of receiving the future we long for will be improved. And if for some reason, by birth or lack of opportunity, we're unable, if or if we try and try but ultimately fail, we shouldn't be surprised to find ourselves cursed as those who simply don't have what's needed to live as real equals with those who succeed, at least as long as they retain their capacity to stay ahead in the game.

For career, fitness and physical appearance, read attitudes to wealth, social networks, shopping, following the right influencers, attaching ourselves to the right causes. None of these things is wrong in and of itself. Paul, remember, was surprisingly relaxed about his readers' *practices* (Gal. 5:6; 6:15). The problem was the expectations that guided them. And here I think the warning lights that were flashing in Galatians should be flashing for us too. Because, without any of the superficial paraphernalia of paganism, the expectations we've just observed in our own world, and the ruthless calculus that underpins them, are transparently the same.

2 Running on the Rails of Ritual

'But even if present-day expectations are similar to ancient pagan expectations,' we might say, 'still none of this *really* brings us into the orbit of Galatians. In Galatians, the problem, was the connection between expectations *and rituals*. It was the connection between believing that actions in the present led to blessings in the future and the rituals that embodied that belief among Paul's readers. That's what made Jewish Christianity so dangerous for them. But we don't have anything like that today.'

And, of course, this argument has some superficial appeal. But it only takes a moment's thought to realize it's grossly overoptimistic.

Jamie Smith's tremendously insightful *Cultural Liturgies* project provides us with the tools we need to explore this question more adequately.[4] For Smith, the entire basis of ordinary human behaviour is bound up with rituals that drive pre-conditioned responses to our environment. This isn't an observation about the norms of specific cultures. It's an observation about basic human

---

4 *Cultural Liturgies* spans three full length books (*Desiring the Kingdom* – Smith 2009; *Imagining the Kingdom* – Smith 2013; *Awaiting the King* – Smith: 2017) complemented by an accessible introduction (*You Are What You Love* – Smith 2016). My summary here draws, in particular, on Smith's interaction with the philosopher, Maurice Merleau-Ponty, and the anthropologist, philosopher and sociologist, Pierre Bourdieu, in the first part of *Imagining the Kingdom*, entitled 'Incarnate Significance: The Body as Background' (Smith 2013: 29–100).

functioning in a complex world. At every moment our senses are bombarded with an unmanageable array of stimuli, far too great to submit to conscious one-by-one decision-making.[5] We survive and thrive thanks to our ability to recognize patterns and deploy pre-formed responses that bypass the process of conscious cognition. Some of the patterns are simple and functional – say, unloading the dishwasher, or responding to a drop shot on a tennis court. We tidy away the plates and glasses, we scamper to the net and make the next shot in the rally, running on rails formed and fettled in the past, our conscious minds providing little more than 'guiding tweaks' along the way. But even complex moral judgments share the same characteristic subservience to pre-formed routines.[6] Across the board, our responses to new circumstances depend to a surprising extent on what we've seen and done *before*.

Absence of outward, organized religious rituals, then, is no argument against the significance of ritualized behaviours in our lives. The neo-pagan expectations that guide our thinking about career, fitness and so many other aspects of contemporary life are reinforced in 'rituals' that escape our notice all the time – whenever we go to the mall, whenever we submit an essay, whenever we get, or fail to get, a pay rise or a promotion. And the connections between our expectations and our actions are so tenacious that even when the stimuli that confront us at any given moment are only obliquely related to those with which a particular expectation was originally associated, that expectation will still rise unbidden to the mind as the best-fitting response available.[7]

The point is brilliantly and poignantly illustrated in Bessel van der Kolk's book *The Body Keeps the Score*, reflecting on the author's long career researching and developing treatments for psychological trauma.[8] At the point of their

---

5 Smith 2013: 49–53.

6 'It's not that beliefs about can-openers and changing diapers are housed in the body while big, ethical, metaphysical beliefs about God and justice are reserved for the mind… practical sense is comprehensive,' Smith 2013: 88.

7 'Every social order systematically takes advantage of the disposition of the body and language to function as depositories of deferred thoughts that can be triggered off at a distance in space and time by the simple effect of re-placing the body in an overall posture which *recalls* the associated thoughts and feelings, in one of the inductive states of the body which, as actors know, give rise to states of mind' (Bourdieu 1990: 69).

8 van der Kolk: 2014. The realization that patterns of thought *attach* to the patterns of action we have associated with them in the past, and that re-exposure to the same or similar patterns of action brings those patterns of thought back to the mind threatens the intellectualist dogma of mind as the master and body as the servant (Smith 2013: 33–35, 57). But it nonetheless forms the basis for an increasingly broad range of effective trauma therapies. EDMR (Eye Movement Desensitization Reprogramming) capitalizes on the close association between REM (Rapid Eye Movement) sleep and the ability to escape well-worn mental pathways and make new, creative connections. By stimulating rapid eye movements in fully conscious subjects, EDMR interrupts the otherwise automatic transition from trauma triggers to the flashbacks associated with them (van der Kolk 2014: 248–262).

original formation, our habits derive from the expectations that form them. The expectation of extreme danger drives a soldier on the battlefield to repeat and repeat the drill of dismantling, cleaning and reassembling his gun. But the connection between expectation and habit becomes so deep-seated that, even after the war is over, any action vaguely resembling cleaning a gun brings the same sensation of fear flooding back into his mind, driven simply by the bodily postures and movements with which it has become entangled. Loud and unexpected sounds trigger flashbacks for the survivor of a car crash. Certain types of rooms, certain types of gestures, reactivate the shame and isolation of the victim of abuse, especially if the abuse happened repeatedly and at an early stage in their development.[9]

None of this should strike us as particularly outlandish.[10] Paul demonstrates his awareness of the same kinds of connections when he urges 'the strong' in Corinth not to take their weaker brothers along with them to eat in idol temples (1 Cor. 8:4–13). He doesn't doubt that the weak share the strong's monotheistic convictions. His fear is just that, if they're put back in the same kinds of situation where their pagan religious expectations formed, they'll find themselves offering devotion to the gods again *irrespective of their convictions*, simply through the power of habit.[11] And the same thing is inescapably true today. If we've grown up, and if young Christians in our churches have grown up, repeatedly reinforcing neo-pagan expectations in the daily patterns of our lives – in the rituals of what we watch, what we aim for and who we follow – exposure to similar patterns in the church can't fail to reactivate the same patterns of thought. Just like the Galatians, we'll find ourselves pursuing Christ with motives that owe less to the Bible than they do to the norms of the world around us, undermining the authenticity of the whole.

---

9 My illustrations in this paragraph synthesize elements from a variety of case studies provided by van der Kolk.

10 See Keener 2016: 260–261.

11 Clearly there is a danger of anachronism here, and it would be a great mistake to rescue Paul from 'The Introspective Conscience of the West' (Stendahl 1963) only to shackle him to a *psychological* alternative. But while we absolutely shouldn't read modern insights and hang-ups back into the experience of Paul and his contemporaries, we absolutely *should* take them seriously as real human beings whose habits influenced their responses to new circumstances just as ours do today. We may have new and more sophisticated ways of *describing* these effects at our disposal, but that doesn't mean *the effects themselves* are new or irrelevant to our understanding of ancient realities.

3 Making It Tangible

So what does this look like in practice? Let me highlight just a few obvious areas where the norms of church are perhaps particularly apt to reawaken the counter-Christian expectations drilled into us by our culture.

Think with me for a moment about sung worship. If we've grown up in the church, perhaps this seems like the most natural thing in the world and all the connections that exist between our actions and expectations are thoroughly conformed to the biblical paradigm of wholehearted devotion to God. For the majority of us, though, given the range of our other influences, I can't help wondering if that's really *all* that's happening when we sing in church. For young Christians just beginning on the journey of discipleship, it's surely reckless to assume that this portfolio of mature reactions will simply snap into place without recognizing the shape and power of the incumbent alternatives.

Where else have we encountered public communal singing and what expectations have become entwined with it in the process? For many, the relevant background here is the rock concert – the crowd energy, the escapism, the sense of buying into a particular musical brand. We go to hear the music *we like* with people *who like it too*, gathering in praise of the performers on the stage. Are those expectations being reawakened in the way we do church? The answer doesn't necessarily have to do with the musical style we adopt, but it certainly has a lot to do with the way we frame it. Or perhaps the relevant background is the sports stadium? The familiar chants cultivating atmosphere and anticipation, the sense of being part of a larger organism. Or perhaps it's the memory of our own attempts at musical performance in the past – singing and being praised, or feeling ashamed because we can't. Not all of this is bad, but there's clearly danger here in any model of church music that doesn't recognize and mitigate the risks associated with the parts of it that are.

Or what about the way we preach? I'm not talking about the content here, so much as the pedagogical model we employ and the expectations associated with it. Obviously, the text itself has to dictate the strategy of the teacher to a large extent, and there are certainly texts that gravitate around lists of virtues to embrace and vices to avoid – we dealt with one in Galatians itself in Chapter 11, hopefully setting it in its larger context in the process. But when *every* sermon has this flavour – when every sermon lands on three ways to change your life, three ways to be a better you, three ways to succeed as a father or a mother, three ways to spruce up your approach to evangelism – I think we're running back into the same problematic territory, quite apart from the larger question of whether these messages really do justice to the overarching story of the Bible.

Where else do we encounter these kinds of narrative? We encounter them *in the mall*. 'Three ways to get a new look and fit in with the crowd this autumn.' We all know it's disposable, it's fast fashion. There's no expectation of commitment, it just signals a deficiency, and a low-hanging way to fix it. Or maybe it's the self-help book. Here at least there's a little more personal investment, but still the idea is that the changes I need to make *lie within my power*. If I follow these three steps and overcome these three obstacles, I'll realize my dreams. And some of the advice is doubtless helpful. But the model is profoundly destructive if it's reactivated in the church. Or what about the workplace annual review? 'Here are the three things you're doing well and the three things you need to improve on if...' If *what*? If you want to get a promotion? Now we've landed in the world of upward increments and rewards, visceralizing the idea that what I have is mine and what I don't have is something I should be ready to compete for. None of this has anything to do with the ethic of grace Paul is seeking to establish and protect.

What about Christian conference publicity? This may seem like a niche issue, but it illustrates a larger problem. Even in the smallest, most culturally insular enclaves of contemporary Christianity we've all seen the way this is done. 'Here is our conference, and here are *our speakers* and here are THEIR PHOTOS. And here are *the issues* they'll be bringing within the realm of our comprehension. (And here, if you're lucky, are the Bible texts they'll be expounding.)'

What pre-formed connections between familiar rituals and their associated expectations is all this triggering? Perhaps it draws on patterns of behaviour and assumptions associated with the business world? We see the flyers and immediately we think, 'These are the people who are higher paid, these are the people who are big successes, these are the people who fly business class.' Or perhaps it's the world of celebrities and fans? 'This is the person I want to be but they'll never stoop low enough to engage in my life. I live out my aspirations *through* them. I don't embrace the sacrifices required to actually move the needle myself. I critique them from a distance and I move from celebrity to celebrity, not surprised by their risings and fallings.'

Are these really the kind of assumptions and expectations we want to trigger in the hearts of God's people when we organize Christian events? What are we thinking? I hate to be so blunt here but aren't these messages profoundly irresponsible? This is like screening adverts for alcohol and cigarettes on children's TV. We have absolutely *no idea* who's reading this stuff and no visibility at all on their backgrounds and their consequent vulnerabilities. Why can't someone organize a conference with the simple message, 'Come and hear Jesus

Christ speaking through his word – we'll do our best not to get in his way,' or at least showcase the churches that are represented ahead of the individuals who lead them?

Paul, I think, would be tearing his hair out if he could see us. There are acute dangers here for the pastors and for the 'fans' involved, as recent church history makes only too clear. And even the way we respond when things go wrong is controlled more by expectations formed in our culture than by the Bible. Where have we suddenly got the idea that social media is an appropriate forum to resolve issues of pastoral malpractice, where every reflex it triggers in us is about being slow to listen, quick to speak and quick to become angry (cf. Jas 1:19)? Our whole approach to the phenomenon of 'the well-known minister' represents a gigantic overestimate of our spiritual resilience, and a gigantic failure to even notice the fact that the expectations of our culture, and of our pre-Christian past, will continue to shape us if we don't recognize them and respond with creative alternatives, embracing the process of spiritual transformation that can help us live in a world that keeps shouting this stuff at us without losing our way.

4 Exhortation

Galatians, I confess, used to be something of a dead letter to me. This was the book of the Bible to go to when we were tempted to start behaving and thinking more Jewishly. And I, for one, wasn't tempted – at least in the terms in which traditional exegeses presented it. It also had a reputation as a preachers' graveyard. Paul comes down incredibly hard on the danger of embracing *Jewish* works in this text. And if that's the point – if that's the enduring lesson – it stretches our ability to explain and apply it week after week beyond the bounds of possibility for most ordinary mortals. In some hands it justifies a witch-hunt against legalism, breeding suspicion of the Old Testament and legalisms of its own along the way. In others it leads to clumsy redefinitions of justification. None of this, I think, really reflects Paul's original intent.

But now I see Galatians as a radical prophetic summons to the church – not just to the church of its time, but to the church of the present day. It speaks – indeed it shouts – to the underlying paganism of the post-modern world. The danger of regressing to the conviction that we can make the future give us what we want has never been more relevant. We live in societies *given over* to this quest, and to the belief that we can accomplish it. And this is a target preachers can *really* get their teeth into.

Paul can't be restricted to speaking through a letter box about the temptation to get circumcised and any spurious parallels we can imagine in the modern world. In this, his most pastorally urgent letter, he's throwing open the barn door and applying the full weight of his gospel concern to the whole of our lives. Paul isn't content for us to press on blindly with the memory of our key moments of commitment to Christ fading into the increasingly distant past, while entrenched assumptions about our capacity to name and cultivate the blessings we desire remain unchallenged within us, subtly pulling the levers of our actions under a deceptively Christian exterior. Paul is looking for radical daily dependence on God as the only controller and loving arbiter of the future he knows we need. He doesn't want Christians who behave like I behaved with my electric toothbrush, carrying on as if I was still using its manual predecessor, directed by the overwhelming power of habit. He wants Christians who will change their posture, challenge the triggers associated with their established expectations, and, with God's Spirit enabling, do whatever it takes to *really live* this new Christian life and help others to do the same.

Galatians 2:20–21 is often identified as a fitting climax to the introductory stanzas of the letter, and after due reconsideration, that assessment still stands:

I have been crucified with Christ and I no longer live but Christ lives in me. The life I now live in the body, I live by faith in the Son of God who loved me and gave himself for me. I do not set aside the grace of God for if righteousness could be gained through the law, Christ died for nothing. (Gal. 2:20–21)

The believer here is no longer a player in the divine–human game. The 'I' is no longer wielding their own spiritual effectiveness and influence. It is Christ whose effective actions draw the blessing and favour of God towards us and who embodies that blessing and favour in himself. That is our gospel. Not going back to what we once destroyed (Gal. 2:18) but relying on the destructive accomplishments of this divine other and yielding ourselves to transformation by his Spirit. Not living as those who are still *of* the world under a Christian veneer, but living distinctive lives *in* the world, aware of the patterns it has impressed on us and others, and seeking with his help to subvert them.

Inscription Corpora

Beichtinschriften – *Die Beichtinschriften Westkleinasiens*, edited by Petzl, Georg. Epigraphica Anatolica: Zeitschrift für Epigraphik und Historische Geographie Anatoliens, vol. 22. Bonn, Germany: Dr. Rudolf Habelt GmbH, 1994.

CMRDM – *Corpus Monumentorum Religionis dei Menis*, edited by Lane, Eugene. Leiden, Netherlands: Brill, 1971.

Hosios kai Dikaios – *Hosios kai Dikaios*, edited by Ricl, Marijana. Epigraphica Anatolica: Zeitschrift für Epigraphik und Historische Geographie Anatoliens, vol. 18. Bonn, Germany: Dr. Rudolf Habelt GmbH, 1992.

I.Pisid.Cen. – *The Inscriptions of Central Pisidia: Including Texts From Kremna, Ariassos, Keraia, Hyia, Panemoteichos, the Sanctuary of Apollo of the Perminoundeis, Sia, Kocaaliler, and the Döşeme Boğazı*, edited by Horsley, G.H.R. et al., Inschriften Griechisher Städte aus Kleinasien, vol. 57. Bonn, Germany: Dr. Rudolf Habelt GmbH, 2000.

IJO – *Inscriptiones Judaicae Orientis: Band II Kleinasien*, edited by Ameling, Walter. Texts and Studies in Ancient Judaism, vol. 99. Tübingen, Germany: Mohr Siebeck, 2004.

The Inscriptions – *The Inscriptions, 1926–1950, Corinth*, vol. 8.3. Princeton, NJ: American School of Classical Studies at Athens, 1966.

MAMA VIII – *Monuments From Lycaonia, the Pisido-Phrygian Borderland, Aphrodisias*, edited by Calder, W.M. et al., Monumenta Asiae Minoris Antiqua, vol. 8. Manchester, UK: Manchester University Press, 1962.

MAMA XI – *Monuments From Phrygia and Lykaonia*, edited by Thonemann, Peter. Monumenta Antiqua Asiae Minoris, vol. 11. London: Society for the Promotion of Roman Studies, 2013.

New Documents From Lydia – *New Documents From Lydia*, edited by Herrmann, Peter et al., Ergänzungsbände zu den Tituli Asiae Minoris, vol. 24. Vienna, Austria: Verlag der Österreichischen Akademie der Wissenschaften, 2007.

New Religious Texts From Lydia – *New Religious Texts From Lydia*, edited by Malay, Hasan et al., Denkschriften (Philosophisch-Historische Klasse), vol. 497. Vienna, Austria: Verlag der Österreichischen Akademie der Wissenschaften, 2017.

PGM – *The Greek Magical Papyri. In the Greek Magical Papyri in Translation Including the Demotic Spells*, edited by Betz, Hans Dieter. Chicago, IL: University of Chicago Press, 1986.

Phrygian Votive Steles – *Phrygian Votive Steles*, edited by Drew-Bear, Thomas et al. Ankara, Turkey: Turkish Republic Ministry of Culture, 1999.

SEG 28 – *Supplementum Epigraphicum Graecum*, edited by Pleket, Henry W. et al. Amsterdam: J.C. Gieben, 1978.

LSAM – *Lois Sacrées de l'Asie Mineure*. Travaux et Mémoires (École Française d'Athènes), vol. 9. Paris: Boccard, 1955.

Bibliography

Agostini, Alessio. "New Perspectives on Minaean Expiatory Texts." *Proceedings of the Seminar for Arabian Studies* 42 (2012): 1–12.

Allen, Leslie, C. *The Books of Joel, Obadiah, Jonah, and Micah*. The New International Commentary on the Old Testament. Grand Rapids, MI: William B. Eerdmans, 1976.

Ameling, Walter. "The Epigraphic Habit and the Jewish Diasporas of Asia Minor and Syria." In *From Hellenism to Islam: Cultural and Linguistic Change in the Roman Near East*, edited by Cotton, Hannah M. et al. 203–234. Cambridge, UK: Cambridge University Press, 2009.

Arndt, William F. et al. *A Greek-English Lexicon of the New Testament and Other Early Christian Literature*, 3rd ed. Chicago, IL: University of Chicago Press, 2000.

Arnold, Clinton E. "'I Am Astonished That You Are So Quickly Turning Away!' (Gal 1.6): Paul and Anatolian Folk Belief." *New Testament Studies* 51, no. 3 (2005): 429–449.

———. "Returning to the Domain of the Powers: 'Stoicheia' as Evil Spirits in Galatians 4:3, 9." *Novum Testamentum* 38, no. 1 (1996): 55–76.

Ascough, Richard S. *What Are they Saying About the Formation of Pauline Churches?* New York: Paulist Press, 1998.

Bandstra, Andrew J. *The Law and the Elements of the World: An Exegetical Study in Aspects of Paul's Teaching*. Kampen: J.H. Kok, 1964.

Barclay, John M.G. "Mirror-Reading a Polemical Letter: Galatians as a Test Case." *Journal for the Study of the New Testament* 10, no. 31 (1987): 73–93.

———. *Obeying the Truth: A Study of Paul's Ethics in Galatians*. Edinburgh, UK: T. & T. Clark, 1988.

———. *Jews in the Mediterranean Diaspora: From Alexander to Trajan (323 BCE–117 CE)*. Hellenistic Culture and Society. Edinburgh, UK: T. & T. Clark, 1996.

———. "Paul, the Gift and the Battle Over Gentile Circumcision: Revisiting the Logic of Galatians." *Australian Biblical Review* 58 (2010a): 36–56.

———. "Paul and the Philosophers: Alain Badiou and the Event." *New Blackfriars* 91, no. 1032 (2010b): 171–184.

———. *Pauline Churches and Diaspora Jews*. Wissenschaftliche Untersuchungen zum Neuen Testament 1. Reihe, vol. 275. Tübingen, Germany: Mohr Siebeck, 2011.

———. *Paul and the Gift*. Grand Rapids, MI: William B. Eerdmans, 2015.

Barnett, Richard D. "Phrygia and the Peoples of Anatolia in the Iron Age." In *Cambridge Ancient History*, 3rd ed., vol. 2, edited by Lewis, David M. 417–442. Cambridge, UK: Cambridge University Press, 1975.

Baron, Salo W. "Population." In *Encyclopaedia Judaica*, vol. 16, edited by Berenbaum, Michael et al. 381–400. Detroit, MI: Macmillan Reference USA in association with the Keter Publishing House, 2007.

Barrett, C.K. *A Commentary on the First Epistle to the Corinthians*, 2nd ed. Black's New Testament Commentaries. London: A. & C. Black, 1971.

Barton, S.C. et al. "A Hellenistic Cult Group and New Testament Churches." *Jahrbuch für Antike und Christentum* 24 (1981): 7–41.

Bauckham, Richard J. "Eschatology." In *New Bible Dictionary*, 3rd ed., edited by Wood, D.R.W. et al. Leicester, UK: Inter-Varsity Press, 1996: 333–339.

———. *Jesus and the God of Israel: God Crucified and Other Studies on the New Testament's Christology of Divine Identity*. Grand Rapids, MI: William B. Eerdmans, 2009.

Baur, Ferdinand C. *Paulus, der Apostel Jesu Christi: Sein Leben und Wirken, seine Briefe und seine Lehre*. Stuttgart, Germany: Becher & Müller, 1845.

———. *The Church History of the First Three Centuries*, vol. 1, edited by Menzies, Allan. London, 1878.

Bergman, Jan. "Religio-Phenomenological Reflections on the Multi-Level Process of Giving to the Gods." In *Gifts to the Gods: Proceedings of the Uppsala Symposium 1985*, edited by Linders, Tullia et al. Acta Universitatis Upsaliensis. 31–42. Stockholm: Academia Ubsaliensis, 1987.

Betz, Hans D. *Galatians: A Commentary on Paul's Letter to the Churches in Galatia*. Hermeneia – A Critical and Historical Commentary on the Bible. Minneapolis, MN: Fortress Press, 1979.

———. *The Greek Magical Papyri in Translation Including the Demotic Spells*. Chicago, IL: University of Chicago Press, 1986.

Blackwell, Ben C. et al. "Paul and the Apocalyptic Imagination." In *Paul and the Apocalyptic Imagination*, edited by Blackwell, Ben C. et al. 3–21. Minneapolis, MN: Fortress Press, 2016.

Blanco-Pérez, Aitor. "Mēn Askaēnos and the Native Cults of Antioch by Pisidia." In *Between Tarhuntas and Zeus Polieus: Cultural Crossroads in the Temples and Cults of Graeco-Roman Anatolia*, edited by De Hoz, María-Paz et al. Colloquia Antiqua: Supplements to the Journal Ancient East and West, edited by Tsetskhladze, Gocha R. 117–150. Leuven, Belgium: Peeters, 2016.

Blinzler, Josef. "Lexikalisches zu dem Terminus τὰ στοιχεῖα τοῦ κόσμου bei Paulus." In *Studiorum Paulinorum Congressus Internationalis Catholicus 1961*, vol. 2. 429–443. Rome: E Pontificio Instituto Biblico, 1963.

Bockmuehl, Markus N.A. *Jewish Law in Gentile Churches: Halakhah and the Beginning of Christian Public Ethics*. Grand Rapids, MI: Baker Academic, 2003.

———. *A Commentary on the Epistle to the Philippians*. Black's New Testament Commentaries. London: Continuum, 2006a.

———. *Seeing the Word: Refocusing New Testament Study*. Studies in Theological Interpretation, edited by Bartholomew, Craig G. et al. Grand Rapids, MI: Baker Academic, 2006b.

Borgen, Peder. "'Yes,' 'No,' 'How Far?': The Participation of Jews and Christians in Pagan Cults." In *Paul in His Hellenistic Context*, edited by Engberg-Pedersen, Troels. 30–59. London: T. & T. Clark, 1994.

Bourdieu, Pierre. *The Logic of Practice*, trans. Nice, Richard. Cambridge, UK: Polity, 1990.

Boyce, Mary. *A History of Zoroastrianism*, vol. 2. Handbuch der Orientalistik. Leiden, Netherlands: E.J. Brill, 1975.

Boyce, Mary et al. *A History of Zoroastrianism*, vol. 3. Handbuch der Orientalistik. Leiden, Netherlands: E.J. Brill, 1975.

Breytenbach, Cilliers. *Paulus und Barnabas in der Provinz Galatien: Studien zu Apostelgeschichte 13f.; 16,6; 18,23 und den Adressaten des Galaterbriefes*. Arbeiten zur Geschichte des Antiken Judentums und des Urchristentums, vol. 38. Leiden, Netherlands: E.J. Brill, 1996.

Breytenbach, Cilliers et al. *Early Christianity in Lycaonia and Adjacent Areas: From Paul to Amphilochius of Iconium*. Arbeiten zur Geschichte des Antiken Judentums und des Urchristentums, vol. 101, edited by Breytenbach, Cilliers et al. Leiden, Netherlands: E.J. Brill, 2018.

Bru, Hadrien et al. "Inscriptions de Pergè." *Zeitschrift für Papyrologie und Epigraphik* 199 (2016): 65–82.

Bruce, F. F. *The Book of the Acts*. New International Commentary on the New Testament. Grand Rapids, MI: William B. Eerdmans, 1988.

Burkert, Walter. *Greek Religion: Archaic and Classical*, trans. Raffan, John. Oxford: Blackwell, 1987.

Burton, Ernest DeWitt. *A Critical and Exegetical Commentary on the Epistle to the Galatians*. The International Critical Commentary on the Holy Scripture. Edinburgh, UK: T. & T. Clark, 1921.

Calvin, John. *Commentaries on the Epistles of Paul to the Galatians and Ephesians*, trans. Pringle, William. Edinburgh: T. Clark, 1854.

Campbell, Douglas A. *The Deliverance of God: An Apocalyptic Rereading of Justification in Paul*. Grand Rapids, MI: William B. Eerdmans, 2009.

———. *Framing Paul: An Epistolary Biography*. Grand Rapids, MI: William B. Eerdmans, 2014.

Carlson, Stephen C. *The Text of Galatians and Its History*. Wissenschaftliche Untersuchungen zum Neuen Testament 2. Reihe, vol. 385, edited by Frey, Jörg. Tübingen, Germany: Mohr Siebeck, 2015.

Cartledge, Tony W. *Vows in the Hebrew Bible and the Ancient Near East*. Journal for the Study of the Old Testament Supplement Series, vol. 147. Sheffield: JSOT Press, 1992.

Chaniotis, Angelos. "Ritual Performances of Divine Justice: The Epigraphy of Confession, Atonement and Exaltation in Roman Asia Minor." In *From Hellenism to Islam: Cultural and Linguistic Change in the Roman Near East*, edited by Cotton, Hannah M. et al. 115–153. Cambridge, UK: Cambridge University Press, 2009.

Charlesworth, James H. *The Old Testament Pseudepigrapha: Apocalyptic Literature and Testaments*, vol. 1. Peabody, MA: Hendrickson Publishers, 2009.

Chester, Stephen J. *Conversion at Corinth: Perspectives on Conversion in Paul's Theology and the Corinthian Church*. Studies of the New Testament and Its World. London: T. & T. Clark, 2003.

———. *Reading Paul With the Reformers: Reconciling Old and New Perspectives*. Grand Rapids, MI: William B. Eerdmans, 2017.

Clark, Ernest P. "*Enslaved Under the Elements of the Cosmos.*" University of St. Andrews, 2018.

Clauss, Manfred. *Kaiser und Gott: Herrscherkult im römischen Reich*. Stuttgart, Germany: Teubner, 1999.

Cohen, Shaye J.D. *The Beginnings of Jewishness: Boundaries, Varieties, Uncertainties*. Hellenistic Culture and Society, vol. 1. Berkeley, CA: University of California Press, 1999.

Collins, John J. *Between Athens and Jerusalem: Jewish Identity in the Hellenistic Diaspora*, 2nd ed. Biblical Resource Series. Grand Rapids, MI: William B. Eerdmans, 2000.

Coogan, Michael David et al. *The New Oxford Annotated Apocrypha*, 3rd ed. Oxford: Oxford University Press, 2007.

Cusack, Carole M. *Conversion Among the Germanic Peoples*. Cassell Religious Studies. London: Cassell, 1998.

Das, A. Andrew. *Solving the Romans Debate*. Minneapolis, MN: Fortress Press, 2007.

Davies, J.P. *Paul Among the Apocalypses?: An Evaluation of the Apocalyptic Paul in the Context of Jewish and Christian Apocalyptic Literature*. The Library of New Testament Studies, vol. 562. New York: Bloomsbury, 2016.

de Boer, Martinus C. *Galatians: A Commentary*. The New Testament Library. Louisville, KY: Westminster John Knox Press, 2011.

———. "Apocalyptic as God's Eschatalogical Activity in Paul's Theology." In *Paul and the Apocalyptic Imagination*, edited by Blackwell, Ben C. et al. 45–63. Minneapolis, MN: Fortress Press, 2016.

Deenick, Karl. *Righteous by Promise: A Biblical Theology of Circumcision*. New Studies in Biblical Theology, vol. 45, edited by Carson, D.A. Downers Grove, IL: InterVarsity Press, 2018.

Delling, Gerhard. *Die Bewältigung der Diasporasituation durch das hellenistische Judentum*. Göttingen, Germany: Vandenhoeck & Ruprecht, 1987.

Devreker, John et al. *Les fouilles de la Rijksuniversiteit te Gent à Pessinonte: 1967–1973*, vol. 1. Dissertationes Archaeologicae Gandenses, vol. 22. Bruges, Belgium: De Tempel, 1984.

Dibelius, Martin. *A Fresh Approach to the New Testament and Early Christian Literature*. International Library of Christian Knowledge. London: Nicholson & Watson, 1936.

Dick, Karl. *Der Schriftstellerische Plural bei Paulus*. Halle, Germany: Niemeyer, 1900.

Dignas, Beate. *Economy of the Sacred in Hellenistic and Roman Asia Minor*. Oxford Classical Monographs. Oxford: Oxford University Press, 2002.

Donaldson, Terence L. *Judaism and the Gentiles: Jewish Patterns of Universalism (to 135 CE)*. Waco, TX: Baylor University Press, 2007.

Drane, John William. *Paul, Libertine or Legalist?: A Study in the Theology of the Major Pauline Epistles*. London: S.P.C.K., 1975.

Drew-Bear, Thomas et al., eds. *Phrygian Votive Steles*. Ankara, Turkey: Turkish Republic Ministry of Culture, 1999.

Dunant, Christiane. "Sus aux voleurs! Une Tablette en Bronze à Inscription Grecque du Musée de Genève." *Museum Helveticum* 35 (1978): 241–244.

Dunn, James D. G. *A Commentary on the Epistle to the Galatians*. Black's New Testament Commentaries. London: A. & C. Black, 1993.

———. *The Partings of the Ways: Between Christianity and Judaism and their Significance for the Character of Christianity*, 2nd ed. London: SCM, 2006a.

———. *The Theology of Paul the Apostle*. Grand Rapids, MI: William B. Eerdmans, 2006b.

———. *The New Perspective on Paul*. Grand Rapids, MI: William B. Eerdmans, 2008.

Dupont-Sommer, André. "L'Inscription Araméenne de Daskyleion." *Istanbul Arkeoloji Müzeleri Yıllığı (Archaeological Museums of Istanbul Report)* 1–14 (1966): 112–117.

Eckstein, Hans-Joachim. *Der Begriff Syneidesis bei Paulus: Eine neutestamentlich-exegetische Untersuchung zum "Gewissensbegriff"*. Wissenschaftliche Untersuchungen zum Neuen Testament 2. Reihe, vol. 10, edited by Frey, Jörg. Tübingen, Germany: Paul Siebeck, 1983.

Ehrhardt, Norbert. *Milet und Seine Kolonien: Vergleichende Untersuchung der kultischen und politischen Einrichtungen*, 2. Aufl. ed. Europäische Hochschulschriften. Reihe III. Geschichte und ihre Hilfswissenschaften vol. 206, edited by Frey, Jörg. Frankfurt: P. Lang, 1988.

Ehrman, Bart D. *The Apostolic Fathers*, vol. 1, translated and edited by Ehrman, Bart D. Loeb Classical Library, vol. 24. Cambridge, MA: Harvard University Press, 2003.

Eisenbaum, Pamela. *Paul Was Not a Christian: The Original Message of a Misunderstood Apostle*. New York: Harper One, 2009.

Elliott, Mark W. "Judaism, Reformation Theology, and Justification." In *Galatians and Christian Theology: Justification, the Gospel, and Ethics in Paul's Letter*, edited by Elliott, Mark W. et al. 143–158. Grand Rapids, MI: Baker Academic, 2014.

Elliott, Susan M. "Choose Your Mother, Choose Your Master: Galatians 4:21–5:1 in the Shadow of the Anatolian Mother of the Gods." *Journal of Biblical Literature* 118, no. 4 (1999): 661–683.

———. *Cutting Too Close for Comfort: Paul's Letter to the Galatians in Its Anatolian Cultic Context*. Library of New Testament Studies, vol. 248. London: T. & T. Clark, 2003.

Eriksson, Anders. *Traditions as Rhetorical Proof: Pauline Argumentation in I Corinthians*. Coniectanea Biblica New Testament Series, vol. 29. Stockholm: Almquist & Wiksell International, 1998.

Fee, Gordon D. *God's Empowering Presence: The Holy Spirit in the Letters of Paul*. Grand Rapids, MI: Baker Academic, 1994.

Feldman, Louis H. *Jew and Gentile in the Ancient World: Attitudes and Interactions From Alexander to Justinian*. Princeton, NJ: Princeton University Press, 1993.

Foster, Paul. "Ignatius of Antioch." In *The Encyclopedia of Ancient History*, edited by Bagnall, Roger S. et al. Oxford: Blackwell, 2012: 3392–3395.

Fredriksen, Paula. *Paul, the Pagans' Apostle*. New Haven, CT: Yale University Press, 2017.

Gager, John G. *The Origins of Anti-Semitism: Attitudes Toward Judaism in Pagan and Christian Antiquity*. Oxford: Oxford University Press, 1985.

———. *Who Made Early Christianity?: The Jewish Lives of the Apostle Paul*. American Lectures on the History of Religions (American Academy of Religion), vol. 18. New York: Columbia University Press, 2015.

Garland, David E. *1 Corinthians*. Baker Exegetical Commentary on the New Testament. Grand Rapids, MI: Baker Academic, 2003.

Gaston, Lloyd. "Paul and the Torah." In *AntiSemitism and the Foundations of Christianity*, edited by Davies, Alan T. 48–71. Eugene, OR: Wipf and Stock, 1979.

Gathercole, Simon J. *Where Is Boasting? Early Jewish Soteriology and Paul's Response in Romans 1–5*. Grand Rapids, MI: William B. Eerdmans, 2002.

Gill, David W.J. "In Search of the Social Elite in the Corinthian Church." *Tyndale Bulletin* 44, no. 2 (1993): 323–337.

———. "Early Christianity and Its Colonial Contexts in the Provinces of the Eastern Empire." In *The Urban World and the First Christians*, edited by Walton, Steve et al. 68–85. Grand Rapids, MI: William B. Eerdmans, 2017.

Glad, Clarence E. *Paul and Philodemus: Adaptability in Epicurean and Early Christian Psychagogy*. Supplements to Novum Testamentum, vol. 81. Leiden, Netherlands: E.J. Brill, 1995.

Gombis, Timothy G. "The 'Transgressor' and the 'Curse of the Law': The Logic of Paul's Argument in Galatians 2–3." *New Testament Studies* 53 (2007): 81–93.

Goodman, Martin. *Mission and Conversion: Proselytizing in the Religious History of the Roman Empire*. Oxford: Oxford University Press, 1994.

Hafemann, Scott J. *Suffering and Ministry in the Spirit: Paul's Defense of his Ministry in II Corinthians 2:1–3:3*. Grand Rapids, MI: William B. Eerdmans, 1990.

Hanfmann, George M.A. et al. *Sardis From Prehistoric to Roman Times: Results of the Archaeological Exploration of Sardis, 1958–1975*. Cambridge, MA: Harvard University Press, 1983.

Hansen, Esther V. *The Attalids of Pergamon*, 2nd ed. Cornell Studies in Classical Philology, vol. 36. Ithaca, NY: Cornell University Press, 1971.

Hardie, Margaret M. "The Shrine of Mēn Askaenos at Pisidian Antioch." *The Journal of Hellenic Studies* 32 (1912): 111–150.

Hardin, Justin K. *Galatians and the Imperial Cult: A Critical Analysis of the First-Century Social Context of Paul's Letter*. Wissenschaftliche Untersuchungen zum Neuen Testament 2. Reihe, vol. 237, edited by Frey, Jörg. Tübingen, Germany: Mohr Siebeck, 2008.

Harnack, Adolf von. *The Mission and Expansion of Christianity in the First Three Centuries*, trans. Moffatt, James. Cloister Library, vol. 92. New York: Harper Torchbooks, 1962.

Hays, Richard B. *Echoes of Scripture in the Letters of Paul*. New Haven, CT: Yale University Press, 1989.

———. *First Corinthians*. Interpretation, A Bible Commentary for Teaching and Preaching. Louisville, KY: John Knox Press, 1997.

———. "The Letter to the Galatians: Introduction, Commentary, and Reflections." In *The New Interpreter's Bible*, vol. 11. 181–348. Nashville, TN: Abingdon Press, 2000.

———. *The Faith of Jesus Christ: The Narrative Substructure of Galatians 3:1–4:11*, 2nd ed. Biblical Resource Series. Grand Rapids, MI: William B. Eerdmans, 2002.

———. "Apocalyptic Poiēsis in Galatians: Paternity, Passion, and Participation." In *Galatians and Christian Theology: Justification, the Gospel, and Ethics in Paul's Letter*, edited by Elliott, Mark W. et al. 200–219. Grand Rapids, MI: Baker Academic, 2014.

———. "The Letter to the Galatians: Introduction, Commentary, and Reflections." In *The New Interpreter's Bible Commentary*, vol. 9, edited by Keck, Leander E. 1019–1173. Nashville. TN: Abingdon Press, 2015.

Hoehner, Harold W. "Did Paul Write Galatians?" In *History and Exegesis: New Testament Essays in Honor of Dr. E. Earle Ellis for His 80th Birthday*, edited by Son, Sang-Won (Aaron). 150–69. New York: T. & T. Clark, 2006.

Horner, Timothy J. *Listening to Trypho: Justin Martyr's Dialogue Reconsidered*. Contributions to Biblical Exegesis and Theology, vol. 28. Leuven, Belgium: Peeters, 2001.

Horsley, G.H.R. et al., eds. *The Inscriptions of Central Pisidia: Including Texts from Kremna, Ariassos, Keraia, Hyia, Panemoteichos, the Sanctuary of Apollo of the Perminoundeis, Sia, Kocaaliler, and the Döşeme Boğazı*. Inschriften Greichischer Städte aus Kleinasien, vol. 57. Bonn, Germany: Dr. Rudolf Habelt GmbH, 2000.

Hübner, Hans. *Law in Paul's Thought*, trans. Greig, James C.G. Studies of the New Testament and Its World, edited by Riches, John K. Edinburgh: T. & T. Clark, 1984.

Hübner, Reinhard M. "Thesen zur Echtheit und Datierung der Sieben Briefe des Ignatius von Antiochien." *Zeitschrift fur Antikes Christentum* 1, no. 1 (1997): 44–72.

Jeremias, Joachim. "Zur Gedankenführung in den paulinischen Briefen." In *Studia Paulina: in honorem Johannis de Zwaan septuagenarii*, edited by van

Unnik, W.C. et al. 146–154. Haarlem, Netherlands: De Ervem F. Bohn N.V., 1953.

Jewett, Robert. *Paul's Anthropological Terms: A Study of Their Use in Conflict Settings.* Arbeiten zur Geschichte des antiken Judentums und des Urchristentums, vol. 10. Leiden, Netherlands: E.J. Brill, 1971.

———. *Dating Paul's Life.* London: SCM Press, 1979.

John, Felix. *Der Galaterbrief im Kontext historischer Lebenswelten im antiken Kleinasien.* Forschungen zur Religion und Literatur des Alten und Neuen Testaments, vol. 264. Göttingen, Germany: Vandenhoeck & Ruprecht, 2016.

Joly, Robert. *Le Dossier d'Ignace d'Antioche.* Université Libre de Bruxelles, Faculté de Philosophie et Lettres, vol. 69. Brussels: Éditions de l'Université de Bruxelles, 1979.

Jones, Christopher P., ed. Philostratus. *The Life of Apollonius of Tyana*, vol. 1. Loeb Classical Library, vol. 16. Cambridge, MA: Harvard University Press, 2005.

Jones, F. Stanley. *The Syriac Pseudo-Clementines: An Early Version of the First Christian Novel.* Apocryphes, vol. 14. Turnhout, Belgium: Brepols, 2014.

Kahl, Brigitte. *Galatians Re-imagined: Reading With the Eyes of the Vanquished.* Paul in Critical Contexts. Minneapolis, MN: Fortress Press, 2009.

Käsemann, Ernst. *New Testament Questions of Today.* The New Testament Library, edited by Richardson, Alan et al. London: SCM Press, 1969.

———. *An die Römer.* Handbuch zum Neuen Testament, vol. 8a. Tübingen, Germany: Paul Siebeck, 1973.

Keener, Craig S. *The Mind of the Spirit: Paul's Approach to Transformed Thinking.* Grand Rapids, MI: Baker Academic, 2016.

———. *Galatians: A Commentary.* Grand Rapids, MI: Baker Academic, 2019.

Kelp, Ute. "Grave Monuments and Local Identities in Roman Phrygia." In *Roman Phrygia: Culture and Society*, edited by Thonemann, Peter. Cambridge, UK: Cambridge University Press, 2013.

Kraabel, A. Thomas. "The Roman Diaspora: Six Questionable Assumptions." In *Diaspora Jews and Judaism: Essays in Honor of, and in Dialogue With, A. Thomas Kraabel*, edited by Overman, Andrew J. et al. South Florida Studies in the History of Judaism, vol. 41, edited by Neusner, Jacob et al. 1–20. Atlanta, GA: Scholars Press, 1992a.

———. "The Disappearance of the 'God-Fearers'." In *Diaspora Jews and Judaism: Essays in Honor of, and in Dialogue With, A. Thomas Kraabel*, edited by Overman, Andrew J. et al. South Florida Studies in the History of Judaism, vol. 41, edited by Neusner, Jacob et al. 119–130. Atlanta, GA: Scholars Press, 1992b.

———. "The Synagogue at Sardis: Jews and Christians." In *Diaspora Jews and Judaism: Essays in Honor of, and in Dialogue With, A. Thomas Kraabel*, edited by Overman, Andrew J. et al. South Florida Studies in the History of Judaism, vol. 41, edited by Neusner, Jacob et al. 225–236. Atlanta, GA: Scholars Press, 1992c.

———. "Paganism and Judaism: The Sardis Evidence." In *Diaspora Jews and Judaism: Essays in Honor of, and in Dialogue With, A. Thomas Kraabel*, edited by Overman, Andrew J. et al. South Florida Studies in the History of Judaism, vol. 41, edited by Neusner, Jacob et al. 237–255. Atlanta, GA: Scholars Press, 1992d.

———. "Impact of the Discovery of the Sardis Synagogue." In *Diaspora Jews and Judaism: Essays in Honor of, and in Dialogue with, A. Thomas Kraabel*, edited by Overman, Andrew J. et al. South Florida Studies in the History of Judaism, vol. 41, edited by Neusner, Jacob et al. 269–291. Atlanta, GA: Scholars Press, 1992e.

Kreider, Alan. *The Patient Ferment of the Early Church: The Improbable Rise of Christianity in the Roman Empire*. Grand Rapids, MI: Baker Academic, 2016.

Lane Fox, Robin. *Pagans and Christians in the Mediterranean World From the Second-Century AD to the Conversion of Constantine*. London: Penguin, 2005.

Levick, Barbara. *Roman Colonies in Southern Asia Minor*. Oxford: Clarendon Press, 1967.

———. "In the Phrygian Mode: A Region Seen From Without." In *Roman Phrygia: Culture and Society*, edited by Thonemann, Peter. 41–54. Cambridge, UK: Cambridge University Press, 2013.

Levinskaya, Irina A. *The Book of Acts in Its Diaspora Setting*. The Book of Acts in Its First Century Setting, vol. 5. Grand Rapids, MI: William B. Eerdmans, 1996.

Lightfoot, J.L. *Saint Paul's Epistles to the Colossians and to Philemon*, 8th ed. Classic Commentaries on the Greek New Testament. New York: Macmillan and Co., 1886.

———. *The Sibylline Oracles With Introduction, Translation, and Commentary on the First and Second Books*. Oxford: Oxford University Press, 2007.

Linders, Tullia. "God, Gifts, Society" In *Gifts to the Gods: Proceedings of the Uppsala Symposium 1985*, edited by Linders, Tullia et al. Acta Universitatis Upsaliensis. 115–122. Stockholm: Academia Ubsaliensis, 1987.

Lipinski, E. "Obadiah 20." *Vetus Testamentum* 23, no. 3 (1973): 368–370.

Littman, Enno. *Lydian Inscriptions*. Publications of the American Society for the Excavations of Sardis, vol. 6. Leiden, Netherlands: E.J. Brill, 1916.

Longenecker, Bruce W. *The Triumph of Abraham's God: The Transformation of Identity in Galatians*. Edinburgh, UK: T. & T. Clark, 1998.

Longenecker, Richard N. *Galatians*. Word Biblical Commentary, vol. 41. Dallas, TX: Word Books, 1990.

Luther, Martin. *Luther's Works*, vol. 26, edited by Pelikan, Jaroslav J. et al. Philadelphia, PA: Fortress Press, 1963.

———. *Luther's Works*, vol. 54, edited by Pelikan, Jaroslav J. et al. Philadelphia, PA: Fortress Press, 1967.

———. *Luther's Works*, vol. 16, edited by Pelikan, Jaroslav J. et al. Philadelphia, PA: Fortress Press, 1969.

———. *Luther's Works*, vol. 47, edited by Pelikan, Jaroslav J. et al. Philadelphia, PA: Fortress Press, 1971.

Ma, John. *Antiochos III and the Cities of Western Asia Minor*. Oxford: Oxford University Press, 1999.

MacMullen, Ramsay. *The Second Church: Popular Christianity A.D. 200–400*. Writings from the Greco-Roman World Supplement Series, vol. 1, edited by Fitzgerald, John T. Atlanta, GA: Society of Biblical Literature, 2009.

Madsen II, Thorvald B. *"Indicative and Imperative in Paul and Ancient Judaism: A Comparative Study."* PhD Thesis, University of Aberdeen, 1998.

Malherbe, Abraham J. "Determinism and Free Will in Paul." In *Paul in His Hellenistic Context*, edited by Engberg-Pedersen, Troels. Studies of the New Testament and Its World. 231–255. Edinburgh, UK: T. & T. Clark, 1994.

Marcovich, Miroslav, ed. Justin. *Iustine Martyris Apologiae Pro Christianis*. Patristische Texte und Studien, vol. 38, edited by Aland, K. et al. Berlin: Walter De Gruyter, 1994.

———, ed. Justin. *Iustine Martyris Dialogus Cum Tryphone*. Patristische Texte und Studien, vol. 47, edited by Aland, K. et al. Berlin: Walter De Gruyter, 1997.

Marek, Christian. "Nochmals zu den Theos Hypsistos Inschriften." In *Juden – Heiden – Christen?*, edited by Alkier, Stefan et al. Wissenschaftliche Untersuchungen zum Neuen Testament 1. Reihe, vol. 400. 131–148. Tübingen, Germany: Mohr Siebeck, 2018.

Marek, Christian et al. *In the Land of a Thousand Gods: A History of Asia Minor in the Ancient World*, trans. Rendall, Steven. Princeton, NJ: Princeton University Press, 2016.

Martin, Neil. *Keep Going: Overcoming Doubts About Your Faith*. Phillipsburg, NJ: P&R, 2008.

———. "Returning to the stoicheia tou kosmou: Enslavement to the Physical Elements in Galatians 4:3 and 9?" *Journal for the Study of the New Testament* 40, no. 4 (2018): 434–452.

215

———. *Regression in Galatians: Paul and the Gentile Response to Jewish Law.* Wissenschaftliche Untersuchungen zum Neuen Testament 2. Reihe, vol. 530, edited by Frey, Jörg. Tübingen, Germany: Mohr Siebeck, 2020.

Martin, Troy. "Apostasy to Paganism: The Rhetorical Stasis of the Galatian Controversy." *Journal of Biblical Literature* 114, no. 3 (1995): 437–461.

Martyn, J. Louis. *Galatians: A New Translation With Introduction and Commentary.* The Anchor Yale Bible, vol. 33A. New York: Doubleday, 1997.

McCaulley, Esau. *Sharing the Son's Inheritance: Davidic Messianism and Paul's Worldwide Interpretation of the Abrahamic Land Promise in Galatians.* Library of New Testament Studies, vol. 608, edited by Keith, Chris. London: T. & T. Clark, 2019.

McCreedy, Wayne, O. "Martyrdom in Accordance With the Gospel." In *Religious Rivalries and the Struggle for Success in Sardis and Smyrna*, edited by Ascough, Richard S. Studies in Christianity and Judaism, vol. 14. 141–155. Waterloo, Belgium: Wilfrid Laurier University Press, 2005.

Meeks, Wayne A. *The First Urban Christians: The Social World of the Apostle Paul*, 2nd ed. New Haven, CT: Yale University Press, 2003.

Meggitt, Justin J. "Meat Consumption and Social Conflict in Corinth." *Journal of Theological Studies* 45 (1994): 137–141.

Meiser, Martin. *Galater.* Göttingen, Germany: Vandenhoeck & Ruprecht, 2007.

Mitchell, Stephen. *Anatolia: Land, Men, and Gods in Asia Minor*, vol. 1. Oxford: Clarendon Press, 1993a.

———. *Anatolia: Land, Men, and Gods in Asia Minor*, vol. 2. Oxford: Clarendon Press, 1993b.

———. "The Cult of Theos Hypsistos Between Pagans, Jews, and Christians." In *Pagan Monthesism in Late Antiquity*, edited by Athanassiadi, Polymnia et al. 81–148. Oxford: Clarendon Press, 1999a.

———. "Greek Epigraphy and Social Change: A Study of the Romanization of South-West Asia Minor in the Third Century AD" In *XI Congresso Internazionale di Epigraphia Greca e Latina: Roma 18–25 Settembre 1997*, vol. 2. 419–433. Rome: Edizioni Quasar, 1999b.

Mitchell, Stephen et al. *Pisidian Antioch: The Site and Its Monuments.* London: Duckworth, 1998.

Moo, Douglas J. *The Epistle to the Romans.* New International Commentary on the New Testament. Grand Rapids, MI: William B. Eerdmans, 1996.

———. *Galatians.* Baker Exegetical Commentary on the New Testament. Grand Rapids, MI: Baker Academic, 2013.

Morales, L. Michael. *Who Shall Ascend the Mountain of the Lord? A Biblical Theology of the Book of Leviticus.* New Studies in Biblical Theology, vol. 37, edited by Carson, D.A. Downers. Grove, IL: InterVarsity Press, 2015.

Morgan, Teresa. *Roman Faith and Christian Faith: Pistis and Fides in the Early Roman Empire and Early Churches.* Oxford: Oxford University Press, 2015.

Moses, Robert E. *Practices of Power: Revisiting the Principalities and Powers in the Pauline Letters.* Minneapolis, MN: Fortress Press, 2014.

Munck, Johannes. *Paul and the Salvation of Mankind.* London: SCM Press, 1959.

Murphy-O'Connor, J. *St. Paul's Corinth: Texts and Archaeology*, 3rd ed. Collegeville, MN: The Liturgical Press, 2002.

——. *Paul: A Critical Life.* Oxford: Oxford University Press, 2012.

Murray, Michele. *Playing a Jewish Game: Gentile Christian Judaizing in the First and Second Centuries CE.* Studies in Christianity and Judaism, vol. 13. Waterloo, Belgium: Wilfrid Laurier University Press, 2003.

Nanos, Mark D. *The Irony of Galatians: Paul's Letter in First-Century Context.* Minneapolis, MN: Fortress Press, 2002.

Nanos, Mark D. et al., eds. *Paul Within Judaism: Restoring the First-Century Context to the Apostle.* Minneapolis, MN: Fortress Press, 2015.

Nollé, Johannes. *Kleinasiatische Losorakel: Astragal- und Alphabetchresmologien der hochkaiserzeitlichen Orakelrenaissance.* Vestigia, vol. 57. München, Deutschland: Beck, 2007.

O'Neill, J.C. *The Recovery of Paul's Letter to the Galatians.* London: S.P.C.K., 1972.

Oakes, Peter. *Galatians.* Paideia Commentaries on the New Testament, edited by Parson, Mikeal C. et al. Grand Rapids, MI: Baker Academic Publishing, 2015.

Overman, Andrew J. "The God-Fearers: Some Neglected Features." In *Diaspora Jews and Judaism: Essays in Honor of, and in Dialogue With, A. Thomas Kraabel*, edited by Overman, Andrew J. et al. South Florida Studies in the History of Judaism, vol. 41, edited by Neusner, Jacob et al. 145–152. Atlanta, GA: Scholars Press, 1992.

Parker, Robert. *On Greek Religion.* Townsend lectures/Cornell studies in Classical Philology, vol. 60. Ithaca, NY: Cornell University Press, 2011.

Petsalis-Diomidis, Alexia. *Truly Beyond Wonders: Aelius Aristides and the Cult of Asklepios.* Oxford Studies in Ancient Culture and Representation. Oxford: Oxford University Press, 2010.

Piper, John. *The Future of Justification: A Response to N.T. Wright.* Nottingham, UK: Inter-Varsity Press, 2008.

Pitre, Brant et al. *Paul, a New Covenant Jew: Rethinking Pauline Theology.* Grand Rapids, MI: William B. Eerdmans, 2019.

Platt, Verity J. *Facing the Gods: Epiphany and Representation in Graeco-Roman Art, Literature and Religion*. Greek Culture in the Roman World. Cambridge, UK: Cambridge University Press, 2011.

Pleket, H.W. "An Aspect of the Emperor Cult: Imperial Mysteries." *The Harvard Theological Review* 58, no. 4 (1965): 331–347.

Potts, Justine. "Corpora in Connection: Anatomical Votives and the Confession Stelai of Lydia and Phrygia." In *Bodies of Evidence: Ancient Anatomical Votives Past, Present and Future*, edited by Draycott, Jane et al. 20–44. London: Routledge, 2017.

Preisendanz, Karl. *Papyri Graecae Magicae: Die griechischen Zauberpapyri*, vol. 2. Leipzig, Germany: Teubner, 1931.

Price, Simon R. F. *Rituals and Power: The Roman Imperial Cult in Asia Minor*. Cambridge, UK: Cambridge University Press, 1984.

Räisänen, Heikki. *Paul and the Law*. Wissenschaftliche Untersuchungen zum Neuen Testament, vol. 29. Tübingen, Germany: J.C.B. Mohr, 1983.

Rajak, Teresa. "Jewish Rights in the Greek Cities Under Roman Rule: A New Approach." In *Approaches to Ancient Judaism: Theory and Practice*, vol. 5, edited by Green, William Scott. Brown Judaic Studies, vol. 32. 19–35. Missoula, MT: Scholars Press, 1985.

Rauer, Max. *Die "Schwachen" in Korinth und Rom*. Biblische Studien, vol. 21. Freiburg im Breisgau: Herder, 1923.

Reynolds, Joyce M. et al. *Jews and God-Fearers at Aphrodisias: Greek Inscriptions With Commentary*. Cambridge Philological Society Supplementary Series, vol. 12, edited by Tannenbaum, Robert et al. Cambridge, UK: Cambridge Philological Society, 1987.

Riches, John K. *Galatians Through the Centuries*, 3rd ed. Blackwell Bible Commentaries. Malden, MA: Wiley-Blackwell, 2008.

Ricl, Marijana. *Hosios kai Dikaios*. Epigraphica Anatolica: Zeitschrift für Epigraphik und Historische Geographie Anatoliens, vol. 18, edited by Akurgal, Ekrem et al. Bonn, Germany: Dr. Rudolf Habelt GmbH, 1992.

———. "The Appeal to Divine Justice in the Lydian Confession-Inscriptions." In *Forschungen in Lydien*, edited by Schwertheim, Elmar. Asia Minor Studien, vol. 17. 67–76. Bonn: Rudolf Habelt, 1995.

Roller, Lynn E. *In Search of God the Mother: The Cult of Anatolian Cybele*. Berkeley, CA: University of California Press, 1999.

Ropes, James Hardy. *The Singular Problem of the Epistle to the Galatians*. Harvard Theological studies, vol. XIV. Cambridge, MA: Harvard University Press, 1929.

Rostad, Aslak. "The Religious Context of the Lydian Propitiation Inscriptions." *Symbolae Osloenses* 81 (2006): 88–108.

Rudolph, David J. *A Jew to the Jews: Jewish Contours of Pauline Flexibility in 1 Corinthians 9:19–23.* Wissenschaftliche Untersuchungen zum Neuen Testament 2. Reihe, vol. 304, edited by Frey, Jörg. Tübingen, Germany: Mohr Siebeck, 2011.

———. "Paul and the Food Laws: A Reassessment of Romans 14:14, 20." In *Paul the Jew: Rereading the Apostle as a Figure of Second Temple Judaism*, edited by Boccaccini, Gabriele et al. 151–181. Minneapolis, MN: Fortress Press, 2016.

Rusam, Dietrich. "Neue Belege zu den *Stoicheia tou Kosmou* (Gal. 4,3.9, Kol 2,8.20)." *Zeitschrift für die Neutestamentliche Wissenschaft und die Kunde der Älteren Kirche* 83, no. 1–2 (1992): 119–125.

Russell, James C. *The Germanization of Early Medieval Christianity: A Sociohistorical Approach to Religious Transformation.* Oxford: Oxford University Press, 1994.

Sanday, W. et al. *A Critical and Exegetical Commentary on the Epistle of the Romans.* Edinburgh, UK: T. & T. Clark, 1898.

Sanders, E. P. *Paul and Palestinian Judaism: A Comparison of Patterns of Religion.* London: SCM Press, 1977.

Saperstein, Marc. *Moments of Crisis in Jewish-Christian Relations.* London: SCM Press, 1989.

Saunders, Nicholas J. "A Dark Light: Reflections on Obsidian in Mesoamerica." *World Archaeology* 33, no. 2 (2001): 220–236.

Schoedel, William R. *Ignatius of Antioch: A Commentary on the Letters of Ignatius of Antioch.* Hermeneia – A Critical and Historical Commentary on the Bible, edited by Köster, Helmut. Philadelphia, PA: Fortress Press, 1985.

Schreiner, Thomas R. *Galatians.* Zondervan Exegetical Commentary on the New Testament. Grand Rapids, MI: Zondervan, 2010.

Schürer, Emil. *The History of the Jewish People in the Age of Jesus Christ*, vol. 3i, edited by Millar, Fergus et al. London: Bloomsbury, 2014.

Schwartz, Daniel R. "Josephus' Tobiads: Back to the Second Century?" In *Jews in a Graeco-Roman World*, edited by Goodman, Martin. 47–61. Oxford: Oxford University Press, 2004.

Schweizer, Eduard. "Slaves of the Elements and Worshipers of Angels: Gal. 4:3, 9 and Col 2:8, 18, 20." *Journal of Biblical Literature* 107, no. 3 (1988): 455–468.

Seager, A.R. "The Building History of the Sardis Synagogue." *American Journal of Archaeology* 76, no. 4 (1972): 425–435.

Shaw, Brent D. "The Passion of Perpetua." *Past and Present* 139, no. 1 (1993): 3–45.

Sherwin-White, A.N. *Roman Foreign Policy in the East, 168 B.C. to A.D.1.* London: Duckworth, 1984.

Smith, James K.A. *Desiring the Kingdom: Worship, Worldview, and Culture Formation.* Cultural Liturgies, vol. 1. Grand Rapids, MI: Baker Academic, 2009.

———. *Imagining the Kingdom: How Worship Works.* Cultural Liturgies, vol. 2. Grand Rapids, MI: Baker Academic, 2013.

———. *You Are What You Love: The Spiritual Power of Habit.* Grand Rapids, MI: Brazos Press, 2016.

———. *Awaiting the King: Reforming Public Theology.* Cultural Liturgies, vol. 3. Grand Rapids, MI: Baker Academic, 2017.

Squire, Michael. *Image and Text in Graeco-Roman Antiquity.* Cambridge, UK: Cambridge University Press, 2009.

Stark, Rodney. *The Rise of Christianity: How the Obscure, Marginal Jesus Movement Became the Dominant Religious Force in the Western World in a Few Centuries.* New York: Harper One, 1996.

Steinleitner, Franz Seraph. *Die Beicht im Zusammenhange mit der sakralen Rechtspflege in der Antike: Ein Beitrag zur näheren Kenntnis kleinasiatisch-orientalischer Kulte der Kaiserzeit.* Leipzig, Germany: Theodor Weicher, 1913.

Stendahl, Krister. "The Apostle Paul and the Introspective Conscience of the West." *Harvard Theological Review* 56, no. 3 (1963): 199–215.

———. *Paul Among Jews and Gentiles, and Other Essays.* Philadelphia, PA: Fortress Press, 1976.

Taylor, Charles. *A Secular Age.* Cambridge, MA: Belknap Press of Harvard University Press, 2007.

Theissen, Gerd. *Psychological Aspects of Pauline Theology,* trans. Galvin, John P. Edinburgh, UK: T. & T. Clark, 1987.

———. *The Social Setting of Pauline Christianity: Essays on Corinth.* Eugene, OR: Wipf & Stock, 2004.

Thiessen, Matthew. *Paul and the Gentile Problem.* New York: Oxford University Press, 2016.

Thiselton, Anthony C. *The First Epistle to the Corinthians: A Commentary on the Greek Text.* New International Greek Testament Commentary. Grand Rapids, MI: William B. Eerdmans, 2000.

Tomson, P.J. "Sources on the Politics of Judaea in the 50s CE: A Response to Martin Goodman." *Journal of Jewish Studies* 68, no. 2 (2017): 234–259.

Trebilco, Paul R. *Jewish Communities in Asia Minor.* Society for New Testament Studies Monograph Series, vol. 69. Cambridge, UK: Cambridge University Press, 1991.

Van der Horst, Pieter W. "Jews and Christians in Aphrodisias in the Light of Their Relations in Other Cities of Asia Minor." In *Essays on the Jewish World of Early Christianity*. Novum Testamentum et Orbis Antiquus, vol. 14. 166–181. Göttingen, Germany: Vandenhoeck & Ruprecht, 1990.

———. "The Jews of Ancient Phrygia." *European Journal of Jewish Studies* 2, no. 2 (2008): 283–292.

———. "Judaism in Asia Minor." In *Studies in Ancient Judaism and Early Christianity*. Ancient Judaism and Early Christianity, vol. 87. 143–160. Leiden, Netherlands: E.J. Brill, 2014.

van der Kolk, Bessel A. *The Body Keeps the Score: Mind, Brain and Body in the Transformation of Trauma*. London: Allen Lane, 2014.

Van Straten, F.T. "Gifts for the Gods." In *Faith, Hope, and Worship: Aspects of Religious Mentality in the Ancient World*, edited by Versnel, H.S. Studies in Greek and Roman Religion, vol. 2. 65–151. Leiden, Netherlands: E.J. Brill, 1981.

Versnel, H.S. "Religious Mentality in Ancient Prayer." In *Faith, Hope, and Worship: Aspects of Religious Mentality in the Ancient World*, edited by Versnel, H.S. Studies in Greek and Roman Religion, vol. 2. 1–64. Leiden, Netherlands: E.J. Brill, 1981.

———. "Beyond Cursing: The Appeal to Justice in Judicial Prayers." In *Magika Hiera: Ancient Greek Magic and Religion*, edited by Faraone, Christopher A. et al. 60–106. Oxford: Oxford University Press, 1991.

Wakefield, Andrew H. *Where to Live: The Hermeneutical Significance of Paul's Citations From Scripture in Galatians 3:1–14*. Academia Biblica, vol. 14. Atlanta, GA: Society of Biblical Literature, 2003.

Weijenborg, Reinoud. *Les Lettres d'Ignace d'Antioche: Étude de Critique Littéraire et de Théologie*, trans. Héroux, Barthélemy. Leiden, Netherlands: E.J. Brill, 1969.

Weima, Jeffrey A.D. *1–2 Thessalonians*. Baker Exegetical Commentary on the New Testament. Grand Rapids, MI: Baker Academic, 2014.

———. *Paul the Ancient Letter Writer: An Introduction to Epistolary Analysis*. Grand Rapids, MI: Baker Academic, 2016.

Weinreich, Otto. *Stiftung und Kultsatzungen eines Privatheiligtums in Philadelphia in Lydien*. Sitzungsberichte der Heidelberger Akademie der Wissenschaften, vol. 16. Heidelberg, Germany: C. Winter, 1919.

Weiss, H. "Paul and the Judging of Days: Unlocking the Theological and Sociological Realities of Pauline Roman Christianity." *Zeitschrift für die Neutestamentliche Wissenschaft und die Kunde der Älteren Kirche* 86, no. 3–4 (1995): 137–153.

Westerholm, Stephen. "The 'New Perspective' at Twenty-Five." In *The Paradoxes of Paul*, vol. 2. Justification and Variegated Nomism, edited by Carson, D.A. et al. 1–38. Grand Rapids, MI: Baker Academic, 2001.

Willitts, Joel. "Context Matters: Paul's Use of Leviticus 18:5 in Galatians 3:12." *Tyndale Bulletin* 54 (2003): 105–122.

Wilson, Stephen G. *Related Strangers: Jews and Christians, 70–170 C.E.* Minneapolis, MN: Fortress Press, 1995.

Wilson, Todd A. *The Curse of the Law and the Crisis in Galatia: Reassessing the Purpose of Galatians*. Wissenschaftliche Untersuchungen zum Neuen Testament 2. Reihe, vol. 225, edited by Frey, Jörg. Tübingen, Germany: Mohr Siebeck 2007.

Winston, David. *The Wisdom of Solomon: A New Translation With Introduction and Commentary*. Anchor Bible vol. 43. New York: Doubleday; Yale University Press, 2007.

Winter, Bruce W. *Seek the Welfare of the City: Christians as Benefactors and Citizens*. First-Century Christians in the Graeco-Roman World. Grand Rapids, MI: William B. Eerdmans, 1994.

———. *After Paul Left Corinth: The Influence of Secular Ethics and Social Change*. Grand Rapids, MI: William B. Eerdmans, 2001.

———. *Divine Honours for the Caesars: The First Christians' Responses*. Grand Rapids, MI: William B. Eerdmans, 2015.

Wittgenstein, Ludwig. *Philosophische Untersuchungen*, 4th ed., trans. Anscombe, G.E.M. et al. Chichester, UK: Wiley-Blackwell, 2009.

Witulski, Thomas. *Die Adressaten des Galaterbriefes: Untersuchungen zur Gemeinde von Antiochia* ad *Pisidiam*. Forschungen zur Religion und Literatur des Alten und Neuen Testaments, vol. 193. Göttingen, Germany: Vandenhoeck & Ruprecht, 2000.

Wright, N.T. *The Climax of the Covenant: Christ and the Law in Pauline Theology*. Edinburgh, UK: T. & T. Clark, 1991.

———. *What Saint Paul Really Said: Was Paul of Tarsus the Real Founder of Christianity?* Grand Rapids, MI: William B. Eerdmans, 1997.

———. *Justification: God's Plan and Paul's Vision*. London: S.P.C.K., 2009.

———. *Paul and the Faithfulness of God*. Christian Origins and the Question of God, vol. 4. Minneapolis, MN: Fortress Press, 2013.

———. "The Letter to the Romans: Introduction, Commentary, and Reflections." In *The New Interpreter's Bible Commentary*, vol. 9, edited by Keck, Leander E. 317–664. Nashville, TN: Abingdon Press, 2015.

———. *History and Eschatology: Jesus and the Promise of Natural Theology*. London: S.P.C.K., 2019.

————. *Galatians*. Commentaries for Christian Formation, edited by Fowl, Stephen E. et al. Grand Rapids, MI: William B. Eerdmans, 2021.

Wyschogrod, Michael. *Abraham's Promise: Judaism and Jewish-Christian Relations*, edited by Soulen, R. Kendall. Radical Traditions. London: William B. Eerdmans, 2004.

Index of Ancient Sources

4. INTRA- AND POST-BIBLICAL JEWISH AUTHORS

5. OXYRHYNCHUS

6. QUMRAN SOURCES

7. GRAECO-ROMAN SOURCES

Aelius Aristides
Hier. Log.
II.1–4 *79*
II.27 *135*
III.16–20 *78*
III.34–36 *78*
IV.16 *79*
IV.45–7 *79, 135*

**Antiochus of
 Athens**
Frag. Ap.
110.17 *123*

Apion
Frag. Glos. Hom.
109 *130*

**Apollonius of
 Tyana**
Let.
26 *79*
43 *79*

Apuleius
Met.
XI.5 *98*

Cicero
Att.
109.2–3 *77*

Flac.
68 *56–57*

Leg.
129 *109*

Tusc.
4.7–8 *161*

Dio Chrysostom
Disc.
38.44 *78*
40.3 *78*

Epictetus
Disc.
1.11.12–13 *60*
1.22.4 *60*
2.8.23 *161*
2.9.19–20 *60, 65*

Epiphanius
Pan.
80.1.5 *59*

Galen
Hipp. Aph.
17b.794.8 *49*

Herodotus
Hist.
1.85–93 *77*

Horace
Sat..
1.4.139–43 *31*
1.5.96–104 *60*
1.9.60–78 *60*
1.9.67–70 *31*

Juvenal
Sat.
3.62–65 *89*
14.96–106 *31, 65*

**Nicomachus of
 Gerasa**
Int. Arit.
I.22.2.24 *49*

Philodemus
Frank Criticism
Fr. *7* 109
Fr. *10* 109
Col. *XXIVa* 109

Plutarch
Lives Ant.
24.1–6 *77*

Lives Brut.
30.1–31.7 *77*

*Mor. Quaest.
 Conv.*
723A *108*

**Seneca the
 Younger**
Brev. Vit.
10.2–4 *161*

Civ.
6.11 *31, 60*

Ep.
50.3 *111*
50.7–9 *109*
50.9 *111*

Sextus Empiricus
Pyrr. Hyp.
3.152 *123*

Strabo
Geog.
12.8.13 *57*
12.8.14 *74*
12.8.19 *78*
13.4.14 *59*
16.2.35–7 *60*

Suetonius'
Aug.
31.1 *72*

Claud.
25.4 *30*

Tacitus
Hist.
5.4–5 *31*
5.5 *60–61*

Zeno of Citium
Test. Frag.
100.2 *123*

Anon.
Hist. Aug.
4.18.5 *67*

Orph. Hym.
5.4 *123*

8. OTHER SOURCES

9. INSCRIPTIONS AND PAPYRI

Index of Modern Authors

Index of Subjects